More
Inclusion Strategies
That Work!

More Inclusion Strategies That Work!

Aligning Student Strengths With Standards

Toby J. Karten

CORWIN PRESS
A SAGE Publications Company
Thousand Oaks, CA 91320

For information:

Corwin Press
A Sage Publications Company
2455 Teller Road
Thousand Oaks, California 91320
www.corwinpress.com

Sage Publications Ltd.
1 Oliver's Yard
55 City Road
London, EC1Y 1SP
United Kingdom

Sage Publications India Pvt. Ltd.
B 1/I 1 Mohan Cooperative
  Industrial Area
Mathura Road, New Delhi 110 044
India

Sage Publications Asia-Pacific Pvt. Ltd.
33 Pekin Street #02-01
Far East Square
Singapore 048763

Printed in the United States of America

Library of Congress Cataloging-in-Publication Data

Karten, Toby J.
More inclusion strategies that work!: Aligning student strengths with standards/
Toby J. Karten.
       p. cm.
Includes bibliographical references and index.
ISBN-13: 978-1-4129-4115-0 (cloth)
ISBN-13: 978-1-4129-4116-7 (pbk.)
    1. Inclusive education—United States. I. Title.
LC1201.K37 2007   371.9'043—dc22

This book is printed on acid-free paper.

07 08 09 10 11 10 9 8 7 6 5 4 3 2 1

Acquisitions Editor:	Allyson P. Sharp
Editorial Assistant:	Nadia Kashper
Copy Editor:	Teresa Herlinger
Typesetter:	C&M Digitals (P) Ltd.
Proofreader:	Anne Rogers
Indexer:	John Hulse
Cover Designer:	Monique Hahn
Graphic Designer:	Lisa Miller

Contents

Preface

Inclusion Poem

Some don't know
The way inclusion will go
One thing is for sure
We definitely need some more
Better classroom ideas
And less teacher fears
More planned strategies
Focusing on abilities
Yes, more inclusion
And less confusion
More parents amicably involved
All conflicts mutually resolved
Less opposition
More transition
To the community
That's the reality
So forget the label
Remember all are able
In different ways to succeed
To count, laugh, smile, and read
Let's give all a turn
To understand and learn
So don't be rude
Figure out a way to include

—© 2005 by Toby J. Karten

How can students succeed in today's standards-based classrooms? How can teachers instruct so that students are successful on high-stakes tests? What does an inclusion classroom look like? Why are some classrooms more successful than others? How do you instruct a student who can barely read, and get him or her to understand about plate tectonics, algebraic expressions, graphing inequalities, global economies, or how to use Excel? Or, do some students even need this knowledge to be included in their world? Well, the basic belief here is that there's a world of knowledge that can be successfully delivered to students. Classroom successes are not limited to those with the most or least skills; rather, the educational goal is to advance the individual levels of all students.

The first thing required by all is a positive attitude. If you believe in all of the philosophical reasons for inclusion, you will find a way to make it work within your own teaching environment. Yes, there are many obstacles that might thwart your march forward, but the bottom line is simply this: Inclusion can and does work! Teachers with accepting attitudes can and do make a difference, when a game plan is followed. Just like a football coach would not allow the players to run onto the field without a strategy in play, teachers must also properly equip their students to successfully tackle each and every lesson.

This book approaches learning objectives from a different viewpoint. It begins with the philosophy of inclusion and standards, and then applies best practices to students' strengths with specific curriculum examples. Research is meant to engage the reader to think beyond the rhetoric and apply the quotes to students, instructional strategies, and the curriculum. Individual subjects each have their own table, broken into grade divisions as shown here in Figure P-1. Standards-based objectives and skills are given for each subject/content area, listing a general fund of knowledge desired for grade divisions. These are shown near each other, allowing teachers across the grades to visually compare prior baseline knowledge in content areas for grades that precede and

Figure P-1

Grades	Content Area/Skills:
K–2	
3–5	
6–8	
9–12	

follow. Regardless of their grade level, individual students might need more, or in some cases less, instruction on some topics.

Vertical and horizontal alignments present current objectives, prior ones, and future goals on the same topic. Hence, students within the same classroom can be learning about one topic, with different objectives. Some students review objectives not achieved from prior grade levels, some work on grade-level objectives, while others are challenged with introductions to higher grade-level objectives. This type of setup combines topic-based learning with student-centered needs. Approaching teaching and learning this way concentrates more on increasing student knowledge, rather than covering individual subjects. Infusion of objectives across subjects and grades is thus an achievable result for teachers instructing and assessing students with different baseline knowledge levels within the same classroom.

Now that those objectives are known, what about moving forward with lessons that promote knowledge and skills with the best types of instructional strategies? All students have varying social, academic, behavioral, perceptual, and cognitive levels. As a matter of fact, all people around the world have these same varying needs and levels. One commonality does exist though, and that is the desire to be included in an accepting world. If teachers can not only deliver subject matter, but also make connections to life with palatable lessons that include spiraling, standards-based objectives that concentrate on students' strengths, everyone will move forward. Learning should not be a chore, but rather an entitlement enjoyed by all. *Joie de learning* is an intrinsic objective for educators to model and instill in their students. Most subjects, although they have specific standards, can also be taught in an interdisciplinary way that prepares students not only for the assessments, but also for lifelong learning.

Researchers support effective teaching practices across subject areas (Colwell, 2005; Downing, 2005; Franklin, 2005; Nunley, 2003; Odom et al., 2005; Ravitch, 2006; Scarpati, 2000; U.S. Dept of Education, 2005b; Wolfe, 2001), while educators have the arduous task of implementing those strategies. The plot thickens, as administrators can tangle or disentangle the accomplishment of these standards-based objectives, translating the learning into classroom realities or bureaucratic nightmares. Ultimately, students embrace or retreat from the instruction, depending upon the meaningful deliveries employed. My, what tangled educational webs we weave! Oh, but Charlotte was a wonderful little spider that managed to weave her web and help others. Inclusion is just as tenacious, with collaborative, masterfully prepared weavers who can capture inclusionary insights for all!

Acknowledgments

This book is possible because of the incredible students I have been fortunate enough to meet and instruct throughout my teaching career. You have inspired me to think more, teach better, and figure out how to match your unique styles with the ever-changing curriculum demands, assessment challenges, and legislative requirements. Classroom teachers who are constantly figuring out ways to improve their strategies to include all learners deserve an enormous round of accolades as well! In addition, kudos to the administrators who go a step beyond the law, by implementing not only *appropriate* strategies in their schools, but also the *best ones* possible, simply because it's what needs to be done. All school personnel who are arduously and consistently collaborating with each other and families deserve acknowledgment as the real *inclusion protagonists* on classroom stages! The production would not be possible without them.

My appreciation to all at Corwin Press who have receptively welcomed my writings. Your encouragement allowed me to realize that I have a lot more to say about this topic of inclusion. Specific thanks go to Robb Clouse for his initial question, "So, is there another book on the drawing board, or was this a one-shot deal?" I think I started writing more that very night! My appreciation goes to Allyson Sharp for her savvy navigation of this book and the streets of Chicago. My gratitude to Nadia Kashper for her artful direction, organization, and flexibility in seeing this project through from the start. Additional thanks to Beth Bernstein, my production editor, and Teresa Herlinger, my copy editor. Glad to have *included* you in round 2, Teresa! Many talk of educational pendulums, but thank goodness, inclusion is not a fad, but most definitely here to stay. Corwin Press is dedicated to that mission!

On a personal note, thanks to Marc and Adam, the best sports I know!

The contributions of the following reviewers are gratefully acknowledged:

Diane Boarman
GT Resource, NBCT, Generalist/Middle Childhood
Patapsco Middle School
Ellicott City, MD

Dolores Burton
Associate Professor of Education
New York Institute of Technology
Old Westbury, NY

Rick Hopper
2005 American Star of Teaching
Special Education Teacher, Grades 4–5
Hampden Meadows School
Barrington, RI

Tina Spencer
Behavior/Inclusion Specialist
Training and Technical Assistance Center,
    College of William and Mary and Virginia Department of Education
Williamsburg, VA

Jacqueline S. Thousand
Professor of Special Education
California State University, San Marcos
San Marcos, CA

About the Author

 **Toby J. Karten** is an experienced educator who has worked in the field of special education since 1976. She has an undergraduate degree in special education from Brooklyn College, a master of science from the College of Staten Island, and a supervisory degree from Georgian Court University. Being involved in the field of special education for the past three decades has afforded Ms. Karten an opportunity to help many children and adults from elementary through graduate levels. Along with being a resource center teacher in New Jersey, Ms. Karten has designed a graduate course titled "Skills and Strategies for Inclusion and disABILITY Awareness." She is an adjunct professor at the College of New Jersey and Gratz College in Pennsylvania. She has presented at local, state, and international workshops and conferences. Ms. Karten has been recognized by both the Council of Exceptional Children and the New Jersey Department of Education as an exemplary educator, receiving two "Teacher of the Year" awards. Her first book, *Inclusion Strategies That Work! Research-Based Methods for the Classroom,* was well received by preservice and inservice special and general educators, as well as administrators and parents who have implemented the pragmatic strategies offered.

Ms. Karten is married, has a son, has two dogs, and currently resides in New Jersey and Vermont. She enjoys teaching, reading, writing, artwork, and, most of all, learning. As the author of this book, she believes that inclusion is a way of life that goes above and beyond the classroom and these pages!

Part I: Fundamentals of Honoring Potentials and Strengths of Students and Teachers

Chapter 1 Concentrating on Students' Strengths and Curriculum Standards	**Chapter 2** Understanding Assessments and Curriculum Standards	**Chapter 3** How Students Learn: Brain Basics	**Chapter 4** How Teachers Teach: Good Practices for All

Part II: Standards-Based Inclusion Strategies That Work

Chapter 5 Standards-Based Reading Objectives	**Chapter 6** Standards-Based Writing, Listening, and Speaking Objectives	**Chapter 7** Standards-Based Math Objectives	**Chapter 8** Standards-Based Science and Technology Objectives

Chapter 9 Standards-Based Social Studies Objectives	**Chapter 10** Standards-Based Art, Dance, Theater, and Music Objectives	**Chapter 11** Standards-Based Health/Physical Education Objectives	**Chapter 12** Standards-Based Career Education and Life Skills Objectives	**Chapter 13** Standards-Based Social/Behavioral/ Emotional Objectives

Part III: Application of Strengths and Standards to Inclusive Environments

Chapter 14 Standards-Based Interdisciplinary/ Cross-Curricular Lessons	**Chapter 15** Attaining Inclusion	**Chapter 16** Rewards for All!

PART I

Fundamentals of Honoring Potentials and Strengths of Students and Teachers

Concentrating on Students' Strengths and Curriculum Standards

This book begins by outlining students' strengths. We all learn best when we are allowed to *show what we know.* By focusing on just the limitations of different disabilities and syndromes, an instructional nightmare will ensue. Yes, there are some characteristics common to different disabilities, but you are not instructing a disability, you are instructing a child. Equally true is that you are teaching a student, not a subject. We as instructors want to challenge all students to achieve their highest potentials with feasible accommodations. Frustrations present themselves most often when there are expectations that do not match the delivery of specific curriculum objectives. As teachers, we know what standards-based objectives we'd like to achieve in a given lesson or unit, but then we are sometimes dismayed to discover that the students have not achieved our expectations. Well, were our expectations realistic? Educators need to be aware of the essential specific baseline knowledge standard for each subject, and then design objectives with accommodations that do not enable, but rather challenge students. Yes, some students might need accommodations or modifications, but these do not replace the plan of each child achieving specific learning objectives. Ultimately, educational professionals need to have high expectations for all students if academic standards are to be achieved.

WHAT ARE THE STANDARDS?

A curriculum is only a guide as to what might be taught. . . . [T]he voluntary national standards do not constitute a program . . . or teaching objectives. . . . [T]he standards contain suggestions about the content that the student might encounter in a complete education. . . . It remains the responsibility of the teacher to develop and instigate an instructional program.

—Colwell, 2005

The latest scientific research shows that students with significant disabilities (approximately 2 percent of all students) can make progress toward grade-level standards when they receive high-quality instruction and are assessed with alternate assessments based on modified achievement standards.

—U.S. Department of Education, 2005b

Planning lesson activities and presenting them to students in a coherent order is a challenging task in standards-based teaching. . . . [W]e need to work together collaboratively.

—O'Shea, 2005

In a truly standards-based approach, students, teachers, teacher-educators, textbook publishers, and testing agencies should know what students are expected to learn (content standards) and what constitutes superior, acceptable, and unacceptable performance (performance standards).

—Ravitch, 2006

There are a number of challenges facing all teachers as they implement standards, assessments, and accountability reforms with students with disabilities. The most significant of these challenges is how to enable each student to access the critical knowledge and skills specified in the standards.

—Nolet & McLaughlin, 2005

Higher and more rigorous expectations of students in schools today pose great implications for students with disabilities.

—Scarpati, 2000

The intense focus on two basic skills (reading and math) is a sea change in American instructional practices, with many schools that once offered rich curriculums now systematically trimming courses like social studies, science, and art. . . . [E]xperts warn that [by] reducing the academic menu to steak and potatoes, schools risk giving bored teenagers the message that school means repetition and drill.

—Dillon, 2006

According to a report by the Rand Corporation, having states set their own proficiency standards has become a controversial issue because some states have set proficiency standards that are easy to achieve, whereas other states have set very rigorous proficiency standards that are difficult to achieve.

—Yell, Katsiyanna, & Shiner, 2006

Standards from different states and associations were reviewed and then divided into disciplines in the curriculum chapters that follow. As an educator, it is imperative to check your state's Web site for more current information on your state and district's content and core standards. More information on assessment and standards will also be addressed in Chapter 2. In no way are these charts encompassing of all topics under each subject, yet they bring to mind the juxtaposition of the huge complexities and simplicities involved within individual subjects. The dilemma or challenge here is how to allow students with disabilities full access to the general education curriculum, while at the same time focusing on individual students' goals and strengths. The conundrum is how to honor and respect varying student abilities within the framework of the standards. In the past, the deletion or overdilution of these standards, when it came to students with disabilities, resulted in a downward spiral of student knowledge. Teachers are now challenged to not only include all students in their classroom, but to also hold them accountable to learning more. It's a road that was at one time less traveled, but with the proper *teaching hiking gear*, it is definitely navigable.

Chapters 2–4 address assessment issues, how students learn, and how teachers teach. Moving forward into the classroom, Chapters 5–14 list specific objectives in reading, writing, mathematics, science, social studies, the arts, physical education, career education, life skills, social areas, and communication as indicated by our national standards and several states across the nation. The objectives are all shown near each other in ranges of grades, to allow for quick viewing of adjacent grades. Teachers can pull from different ones to allow students of higher and lower levels within the same class to learn about a topic or concept, on varying levels, with vertical and horizontal alignments. Baseline, advanced, and more challenging assignments are also included on primary, intermediary, and secondary levels. Following that, possible accommodations are listed for students with differing emotional, physical, cognitive, and sensory abilities. The question here is not whether students with differing academic, motoric, behavioral, perceptual, or physical needs can learn the same topics or concepts, but rather, what are the best strategies or tools to assist teachers with their endeavors. Baseline, advanced, and more challenging assignments try to mimic actual classroom lessons. The purpose here is to replace the thinking of impossibilities with a mentality that supports a *feasibility approach!*

The following on line sources were consulted:

Online Sources for Standards

Mid-Continent Research for Education and Learning: www.mcrel.org/standards-benchmarks/

Education World: www.education-world.com/standards/national/ and

http://www.education-world.com/standards/state/index.shtml

Illinois Learning Standards: http://www.isbe.state.il.us/ils/social_emotional/standards.htm

---

(Continued)

(Continued)

New Jersey Core Curriculum Content Standards: http://www.state.nj.us/njded/cccs/Standards

Texas Assessment of Knowledge and Skills (TAKS): http://www.tea.state.tx.us/student.assessment/

Music Educators National Conference (MENC), The National Association for Music Education: http://www.menc.org

Science Content Standards Developed by the National Research Council: http://www.nsta.org/standards

Content Standards for Mathematics Developed by the National Council of Teachers of Mathematics (NCTM): http://standards.nctm.org

Content Standards for Social Studies Developed by the National Council for the Social Studies (NCSS): http://www.ncss.org

Content Standards for the English Language Arts Developed by the National Council of Teachers of English (NCTE) and the International Reading Association (IRA): http://www.ncte.org

National Standards for Physical Education—American Alliance for Health, Physical Education, Recreation and Dance: http://www.aahperd.org/NASPE/publications-national standards.html

The Kennedy Center ArtsEdge: http://artsedge.kennedy-center.org/teach/standards.cfm

Before generic standards are applied, students' varying abilities must be known. The following pages list syndromes by name and concentrate on possible strengths, instead of looking at a deficit paradigm. Teachers can apply the standards to match students' strengths when equipped with the facts. This allows for a feasible and realistic approach to deliver learning objectives instead of just trying to follow standards without knowing and valuing your special audience!

POSITIVE CHARACTERISTICS OF DISABILITIES

The best teachers never lose sight of their students' potential. They believe in the brilliance and ability of all their students.

—Landsman, 2006

Even though many disabilities or syndromes have weak areas, individual strengths exist as well. Classroom instruction that focuses on what students are capable of accomplishing recognizes how students' strengths can surpass their deficits. Placing energy and attention on students' current levels and potentials yields many positive results. Disabilities have common characteristics, yet they do not describe an individual child's likes or dislikes. Consequently, there are no blanket teaching lessons that promote the mastery of the same objective for all students, without recognizing individual differences. In addition, teachers must challenge, not enable, their students by incorporating appropriate and feasible accommodations. The second step would be to modify or change the curriculum or expectations if accommodations are not sufficiently addressing individual needs. The third option, deleting the concept, is a last resort that if consistently employed has a cumulative negative spiraling effect throughout a child's years in school and future as an adult.

Quite often, teachers set themselves and their students up for many frustrations by not realizing the individual characteristics and strengths of their students. It's not an easy task to recognize these traits, but not an impossible one either. The goal here is to combine topic-based learning with student-centered needs and abilities. Check out the possible strengths and some supportive research of the alphabetically listed categories described below. Quite often, it's your positive perspective that determines that the glass is half-filled, or, in this case, ensures more positive student learning outcomes! Cheers!

Remember, of course, that diversity exists within each underlined category.

Positive Characteristics

Many students with *above average skills*

- Are proud of their achievements
- Have strong parental support
- Respond to challenging assignments
- Have high levels of curiosity
- Have excellent critical-thinking skills
- Like independent projects
- Use creative outlets (e.g., music, art, chess, etc.)
- Respond to project-based learning assignments
- Are introspective
- Are goal oriented
- Are willing to share their knowledge
- Are eager to improve grades with additional assignments
- Prefer open-ended questions with multiple responses
- Do well with options and self-directed learning
- Thrive with differentiated pacing of assignments
- Learn new material in less time
- Remember what they learn
- Multitask simultaneous classroom activities

Research/literature about students with above average skills says the following:

> [G]ifted students often resist doing their assigned work because it is designed for age-appropriate learners and usually cannot provide the challenge and sense of accomplishment that would keep gifted learners motivated to work. . . . [T]hese students are entitled to receive the same types of differentiation so readily provided to students who struggle to learn.
>
> —Winebrenner, 2000

Being gifted academically means that you are achieving or have the potential to achieve at rather high levels when compared with other students of your age and/or grade level. It would be a sad waste of your school days to be studying curriculum you already know or spending a lot of your time tutoring classmates.

—from a student, quoted in Callard-Szulgit, 2005

Many students with *Asperger's syndrome* (AS)

- Possess an affinity for routines
- Have a good handle on their own interests
- Work well with written assignments (e.g, graphic organizers, social skills notebook)
- Respond to behavior modification approaches
- Have sensory preferences (tactile learning, visual cues)
- Motorically demonstrate their learning
- Pick up cues by watching others
- Have a high verbal IQ
- Advance with direct skill instruction
- Have good relationships with adults

Research/literature about Asperger's says the following:

Reasonably normal language development (specifically, two-word phrases by age 2 and three-word phrases by age 3) is a distinguishing feature of Asperger's (compared to children with true autism or high-functioning autism). . . . [Children with Asperger's] often have impaired social interactions, stereotyped behaviors, preoccupations or interests, motor delays or clumsiness. . . . Neuropsychiatry testing also shows that children with Asperger's consistently score higher on verbal rather than performance IQ.

—Klass & Costello, 2003

Many teachers fail to recognize the special academic needs of children and adolescents with AS because these students often give the impression that they understand more than they do.

—Myles, 2005

Incorporating special interests of students with AS into the curriculum is one way to make interesting a task that may initially seem overwhelming or lack meaning to a student with Asperger's.

—Myles, 2005

Many students with *attention deficit/hyperactivity disorder* (AD/HD)

- Are responsive to immediate teacher feedback
- Have the ability to move and learn
- Thrive in a nonthreatening environment

- Possess good cognitive levels
- Model appropriate behaviors with guided practice and application
- Are able to develop increased self-awareness under teacher's auspices
- Can multitask in a well-organized environment
- Learn well with kinesthetic activities
- Like when notebooks and text covers are color coded
- Advance when given clear expectations and immediate feedback
- Complete assignments that are broken down into their smaller components

Research/literature about AD/HD says the following:

Diagnosing and helping students with AD/HD requires the collaboration of parents, clinicians, teachers, and students.

—Schlozman & Schlozman, 2002

Children with AD/HD are not all the same. . . . However, they need reassurance that the problems they have are not unique to them. They benefit from a sense that help is available and that they themselves can be a powerful force in their own treatment.

—Quinn & Stern, 2001

Although AD/HD can generate a host of problems, there are also advantages to having it . . . such as high energy, intuitiveness, creativity, and enthusiasm, and they are completely ignored by the disorder model.

—Hallowell & Ratey, 1995

In addition, clinical psychologist Stephen Faraone of Harvard University says, "My hope is that once we've discovered those genes, we'll be able to do a prospective study of kids at high versus low genetic risk. Eventually . . . environmental changes could play an important role in treating some AD/HD patients" (Brown, 2003).

Many students with *auditory processing* disabilities

- Have good focus with written and visual directions and cues
- Understand better when allowed to intermittently paraphrase
- Have excellent response to technology tools such as interactive white boards, along with ones that offer word processing programs that include accompanying graphics
- Learn well with structured phonetic and linguistic programs
- Attend well to lectures when given outlines or graphic organizers to follow
- Exhibit increased auditory responses when eye contact is established with speaker
- Make excellent progress when metacognitive strategies are learned and applied
- Experience advances when hooked up with a peer coach to model and consult

Research/literature about auditory processing disabilities (APD) says the following:

A child with APD is often described as a "visual learner," who learns best when material is presented through pictures and hands-on demonstrations. . . . [I]f multisensory cues seem to confuse the child, the possibility of an interhemispheric disorder should be considered.

—Bellis, 2002

Auditory processing problems won't show up on standard hearing tests since the problem is not the ability to hear sounds, but the ability to process verbal information. . . . [These students] have trouble hearing in a crowded classroom . . . [have trouble understanding] multi step directions . . . [and] need to receive instructions in writing not just auditorily.

—Warshaw, 2004

Many students with *autism*

- Have focused interests
- Are able to continue ongoing tasks
- Respond to directed social play through structured play groups
- Follow routines well when there is consistency in scheduling
- Achieve understandings through concrete experiences
- Have an affinity for tactile stimulation such as different textures, or even water therapy
- Like step-by-step explanations in learning
- Use pictures to communicate needs and thoughts
- Have different reactions to noises and lights
- Benefit when academics are related to life skills
- Make excellent strides when given appropriate early interventions

Research/literature about autism says the following:

Through play, children experience cognitive, social, linguistic, motor and emotional growth . . . with typical peers as role models . . . in natural settings that promote generalizations.

—Lantz, Nelson, & Loftin, 2005

I THINK IN PICTURES. Words are like a second language. . . . I translate both spoken and written words into full-color movies, complete with sound, which run like a VCR tape in my head. When somebody speaks to me, his words are instantly translated into pictures.

—Grandin, 1995

High-functioning autism (HFA) is a term sometimes used interchangeably with Asperger's syndrome, but these individuals are in fact a distinct group . . . slower to acquire language and have weaker verbal scores and stronger integrative skills (visual-spatial skills). . . . One distinction is that children with HFA are not particularly interested in social relationships, whereas children with Asperger's are deeply interested though unable to understand the rules.

—Klass & Costello, 2003

Typically developing peers may provide a role model for well-adjusted social behavior, with possible implications for the social competence of the child with autism.

—Bauminger, Shulman, & Agam, 2003

Practitioners working with students with ASD (Autism Spectrum Disorder) have found that these individuals learn best when they have visual aids and other forms of structure to assist them in understanding rules, time frames, sequences, time allocations, and task completion . . . which will enable students with ASD to be more independent and productive in their lives.

—Simpson et al., 2005

Many students with *communication disorders*

- Have better receptive than expressive language skills
- Exhibit excellent responses to timely and structured speech interventions
- Experience advancements when learning is coordinated between school and home environments
- Experience gains with modeling, rewards for approximations, and meaningful praise
- Make headway when communication skills are combined with more visuals (e.g., pictures, mirrors) and technology tools such as computer programs and digital recorders
- May need a personalized PECS (Picture Exchange Communication System) if more severely disabled
- Improve speech in inclusive environments that relate speech to children's experiences, such as speech through *conversational instruction* and *peer osmosis*

Research/literature about communication disorders says the following:

Communicative impairments can occur in association with a syndrome (speech production, voice, language, resonance, and hearing) as well as feeding disorders.

—Shprintzen, 2000

An estimated 18.4% of children ages 5–17 speak a language other than English. Of the total number of students receiving services in special education, 18.9% have a speech or language impairment.

—Data from U.S. Census Bureau, 2000

Children with dyspraxia or apraxia . . . have the capacity to say speech sounds but have a problem with motor planning. They have difficulty making the movements needed for speech voluntarily.

—Bowen, 1998

The more individuals with significant disabilities are provided with ways to express their thoughts and feelings, the more they will be engaged in establishing basic literacy skills.

—Downing, 2005

Many students with *conduct disorders*

- Respond to behavioral charts that reward positive strides
- Improve behavior within structured, consistent environments
- Establish a rapport with a trusting adult
- Want other ways to feel good about themselves (e.g., art, music)
- Like physical outlets such as yoga or exercise
- React appropriately when given fair, yet consistent limits and consequences
- Desire peer acceptance
- Are not all about the surface behavior, but are complex caring individuals
- Have positive interactions when allowed meaningful and guided opportunities to contribute/share thoughts with peers
- Display responsibility under teacher's auspices
- Increase progress when parents are given guidance about managing behavior issues

Research/literature about conduct disorders says the following:

Problem-solving and social skills training may offer promise to students with conduct disorder. Proceeding step by step, using games and stories that gradually approach real-life situations, the therapist teaches the child how to exercise self-control, see other people's point of view, anticipate their reactions, and understand the consequences of their own actions. This method works best with children of mild disturbance. . . . Many experts believe the most promising approach . . . is parent management training. . . . Parents are taught to issue and enforce stable rules, negotiate compromises, and substitute sensible discipline for inconsistent harshness.

—"Child and Adolescent Conduct Disorder," 2005

[P]unishment shouldn't be the final step in handling aggressive students. . . . Educators should look for ways to help aggressive kids change their behaviors . . . critically examining . . . the school's culture and climate—including classrooms, corridors, and cafeterias—to identify conditions that provoke students to display anger and aggression.

—Black, 2003

Many students with *deafness/hearing loss*

- Are of average or above average intelligence
- Can use "alternative" ways of communicating, such as oral (using speech, lip reading, and any residual hearing), manual (signs, finger spelling), or total communication (oral method plus signing and finger spelling)
- Learn well with more visuals, outlines, and handouts of teacher's notes
- Benefit from technological advances, such as a laptop, amplification systems, or even cochlear implants, if appropriate
- Possess more introspective qualities
- Desire to be included with peers, family, and community
- Have strong capacities for learning

Research/literature about deafness/hearing loss says the following:

The Association Method is a systematic, multisensory approach for teaching spoken language, reading, and writing for students with hearing loss and other populations with speech, language, and reading difficulties. . . . [I]t benefits students with a step-by-step, repetitive, and cumulative approach, learning each sound, word, sentence, and story.

—Sullivan & Perigoe, 2004

Short periods of exposure to amplified sound may not cause permanent hearing loss, but damage from long-term exposure can be cumulative. This means a slight hearing loss in childhood can become a substantial loss later on.

—"Most Teens Oblivious to the Threat," 2005

There is no doubt that hearing loss alters lifestyle. While we have not reached the age of reversing all hearing loss, we are in an age of technology that enables better hearing than ever before. Hearing loss is an "invisible" disability. . . . [T]he stigma associated with hearing aid use leads to poor use of hearing aids. Individuals with hearing loss who do not use hearing aids report higher rates of depression, sadness, anxiety, and paranoia . . . [and tend to be] less socially active and experience greater emotional insecurity . . . [and may have] stopped attending social events and avoided family gatherings, simply because it was too difficult to hear and understand conversation.

—Sherlock, 2005

Unlike a hearing aid, which amplifies sound, a cochlear implant digitizes sound and sends it via magnets and electrodes to the brain. . . . The success stories amazed us: implanted children in mainstream classrooms speaking beautifully, nearly indistinguishable from hearing classmates.

—Denworth, 2006

When appropriate, use of a student's residual hearing can be utilized to gain phonological information about spoken language.

—Neff, 2006

Many students with *depression*

- Respond well to individual counseling, modeling, and coaching
- Advance with behavioral interventions, strategies, and support
- Like to play with toys to resolve conflicts when younger
- Recognize their own mood swings when older
- Seek transitional plans and more career guidance when adolescents
- Establish comforting relationships with pets
- Cathartically benefit when allowed to role-play *hypothetically* stressful situations
- Can use nonverbal modes of expression like art, dance, writing, or music

Research/literature about depression says the following:

Children with intense anxiety or depression are particularly likely to have problems that appear similar to AD/HD, and evidence also exists that suggests that symptoms of depression—as the child's "self-esteem" suffers in the face of continuing social and developmental failures—can complicate AD/HD.

—Zametkin & Monique, 1999

Regular exercise is a potent mood lifter. [An] American Journal of Preventive Medicine *article by Andrea Dunn found that an exercise regimen of 180 minutes a week could rouse depressed subjects out of the doldrums and keep them that way, if they stuck with the program.*

—Dunn, 2005

Educators are beginning to recognize that mental health is essential to learning. . . . With emotional disorders such as depression . . . students need to think in a more positive way. Educators can teach anger management, social skills, conflict resolution, mediation skills, relaxation techniques. . . . General educators need to work with special education teachers, watch students in lunchroom, playground, classroom and have opportunities for more staff development to help students achieve more in their lives.

—Vail, 2005

Many students with *developmental disorders*

- Have the ability to understand concrete concepts
- Possess an affinity for repetition in learning
- Desire to be included with peers
- Have a strong determination to succeed
- Have concerned parents
- Respond well to early intervention
- Experience success with related services such as speech, occupational, physical, and play therapies
- Are able to make gains with structured academic and behavioral interventions
- Have individual needs, goals, and aspirations

Research/literature about developmental disorders says the following:

A genetic disorder predisposes individuals to a variety of behavioral characteristics.

—Hodapp, 2004

Over time and as students with significant disabilities accessed the core curriculum, we began to notice that students were exceeding our expectations.

—Downing, 2005

Many students with *dyscalculia*

- Have better reading/language skills
- Have success with numbers when using a step-by-step approach
- Respond to kinesthetic approaches; e.g., Touch Math, physical demonstration and manipulation of concepts
- Experience better understandings when math procedures are connected to their own lives; e.g., *Everyday Mathematics*
- Have good computational skills when conceptual background is concretely or pictorially explained
- Have success with intermittent repetition of prior learning
- Achieve progress when instruction teaches the language of math
- Develop a desire to succeed when given frequent, yet realistic praise and encouragement

Research/literature about dyscalculia says the following:

Children with dyscalculia can usually learn the sequence of counting words, but may have difficulty navigating back and forth, especially in twos, threes or more. . . . [E]stimating numbers is impaired in comparison to that of their peers. . . . [A]n intuitive grasp of number magnitudes typical of children in the age group of 7 to 11 is absent in the child with dyscalculia.

—Vaidya, 2004

Visualization, focusing strategies, guidance with seriation, classification and reading word problems are part of best practices for students with dyscalculia.

—Vaidya, 2004

Many students with *dysgraphia*

- Work well with computers and specialized software programs
- Like voice recognition and prediction programs, which translate words into written form

- Benefit from tactile stimulation such as salt, felt, clay, or raised lettering
- Make more strides when a peer or adult acts as a scribe to help with lecture notes
- Experience increased understanding when allowed to listen to taped class lectures
- Need graphic organizers such as outlines or webs to minimize hand strain while maximizing writing pace
- Respond to increased awareness, reminders, and corrections for improved body posture; e.g., sitting upright, and proper location of fingers and appropriate pencil grip when writing
- Improve with eye–hand coordination and visual fine motor integration practice
- Work well with occupational therapists
- Make strides with explicit written language instruction that views writing as a process
- Demonstrate written work best in an untimed, nonthreatening environment

Research/literature about dysgraphia says the following:

For kids with dysgraphia, it is important to disentangle the mechanics from generation of content. . . . [U]se dictation at first, then keyboarding . . . to share their ideas without their physical limitations getting in the way.

—Warshaw, 2004

Students with disabilities often experience particular difficulties with handwriting, and these problems can hinder their development both in school and in postsecondary settings. The importance of an ongoing and consistent program of handwriting instruction is stressed, especially for students with disabilities who need to fight negative first impressions.

—Greenland & Polloway, 1994

Many students with *dyslexia*

- Like textbooks-on-tape or high-tech reading machines
- Exhibit excellent cognitive thought processes
- Have academic and social strengths
- Have stronger oral comprehension
- Have better math skills
- Are able to compensate for reading/language weaknesses
- Desire to complete same work as peers
- Have a conceptual understanding of content
- Respond well to low-level but high-interest books
- Are motivated learners when given praise for strides

- Are able to break the phonetic code when given direct and consistent skill instruction
- Have excellent responses to multisensory reading approaches; e.g., the Orton-Gillingham method

Research/literature about dyslexia says the following:

In teaching reading . . . the objective is not multisensory teaching from the teacher; the objective is multisensory learning within the learner.

—Broomfield & Combley, 2003

Intensive phonics instruction literally gets into the heads of adults with dyslexia, according to a new brain-imaging study. After completing such training, these individuals display modified brain activity that apparently fosters their improved performance on reading tests, concludes a team of neuroscientists led by Guinevere F. Eden of Georgetown University Medical Center in Washington, D.C.

—Bower, 2004

Many students with *executive dysfunction*

- Are able to set goals with adult assistance and modeling
- Respond well when given step-by-step directions
- Have better sequencing and organizational skills when using checklists
- Experience increased understandings when verbal directions are repeated and continually accompanied by easy-to-follow, terse written ones
- Progress to retraining and sharpening cognitive abilities when given applicable bypass strategies to use in all content areas
- Respond well to technology programs
- Advance when given appropriate accommodations to regulate attention, set goals, and monitor achievements

Research/literature about executive dysfunction says the following:

What comes to most of us fairly unconsciously must be explicitly taught to folks with Executive Dysfunction. A combination of cognitive training and appropriate accommodation can make a difference.

—Kight, n.d.

Many students with *mental retardation/intellectual disabilities*

- Benefit from family support that continues school efforts at home
- Feel a sense of loyalty to peers and loved ones
- Appreciate supportive staff

- Possess a desire to learn
- Are able to succeed in school and life
- Have strong social needs
- Have trusting personalities
- Respond well to concrete learning
- Have the same thoughts and desires as peers of different intellectual levels
- Have better receptive than expressive language skills

Research/literature about mental retardation/intellectual disabilities says the following:

> *In the case of students with mental retardation, it appears that those who need physical education the most to develop fitness may be prone to receive less instruction in many schools.*
>
> —Ayvazoglu, Ratliffe, & Kozub, 2004

> *Students with mild retardation seem to be at risk for depression because they often can perceive that their peers without disabilities are able to accomplish tasks that they themselves cannot.*
>
> —Stough & Baker, 1999

> *People with intellectual disabilities are showing they not only can work on landscaping crews or as baggers in supermarkets but also can serve as cashiers, office aides or technical assistants. . . . [V]arious organizations stand ready to provide job counseling and other services for employers and their workers with intellectual disabilities. Moreover, the accommodations needed for such workers are typically small, and sometimes prove beneficial to other employees.*
>
> —Shea, 2005

> *The term* highest achievement standards possible *is intended to reflect that the alternate achievement standards should be no less challenging for students with the most significant cognitive disabilities than the standards set for all other students.*
>
> —U.S. Department of Education, 2005b

Many students with *obsessive-compulsive disorder* (OCD)

- Follow cues for self-management programs
- Have a strong affinity for perfection
- Have good hygiene practices; e.g., clean hands
- Respond well to self-awareness/behavioral programs
- Are able to learn when given acceptable positive outlets to channel obsessions
- Have age-appropriate cognitive levels

- Have high organizational skills
- Desire to control obsessions and compulsions

Research/literature about obsessive-compulsive disorder says the following:

A large proportion of adults with OCD, perhaps as high as 80%, have their onset during childhood or adolescence. . . . Obsessions and compulsions should be explored in relation to the age of onset, and the degree of interference with daily activities, as well as the degree of distress caused by the complaints. . . . Early intervention and preventive strategies, aided by the new surge of family, genetic, immunological and neurophysiological studies, pose the best hope for the improved treatment of OCD in children.

—Grados, Labuda, Riddle, & Walkup, 1997

Cognitive behavioural therapy (CBT), including exposure and response prevention (ERP), should be offered as first-line therapy for children, young people and adults with mild to moderate OCD.

—Reed, 2005

An accurate and developmentally sensitive conceptual model of the development and maintenance of OCD during childhood and adolescence would lead to the refinement of current assessment procedures and treatment guidelines, to the benefit of children and adults.

—Farrell & Barrett, 2006

Many students with *oppositional defiant disorder*

- Have strong goals
- Possess a drive for independence
- Respond well to learning when allowed to be active participants
- Make strides when individual behavior management programs are implemented by a caring adult that they trust
- Learn how to circumvent self-imposed interferences
- Achieve gains with individual counseling/therapy/coaching
- Experience greater benefits when home reinforces school's behavioral plan

Research/literature about oppositional defiant disorder says the following:

Treatment seeks to identify and connect with unmet emotional needs . . . [and] capitalize on the adolescents' healthy drive for independence by identifying the emotional truths that inform their acting out and by coaching them to find ways to actualize their emotional goals. . . . [Treatment also] coaches the parents to avoid counterproductive kinds of interference with learning from trial and error. The author helps parents learn from their failures, too.

—Bustamante, 2003

[T]erms such as oppositional defiance disorder locate problems within students rather than within the educational system. . . . [Teachers and staff should strive to become] knowledgeable about [students'] unique characteristics . . . establish and teach rules, build relationships with students . . . [and] collaborate and communicate with students' families to strengthen the connection between the school and home.

—Salend & Sylvestre, 2005

Many students with *physical impairments*

- Have excellent cognitive levels
- Experience positive interactions with peers
- Possess good communication skills
- Have strong self-advocacy abilities
- Have supportive families
- Are able to maximize potentials
- Possess metacognitive and compensatory skills to circumvent physical weaknesses
- Make good use of technology options
- Possess a keen awareness of how to modify their environment to best meet physical needs
- Desire to be treated on a par with students who do not have noticeable disabilities

Research/literature about physical impairments says the following:

This study highlights the importance of conducting a careful assessment of social needs and competencies for elementary school students with physical impairments and documenting socially focused IEP goals and intervention plans when difficulties are identified. . . . With consistent provision of needed supports and interventions in these areas . . . more students can achieve optimal outcomes from their educational experiences.

—Coster & Haltiwanger, 2004

Computer technology in recent decades has opened up worlds of opportunity for people who face physical limitations.

—Teicher, 1999

Many students with *sensory impairments*

- Are able to compensate through stronger modalities
- Maximize self-regulatory strategies
- Are motivated to succeed
- Get good results with early sensory training
- Make excellent advances with peer modeling
- Possess the same emotional/academic/cognitive levels as other students in class
- Can obtain remediation with assistive technology

Research/literature about sensory impairments says the following:

A person with sensory impairments has a reduced or lack of ability in using one or more of three senses—vision, touch, and hearing . . . [that] range from slight to complete loss of ability to use the sense. . . . [The impairment] may be present with other disabilities such as mobility impairments or learning disabilities. . . . While the use of assistive technology does not remove a sensory impairment, it can remediate its effects so that a person is able to . . . demonstrate and apply her knowledge.

—University of Washington, 2001

Although schools commonly use them to support students with sensory impairments and learning disabilities, these features (e.g., closed captioning of video, text-to-speech, speech recognition, computer-based graphic organizers) can help a broad range of students. Research is beginning to show the benefits of giving all students access to these capabilities.

—Silver-Pacuilla & Fleischman, 2006

In addition, *The Sensory Profile* by Winnie Dunn (n.d.) is an evaluation tool for professionals to gather information about children's sensory-processing abilities that support or interfere with functional performance.

Many students with a *specific learning disability*

- Achieve results with appropriate help
- Complete work when given more time
- Perform well when tasks are broken down into steps
- Like to be tested in a quieter place that is free from distractions
- Make strides with multisensory approaches to learning
- Learn to compensate for learning difficulties
- Respond well to appropriate educational interventions
- Have untapped strengths
- Go on to live successful and productive lives as adults

Research/literature about specific learning disability says the following:

[T]he biggest challenge for us was not overcoming our weaknesses as Specific Learning Disabilities/ADHD thinkers but transcending the biases and oppression of the institution of education.

—Mooney & Cole, 2000

With careful planning, students with learning disabilities can choose appropriate postsecondary programs, be successful, and subsequently graduate. . . . A critical step is to know their rights and responsibilities . . . [and] be aware of accommodations needed . . . [so as to] make well-informed decisions.

—Beale, 2005

Students need to know that they're accepted. I had one student with a learning disability; everyone told him what was wrong with him, but no one tried to help him realize what was good in him.

—Tomlinson, quoted in *ASCD. Education Update*, 2002

A learning disability can really affect the way you feel about yourself. Now I know that even if a person learns differently, he or she can still be filled with greatness. Every one of us has something special inside. It's our job to figure out what that is. Dig deep, get it out, and give it to the world as a gift.

—Winkler, 2005

Many students with *Tourette's syndrome* (TS)

- Can make advancements in environments with reduced visual distractions
- Experience increased understandings when given ample time to respond
- Have more self-confidence when given realistic praise
- Have good social interactions when peers are better educated about Tourette's
- Have average or above average cognitive levels
- Make excellent progress with word processing programs
- Have unique movements that can be refined with structured programs/therapy; e.g., handwriting, occupational therapy
- Improve behavior/attention with proper classroom scaffolding
- Require optimum classroom seating (e.g., not in front of class if student has extra motor movements)
- Have better self-control and less embarrassment if allowed to inconspicuously release extra energy or fidgetiness; e.g., go on an errand, walk out into the hallway

Research/literature about Tourette's syndrome says the following:

Dr. Samuel Johnson, famous for his dictionary and wit, had classic TS symptoms that have been recorded in detail. Mozart also exhibited the symptoms. Many Touretters are enormously creative and smart.

—Kramer, 2004

Educators who foster openness and understanding to students with Tourette's help them feel included and academically adept by applying simple interventions . . . [such as] praise, multiple breaks, dictate[d] assignments, computers for written work if handwriting is an issue, related services such as OT or physical therapy, giving guidance for independence, self-care skills, and self-confidence.

—Prestia, 2003

Many people with Tourette's are never diagnosed, because they are embarrassed by their tics, and able to suppress them during visits to the doctor. . . . [Tourette's is] mainly a disorder of childhood and

*adolescence. . . . [M]ost tics fade by age 18. . . . [I]t's important to remember
that in many cases the symptoms are mild and require nothing more than
explanation and reassurance.*

        —"Child and Adolescent Conduct Disorder," 2005

Many students with *traumatic brain injury* (TBI)

- Make progress in school using a step-by-step approach
- Increase understandings when learning is tied to themselves with personal connections
- Have good results with repeated practice
- Advance further when there is collaboration and coordination of programs between school and home
- Apply strategies to compensate for memory issues; e.g., mnemonics, advance notice/study guides for assessments
- Make positive strides by reducing distractions in structured and supportive environments

Research/literature about traumatic brain injury says the following:

*Inflicted traumatic brain injury (TBI) is the leading cause of death among
children, as a result of abuse.*

        —Runyan, Marshall, Nocera, & Merten, 2004

*If you are a medical professional, it is your responsibility, if not your duty,
instead of trying to fit a square peg into a round hole, you should foster and
help this budding individual-to-be to grow into who they can be . . . and are.*

        —Harvey, 2006

Many students who are *twice-exceptional*

- Make more strides when praised for accomplishments
- Maximize areas of strength to circumvent weaker issues
- Accomplish more when they possess high yet realistic confidence levels
- Have unique levels in social or academic areas
- May have dual exceptionalities
- Have self-driven motivation
- Have a strong, resilient inner core
- Understand ways to compensate for weaker areas to reach potentials
- Will experience more self-awareness by keeping class portfolios of work completed
- Achieve positive results when environmental and instructional resources are orchestrated, maximized, and implemented
- Have strong advocates; e.g., parents, school personnel
- Do well with a growth vs. deficit paradigm
- Fare better without assigned labels
- Show what they know with authentic and varied assessments

Research/literature about twice-exceptional children says the following:

When giftedness is identified in a population of people with disabilities, conflict[s] concerning what constitutes adjustment and conformity arise.
—Cline & Hegeman, 2001

Many eminent individuals throughout history have shown evidences of a learning disability in conjunction with giftedness; e.g., Albert Einstein, Winston Churchill, Thomas Edison.
—Little, 2001

Many students with *visual impairments*

- Have stronger auditory or kinesthetic/tactile orientations
- Achieve better understandings with accompaniment of verbal instructions
- Experience successes with technology and adapted materials
- Acquire independent living skills with mobility training
- Progress when given visual parameters (e.g., outlines, graphic organizers)
- Have good experiences when manipulatives accompany learning of abstract concepts
- Have the same social needs and academic levels as peers with better vision

Research/literature about visual impairments says the following:

The inclusion movement has not eliminated the need for specialized schools for students who are blind. . . . [S]pecialized services enable children with visual disabilities to succeed in regular classrooms . . . providing a continuum of service options. . . . [This may be] considered to be a more restrictive environment, but [is in fact] a potentially more productive setting.
—Bina, 1999

There's a tremendous amount of technology available to students with visual impairments. . . . A cooperative effort between ViewPlus Technologies and Hewlett Packard Specialty Printing Systems has resulted in a machine that can produce Braille, and tactile graphics all on the same page. . . . Talking Book devices now offer better audio quality, easier navigation by page and chapter, and the ability to bookmark favorite passages.
—"Talking Book Machines," 2005

Itinerant Teaching: Tricks of the Trade for Teachers of Students with Visual Impairments *has suggestions for keeping up with students' equipment, organization, scheduling, travel demands . . . planning a typical day, resources [and so forth].*
—Prause, 2005

Talking computers have brought the blind to the world and the world to the blind. . . . The proponents of Braille always fall back on the same argument: If reading and writing is important to the sighted, they are important to the blind.

—Faherty, 2006

To summarize this section on disabilities, the power of positive thinking is enormous. Rather than concentrating on weaknesses, search for what students can do, giving their lives a positive rather than negative spin. This is a way to build self-esteem which often goes hand in hand with academics. Students' strengths are often neglected when their weaknesses are magnified and dissected. The following quote poignantly states the significance of concentrating on students' abilities.

If we want to prepare kids for adulthood, one of the most important things we can do is celebrate their strengths, those assets with which they're going to find meaning in life and be able to make contributions. (Levine as quoted in Scherer, 2006)

Let's celebrate the positive by connecting students' strengths to the standards. This is a way to honor both their present levels and future potentials!

ENABLING VERSUS CHALLENGING YOUR STUDENTS

Students with disabilities need varying accommodations, depending upon factors such as

- Complexity of the assignment
- Prior knowledge
- Interest level
- Class size
- Physical needs
- Social skills
- Type of presentation (concrete vs. abstract)
- Type of disability
- Individual Education Program (IEP) requirements
- Social history
- Psychological needs
- Cognitive levels
- Home support
- Individual motivation

Feasible Accommodations

Accommodations must help students master skills and standards-based curriculums, not circumvent learning the concepts. Yes, *accommodations and modifications may be necessary, but they do not replace remediation.* Teachers need to focus upon the purpose or objectives of the assignment before they plan just how they

will implement students' accommodations or modifications, if necessary. For example, what if students are asked to make a collage of magazine pictures of items that they use for good hygiene, but some students in the class do not have the fine motor coordination to use a pair of scissors? Would placing already-cutout pictures in a pile for them to choose from be an appropriate accommodation? What about using visual images on the computer? They'd still have to select appropriate pictures of hygiene items for their collage from a group of pictures. In this case, the final product will be the same, but the means of getting there is somewhat modified.

How about a student who was asked to solve a word problem on a high-stakes examination, and did all of the correct processes, but then made a careless error in the computation part? Should that student be allowed to use a calculator as an accommodation, or be given partial credit for choosing the correct problem-solving strategy? That's a call that needs to be made by individual teachers. Maybe the teacher could give that child a second try with a calculator so he or she could check the accuracy of the computation. Is the expectation to know how to solve the word problem, implementing the correct strategies, or is it to also know how to correctly perform mathematical operations, or is it both? Here the teacher needs to decide whether the accommodation of a calculator or a multiplication chart is a feasible accommodation or an enabling one. Will the accommodation or grade modification dilute the grade, or promote self-mastery and more reflections? What do the district and state recommend concerning how to accommodate the students?

How about a student that needs to perform a scientific experiment in a lab setting, but has difficulties reading grade-level vocabulary in the written directions? Would assigning a peer coach to help this student read the words or allowing the student to listen to a tape with oral directions and procedures be examples of appropriate accommodations? What about a paraeducator or educational assistant reading the directions to the student? Just what level of support would be appropriate here?

What about students with dysgraphia who are asked to demonstrate writing skills? If they struggle with the handwriting, but their thinking process is good, would it be okay if they dictated their compositions to a scribe or write with a keyboard such as an Alpha Smart? What about the child who is poor in encoding (spelling)? Should he or she be penalized for errors or given an accommodation such as a handheld electronic speller or a list of commonly misspelled words?

All of these scenarios require teachers to ask themselves,

- What are the expectations of the assignment?
- Will the accommodations provided sacrifice these expectations?
- Is the student learning?
- Are the results skewed, compromised, or legitimate?
- Do the accommodations enable the student?
- Have the student's individual needs been met?
- Am I teaching a topic or teaching individual students to learn *about* that topic?
- Will the student be assessed? If so, how?

The chart that follows allows educators to visually compartmentalize accommodations for individual students with disabilities. There's a crossover of accommodations that are applicable for different students' needs depending upon the complexity of the assignment, prior knowledge, interest, and home support. It's a guideline that brings to mind the idea that, since abilities and strengths vary, teaching strategies, accommodations, and modifications must vary as well.

(text continues on page 32)

Accommodations for Students With . . .	Learning Needs	Emotional/Social/ Behavioral Needs	Physical/ Perceptual/ Sensory Needs	Teacher/Student Concerns and Online Resources
Above Average Skills	Individualized and independent assignments with realistic and attainable goals	Lessons need to match maturity level and be age appropriate despite students' higher intelligence	Dependent upon students; observe and assess accordingly	Ongoing classroom assignments/ centers set up that honor students' advanced levels; www.cectag.org www.nagc.org
Asperger's Syndrome	Structured instruction with routines clearly explained and consistently followed; e.g., lists, graphic organizers, classroom rules	Guided social-skills training during cooperative assignments	Limit distractions, yet honor other kinesthetic/ tactile and visual presentations	Can perseverate on own interests, need to be drawn back into lessons with more reflection; www.asperger.org
Attention Deficit/ Hyperactivity Disorder	Step-by-step presentations in a structured environment with organization/ study skill instruction	Need monitoring and reinforcement for positive behavioral/social interactions	More chances to move about through *active learning*	May be on medication to control impulses, be aware of possible side effects; www.chadd.org
Auditory Processing Disabilities	Accompany verbal instruction with written models and appropriate technology	Same opportunities as peers	Increase eye contact with students when giving oral directions	May need additional time to respond; www.ncapd.org/php/
Autism	Functional vs. more advanced academics dependent upon cognitive levels	Social stories with hypothetical, yet realistic role-playing of everyday encounters with peers and adults	Tactile stimulation with concrete examples of abstract concepts; usage of more visuals	Link students with peer mentors as role models in inclusive environments; www.autism-society.org

(Continued)

(Continued)

Accommodations for Students With . . .	Learning Needs	Emotional/Social/ Behavioral Needs	Physical/ Perceptual/ Sensory Needs	Teacher/Student Concerns and Online Resources
Communication Disorders	Clear, explicit directions for academic assignments with more visual aids; e.g., visual dictionaries, videos, computer graphics	Inclusion in all social class groups; be aware of frustrations	Face student when speaking and talk in conversational tone. Ask student to paraphrase understandings	Collaborate with speech pathologists; www.asha.org
Conduct Disorders	Consistent, structured class environment with rules outlined and enforced	Behavioral/social contracts with more student metacognition; proactive approach to deter negative effect on classroom dynamics	Check students' perceptions; e.g., diary, log of thoughts, student–teacher conferences	Communicate with parents of students; behavioral strides with school–home coordination; www.nmha.org www.nimh.nih.gov
Deafness/ Hearing Loss	Optimize students' abilities; e.g., more visuals for vocabulary, outlines, copies of teacher's guides and lessons	Opportunities to effectively socialize with peers in class and extracurricular activities	Match technology with individual student needs; e.g., PECS; interactive board for easier note taking	Be aware of individual preferences; e.g., total communication, speaking, lip reading, finger spelling, or signing; www.agbell.org www.shhh.org www.deafchildren.org
Depression	Allow alternative assignment if you think academic performance was negatively influenced by emotions at time of observation, instruction, or evaluation	Have available *feel good* emotional outlets; e.g., intersperse exercise, art, or music with learning	Encourage more metacognition for students to accurately reflect on perceptions and trigger points; e.g., graph daily moods	Monitor quieter students who reach out in *silent ways*; e.g., writings, art, absences, self-care, dress; www.nimh.nih.gov

Accommodations for Students With . . .	Learning Needs	Emotional/Social/ Behavioral Needs	Physical/ Perceptual/ Sensory Needs	Teacher/Student Concerns and Online Resources
Developmental Disorders	Patient, repetitive, concrete learning presentations with concentration on functional academics	Age-appropriate activities, direct social-skill instruction; e.g., social stories	Check with school nurse for possible medical concerns	Introduce learning with high expectations for all students; www.devdelay.org www.thearc.org www.aaidd.org/
Dyscalculia	Step-by-step kinesthetic approach with real-life connections	Try to focus on other strengths to bypass math weakness; e.g., draw or write a math story	Do not penalize students for number reversals, allow and teach usage and functions of calculators	Have students record and graph their math strides; www.dyscalculia.org www.ldinfo.com
Dysgraphia	Maximize and utilize technology; e.g., from pencil grips to word prediction programs	Encourage written communication by not penalizing students for illegible thoughts	Ease fine motor strains by allowing alternative responses; e.g., express thoughts in dance or pantomime, give more frequent breaks	Decide if oral communications to a scribe or digital recorder are acceptable accommodations; www.ldinfo.com
Dyslexia	Multisensory, systematic, direct phonetic skill instruction across curriculum areas; e.g., breaking up more difficult multisyllabic vocabulary words, classifying vowel types in literature and texts	Do not embarrass students by asking them to read in front of peers, allow wait time, increase praise for reading progress, use age-appropriate materials	Increase individual student awareness of letter reversals; e.g., self-corrections and highlighters; allow students to use a ruler, blank paper, or thin overlays as line guides in readings; enlarge smaller text	Maximize technology for students to ease frustrations; e.g., books on tape, Recording for the Blind & Dyslexic; www.rfbd.org www.interdys.org www.ortonacademy .org

(Continued)

(Continued)

Accommodations for Students With . . .	Learning Needs	Emotional/Social/ Behavioral Needs	Physical/ Perceptual/ Sensory Needs	Teacher/Student Concerns and Online Resources
Executive Dysfunction	Set up checklists for students to organize, prioritize, and complete assigned learning tasks	Teacher-student conference to assess, motivate, personalize, and encourage goal setting	Step-by-step modeling helps students with sequencing, perceptual overload, and memory issues	Appropriate and realistic accommodations help students to compensate for weaker areas; www.school behavior.com http://www.tourette syndrome.net/ef_ overview.htm
Mental Retardation/ Intellectual Disabilities	Concrete, step-by-step learning presentations with modeling and repetition of specific requirements	Circumvent frustrations by rewarding approximations toward learning goals; encourage relationships with peer mentors	Ongoing communication with school nurse and families for pertinent medical history and other physical concerns	Relate learning to individual interests while trying to focus on functional and independent daily living skills; www.thearc.org www.aaidd.org/
Obsessive-Compulsive Disorder	Channel student concerns for perfection as well as possible ritualistic behavior into appropriate academic/ behavioral tasks; e.g., class sharpener or other productive daily chores	Appropriate preventive classroom interventions/ strategies; e.g., behavioral monitoring, *quiet* signals	Awareness of possible school triggers, physical effects, and emotional stress exhibited as a result of compulsions and obsessions	Understanding and patient environments that accept and do not ridicule students; www.ocfoundation.org www.adaa.org
Oppositional Defiant Disorder	Empower students with acceptable learning direction/ choices; e.g., choose 3 of these 5 listed assignments	Like the child, but dislike the behavior; try to establish ongoing, nonjudgmental, and trusting relationship	Be certain students' sensory perceptions are accurate by asking them to paraphrase rules and interactions	Do not engage in power struggles with students, but be firm, consistent, and fair; www.nmha.org www.mentalhealth.com

Accommodations for Students With . . .	Learning Needs	Emotional/Social/ Behavioral Needs	Physical/ Perceptual/ Sensory Needs	Teacher/Student Concerns and Online Resources
Physical Impairments	Realize that physical difficulties and learning deficits are not synonymous! Maximize technology options from pencil grips to paper stabilizers, bookstands, word prediction software, and more	Allow students same access and opportunities to meaningfully participate in all activities with peers	Coordinate and communicate with physical, occupational, and speech therapists to gain information and strategies to provide and maintain a safe, productive classroom environment	Ease physical fine or gross motor requirements, but do not dilute academic assignments; www.disabilitysite .net/s/physical_ disability www.ucpa.org
Sensory Impairments	Informally assess and observe students and then appeal to stronger modalities	Comparable emotional/ behavioral/social needs as peers	Depending upon individual sensory needs, lessen or increase visual/auditory elements	Use appropriate assistive technology and materials to maximize vision, hearing, and/or touch; www .devdelay.org/
Specific Learning Disability	Use task analysis to determine how to proceed and tailor remediation; challenge students but do not frustrate; increase practice and application	Vary direct skill instruction with cooperative learning to increase social skills and class cohesiveness	Address letter reversals, auditory processing issues, and visual or fine motor weaknesses that may interfere with reading, writing, and math performance	Appeal to untapped strengths and interests to motivate students and boost self-esteem; www.ldanatl.org www.ncld.org
Tourette's Syndrome	Give students multiple breaks, lessen writing requirements, be sensitive to individual needs	Educate other students and adults in the school environment about Tourette's; e.g., tics, blinking, grimaces	Allow students acceptable motoric releases of extra energy; e.g., going on errands or to another temporary private setting without peer ridicule or embarrassment	Scaffold as needed to address behavioral/ attention issues; www.tsa-usa.org http://www.tourette syndrome.net/

(Continued)

(Continued)

Accommodations for Students With . . .	Learning Needs	Emotional/Social/ Behavioral Needs	Physical/ Perceptual/ Sensory Needs	Teacher/Student Concerns and Online Resources
Traumatic Brain injury	Employ mnemonics and study guides, repetitive instruction with a step-by-step approach	Realize students' learning frustrations; praise approximations	Utilize memory-strengthening activities that appeal to multiple modalities	Determine individual students' stamina and daily thresholds; www.biausa.org
Twice-Exceptional	Vary types of instruction and assessments, using multiple intelligences and brain-based learning principles	Reward both growth and accomplishments, honoring unique social/behavioral/ emotional/ academic levels	Address various sensory, physical, and perceptual needs evidenced; enlist help of school-related services	Concentrate on growth vs. deficit paradigm http://content.bvsd .org/tag/Twice Exceptional.htm
Visual Impairments/ Blindness	Appeal to auditory and kinesthetic/ tactile modalities with increased written directions and more learning manipulatives across the subject areas	Include students in all activities with peer education for classmates about students' visual needs, interests, and areas of strengths	Eliminate frustrations by removing physical barriers in the classroom environment and school; work with mobility trainers	Optimize available technology; e.g., talking Web sites, tactile outlines; www.afb.org www.rfbd.org

Now it's time to incorporate these accommodations into students' individually written educational programs. The IEP can be thought of as a learning roadmap. Sometimes different vehicles will help educators transport students to the learning outcomes and the ultimate achievement of the standards! In addition to instructional accommodations, the IEP should specifically state the exact kind of test-taking accommodations. These accommodations include but are not limited to extra time, alternative smaller setting, someone reading directions, and larger print. Realistic instructional and testing supports may accommodate students' needs, but should remediate as well!

IEPs: BEFORE AND BEYOND THE PAPERWORK

The Individual Education Program is a living document that is meant to be revised if goals are unrealistic or inappropriate matches for students. IEPs can be just as changing as the weather. Suppose you always carry an umbrella?

Yes, it gives you increased protection during a thunderstorm, but what if it's not raining? Do students always need the same modifications in each subject area? That, too, would depend upon the changing classroom climate.

The acronym *IEP*, besides the Individual Education Program, also translates to It's Educationally Prudent. Prudence involves all students! The staircase goes up and down, with students on all levels. Sometimes students advance one step at a time, while others might learn some concepts more quickly than others. Some students have achievement strides, and then regress, or some students might even need to take an elevator instead of the stairs! The point here is that the IEP is written, and yes it must be followed, but without considering the varying student needs, you could find yourself toppling down the steps, stuck between floors, or standing in the rain without an umbrella!

Accommodations mean that students are achieving the same objectives and learning, but need adjustments to achieve those objectives; e.g., larger font or uncluttered worksheets. Modifications change the learning objective; e.g., if the class was learning about decimals, students may only learn to name decimals up to the thousandths or hundredths place, rather than the millionths place. The next chart brings these points to the top of the landing.

This chart asks teachers to look at accommodations or modifications given and see how students perform, noting specific discrepancies from prior expectations. The last column wants teachers, students, and parents to be cognizant of specific concerns and discrepancies between needed levels as the breadth of the topic broadens.

Here are some questions that can guide teachers as they plan and implement their lessons:

- Do the accommodations/modifications need to be increased?
- Do the accommodations/modifications need to be decreased?
- Are the accommodations/modifications appropriate?
- How will the student be assessed?

I would be totally remiss if I did not include the most important people in the IEP process, and they are the students and their families! The students are integral IEP members who must not be overworked, undervalued, unappreciated, or overlooked. Self-determination is a goal that needs to be developed at an early age and nurtured throughout all phases of the educational process. The amount of participation will be contingent upon factors such as the student's age, maturity level, extent of disability, and parental acceptance. However, an appropriate inclusion level is an imperative foundation for self-advocacy skills to develop.

> To many students, the IEP process and meeting may appear as alien and awkward as an annual birthday party that they do not plan or attend. (Dycke, Martin, & Lovett, 2006)

The above quote is from an article in which the authors draw an analogy between an IEP and a birthday party. They poignantly describe a child hearing about an annual event (the IEP) for years and sometimes decades, but not being a part of the *inner circle*, always viewing things from the outside. They go on to say that students need to "blow out the candles of success" instead of watching the candles burn!

Student/Dates	IEP Accommodations/ Modifications	Classroom Performance Assessments/Dates Mastery Level	Discrepancy/Concerns Comments

WHERE SHOULD CHILDREN BE PLACED?

Resources to Consult

Families, teachers, all support staff, and students require access to the information and organizations that are catalytic keys to educational/emotional success for their children, students, and themselves. All parties involved need to learn more about specific disabilities, learning strategies, how to help themselves and others, and how to network.

Specialists such as music, gym, art, and world language teachers need to be aware of the special services students with IEPs in place require in the general education classroom. This type of communication helps children succeed in all environments. Dialogue with the special education teacher responsible for that student's IEP goals must be ongoing to match necessary curriculum adaptations, behavior modifications, study skills support, help with classroom management, test-taking requirements, or even the physical setup of the class. This way the goals are not ignored, but honored in all

CHILDREN BELONG INSIDE THE LEARNING CIRCLE, NOT ON THE OUTSIDE LOOKING IN!

settings by informed and prepared staff that proactively collaborate, communicate, accommodate, or modify lessons that match students' individual needs. Administrative support must allow and slot ongoing planning and conference times between staff and families for this to be achieved.

The mentality that they are not alone in their thoughts and circumstances is a comfort to families of students with disabilities, who think that the road they are now on is not the journey they planned to embark upon or choose. It does not have to be a frustrating journey, on an unpaved road, but rather can be a smooth one. Parents and teachers should never find themselves in a tug-of-war match with school officials either. Everyone need not agree on all points, but together

the parties can compromise and decide upon the best plan for proactive home–school interventions—families, teachers, students, and all who are involved need access to this type of "educational EZ Pass" that replaces former roadblocks. Information is like a suspension bridge that connects individuals with knowledge, along with the support and confidence to move onward.

Furthermore, most teachers are willing to include students with special needs in their classrooms, but do not know enough about certain disabilities. They can't be left stranded on a deserted classroom island either. In addition, students should also be enlightened and privy to their own strengths, needs, and outlooks for the future. The following organizations' online sites and other resources for families, educators, students, and more are just a few that are out there to assist and to advance the knowledge of diversities, creating and widening learning roads and the many positive options that exist for all!

The Council for Exceptional Children (CEC)

> 1110 North Glebe Road, Suite 300, Arlington, VA 22201
> (703) 620-3660 TTY: (703) 264-9446
> www.cec.sped.org

Exceptional Parent

> 65 East Route 4, River Edge, NJ 07661
> (201) 489-4111
> www.eparent.com

Exceptional Parent Library

> (800) 535-1910
> www.eplibrary.com

HEATH Resource Center (Higher Education and Adult Training for People with Disabilities)

> 2121 K Street, NW, Suite 220, Washington, D.C., 20037
> (202) 973-0904 (800) 544-3284
> www.heath.gwu.edu

LD: Online Web site on learning disabilities for parents, teachers, and other professionals

> www.ldonline.org

Nonverbal Learning Disorders, NLDline

> www.nldline.com

> Includes information about nonverbal disorders (NLD) and neurological syndromes including deficits in motoric, visual-spatial-organizational, social, and sensory areas.

Recording for the Blind & Dyslexic (RFB&D)

> 20 Roszel Road, Princeton, NJ 08540
> (800) 221-4792
> www.rfbd.org

> Library of textbooks for students with print disabilities, from kindergarten through graduate school and beyond. Those with learning disabilities must complete certification requirements, submitting appropriate documentation.

Schwab Learning

1650 South Amphlett Boulevard, Suite 300, San Mateo, CA 94402
(650) 655-2410 (800) 230-0988
www.schwablearning.org

Developed especially for parents of children who are newly identified as having a learning difference, it is designed to be a parent's guide through the new and unfamiliar landscape of LD.

National Dissemination Center for Children With Disabilities (NICHCY)

Basics for Parents: Your Child's Evaluation is a publication of NICHCY
P.O. Box 1492, Washington, D.C. 20013
(800) 695-0285 (Voice/TTY) (202) 884-8200 (Voice/TTY)
www.nichcy.org
E-mail: nichcy@aed.org

Also offers an array of information on disabilities, the special education laws, networking opportunities, and more.

American Speech-Language-Hearing Association (ASHA)

10801 Rockville Pike, Rockville, MD 20852
(800) 638–8255
www.asha.org

National Parent Network on Disabilities

1130 17th Street NW, Suite 400, Washington D.C. 20036
(202) 463-2299
www.npnd.org

Developmental Delay Resources (DDR)

6701 Fairfax Road, Chevy Chase, MD 20815
(301) 652–2263
www.devdelay.org

Provides information and networking opportunities to parents and professionals working with children with delays in motor, sensory-motor, language, and social emotional areas.

Parent Training and Information (PTI) Centers

Contact information may be obtained from NICHCY's individual state resource sheets. Each state has a department with a division for special education, giving information and help.

You Will Dream New Dreams (2001), by Stanley Klein and Kim Schive

New York: Kensington Books
Excellent inspirational parental resource

National Parent Teacher Association

330 N. Wabash Avenue, Suite 2100, Chicago, IL 60611
(800) 307-4PTA (4782)
www.pta.org

National Center for Family Literacy

325 West Main Street, Louisville, KY 40202
(877) FAMLIT-1
www.famlit.org

Chapter Review Questions/Activities

Choose 5 disabilities from the ones in this chapter and list at least 3 possible *positive* characteristics for each one in the table below.

DisABILITY	Positive Characteristics

1. P.A.Y. (Paraphrase, Analyze, You):

   Paraphrase, analyze, and think more about the personal connection of two research/literature quotes from this chapter.

Research/Literature Quote:	_Paraphrase_ (Can you express this quote in your own words?)	_Analyze_ (Break it up; what makes the quote tick?)	_You_ (How does this information relate to your current or future student interactions?)

2. Compare and contrast applying these philosophies to challenging class-room work. Tell about the possible benefits and pitfalls for each:

Accommodations

Modifications

Deletion of content/instruction

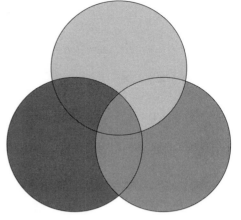

2

Understanding Assessments and Curriculum Standards

U h, oh! It's testing time, and panic permeates from teachers' pores. It prevails in the hallways, classrooms, administrative offices, and students' homes as well. *What if we don't succeed?* This question could be from school district boards of education, administrators, curriculum directors, supervisors, teachers, students, or families. Assessments are a complex process, probably as clear cut as a winding labyrinth of a road.

Now testing issues are not just up to local districts and states. With No Child Left Behind (NCLB), the assessment stakes and accountability have increased.

NCLB, which was signed into law in 2002, has four overall pillars:

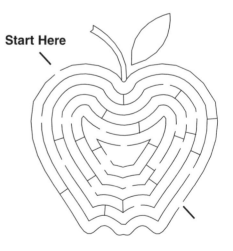

Start Here

1. Stronger accountability for results with state and local report cards, corrective options such as tutoring, along with specified time deadlines to achieve AYP (Annual Yearly Progress)

2. Flexibility for states and school districts to use money as needed; e.g., teacher training, hiring new staff

41

3. Usage of research-based educational teaching methods and programs to boost student achievements

4. More options for families of students attending low-performing or unsafe schools

---

SOURCE: www.ed.gov/nclb/overview/intro/4pillars.html

GRADING ISSUES

Since NCLB specifies research-based interventions, here's a sampling of some pertinent ones that indicate the complexities and assessment dilemmas.

Research about grading says the following:

The purpose of grading adaptations is not to make it easier for students to get higher grades, but to produce accurate, meaningful, and fair grades.

—Munk & Bursuck, 2003

When students with disabilities are part of the accountability system, educators' expectations for these students are more likely to increase. . . . Research suggests that excluding students with disabilities from school accountability measures may lead to dramatically increased rates of referral of students for special education.

—National Center on Educational Outcomes, 1997

In general, the Department estimates that about 9 percent of students with disabilities (approximately one percent of all students) have significant cognitive disabilities that qualify them to participate in an assessment based on alternate achievement standards. . . . [The] task of defining alternate achievement standards in reading/language arts, mathematics, or science for these students should begin with consideration of the State's academic content standards to reflect instructional activities appropriate for this group of students.

—U.S. Department of Education, 2005a

If you stand up for the kids and provide better instruction and assessment, we will stand by you.

—U.S. Department of Education, 2005b

Teaching for meaning is an engaging idea, but many teachers find it problematic in this age of mandates and standardized tests.

—McTighe, Seif, & Wiggins, 2004

Remember, never let teaching take a back seat to testing. When in doubt, teach. Testing is just a way to see if your teaching has been effective.

—Nolet & McLaughlin, 2005

A good education makes knowledge, skill, and ideas useful. Assessment should determine whether you can use your learning, not merely whether you learned stuff.

—Wiggins, 2006

STUDYING AND TEACHING FOR MORE THAN THE TEST

The following are some assessment questions for general and special educators to consider:

- Are the students thinking?
- Are assessments ongoing, frequent, and varied?
- Is my instruction test- or student-oriented?
- Are individual levels and interests respected and acknowledged?
- Will I vary ways for students to display competencies?
- Does my grading system give merit to efforts and progress over time?
- Do I give my students enough response time?
- Have I allowed different ways for students to show what they know (e.g., portfolios, art or music projects, oral presentations, research papers, projects, skits, WebQuests)?
- Are my tests composed of open-ended questions, or do they just require a regurgitation of facts?
- Do I have a contingency plan if a student does not test well?
- Does the atmosphere in my classroom value the merits of learning or is it all about achieving good grades?
- Do I keep individual student learning/assessment profiles?
- Do I tap into my students' strengths?
- Are my tests sensitive to culturally and linguistically diverse students?
- Do I realize that grading has multiple purposes for students, teachers, administrators, and parents?
- Can the final grade be broken down into components?
- How frequently will I test students?
- Can modifications or different weighting be made for students who struggle with tests, but put forth excellent efforts in class participation, cooperative groups, and homework assignments?
- Do I have high expectations for all students?
- Have I allowed my students to walk away feeling successful?

OTHER ASSESSMENT OPTIONS

Here are some possible options regarding alternative assessments:

- No typical format
- Portfolios of students' work
- Teacher observation

- Work samples demonstrating knowledge on alternative assessments
- Assessments based on grade-level standards
- Questions may be modified or simpler than regular assessment
- May be less complex, but still challenging with rigorous content
- Documented and validated standards-setting process
- Inclusion of alternative achievement standards for students with the most significant cognitive disabilities
- Bias-free test items
- Simple, clear instructions and procedures
- Maximum readability and comprehensibility
- Standardized scoring methods
- Professional development for teachers on how to include students with the most severe cognitive disabilities in the general education curriculum
- Guidance in the use of accommodations and administration
- Desired outcome: Production of valid and meaningful results

Again, accommodations can vary to incorporate extra time, a different setting, a modified presentation, or someone inscribing for the student. Each student has specific guidelines for testing that are directly stated in their IEP. The Individuals with Disabilities Education Act (IDEA) requires students with disabilities to participate in *all* state assessments. For purposes of IDEA compliance, a student whose score may be invalid for AYP may still be considered to be a participant in a statewide assessment. Education is not primarily about the assessments and accommodations, but hopefully about remediation as well. In the past, students with special needs were often left behind; now they are expected to achieve the same standards as peers. It's good to have high expectations, but they should be realistic ones set forth in doable timetables too! (Note: above information came from U.S. Department of Education, 2005a.)

TESTY LANGUAGE

Sometimes it's not the content of the test, but the language or format that is confusing. Even a word like *identify* can confuse students, if they do not know that it means to tell, pinpoint, locate, or recognize.

INTERPRETING DATA

What do the data mean? If a student fails a test, has he or she learned anything at all? Maybe the student's level does not meet the criteria required for a passing grade, but has the student jumped over his or her own learning hurdles? If a student scores a 62% on a test, is he or she a failure, if initially the child only understood 30% of the material before instruction began? Some teachers argue that failing test scores from students prove that these students do not belong in the "regular" classroom. Does that make them "irregular" learners who once again

Table 2.1   Understanding *Testy* Words

Words	Interpretation
Mainly about	Subject or topic of a passage
Topic sentence	Sentence that sums up the main idea
Passage or selection	May be a few paragraphs, a poem, news article, advertisement, and more
Most	↑
Least	↓
Except	Not ≠
Probably	Most likely
Tone	Feeling, emotion, or mood
Positive tone	☺
Negative tone	☹
Neutral tone	😐
Fact	True, can include details
Opinion	What you think, can't be proven
Sequence	Order of events, such as first, next, later, after, finally
Out of sequence	Not in order, mixed-up events
Omitted	Oops! Left out, not included
Table of Contents	TOC At the beginning of a book, listing of chapters with topics and page numbers
Index	Located at the back of a book, alphabetical listing of subjects
Glossary	Dictionary defining vocabulary words, located at the back of a book

belong in "irregular" classrooms? The goal of special education or *any* education is to prepare students to lead independent lives as productive members of the community. The data in the next chart, released by the U.S. Department of Education in August of 2005, support the fact that students with disabilities have made excellent transitional gains. What a coincidence that these gains were made during a time period when inclusion became more prevalent! Or, maybe it's not a coincidence, but an educational plan that worked. Many educators are doing something right here! The data speak for themselves.

Table 2.2 Changes Over Time in the Early Post School Outcomes of Youth With Disabilities

National Longitudinal Transitions Study	1987	2003
Students completing high school	53.5%	70.3%
Students enrolled in postsecondary education	14.6%	31.9%
Two-year college	3.6%	20.8%
Four-year college	1.3%	9.6%

SOURCE: Samuels, C. (2005, August 10). Disability less likely to hold back youths following high school. *Education Week, 24*(44), 1–19.

This study is promising, but there are some other things to consider as well. African Americans and Hispanic/Latino youth still need to show more improvements. In addition, students with emotional disturbances and other health impairments made fewer achievements than other disability groups. Students with physical, hearing, and visual impairments made the most gains in college attendance. (Samuels, 2005.)

The following ideas can assist educators in their quest to help students with cultural diversity and emotional differences achieve equitable gains as well:

- Realize that family dynamics often differ from school values.
- Accept that students with cultural or emotional differences have distinct needs that may vary from teachers' academic agendas.
- Teaching the whole child acknowledges students' differences.
- Differences can not only be acknowledged, but also honored and treated as strengths, not deficits.
- Activities that promote more self-awareness of academic and social levels need to be infused in classrooms.
- Peers often isolate those who do not conform to a *group mentality.* To circumvent this, teachers need to include and model more classroom team-building activities.
- Students need practice with the language of standardized testing since varying interpretations can interfere with a test's intended meaning and validity.
- Realize that emotional factors may interfere with testing performance.
- Include more visuals in instruction and evaluations.
- Classroom needs to embrace, not isolate, differences in a *mixed salad atmosphere* that nutritionally tosses together students to achieve a sense of belonging vs. isolation.
- Include literature from cultures and realistic viewpoints that match those of students, thereby validating more than just the mainstream culture.

EMPOWERING STUDENTS BY DEMYSTIFYING THE GRADING SYSTEM

Teachers that share their grading system with students hand over the keys to the car with a license to succeed since the students now know the rules of the road. The next pie chart is a sample classroom division indicating just what counts toward a grade.

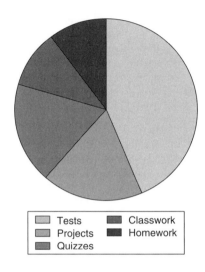

Tests	Projects	Quizzes	Classroom Participation	Homework
40%	20%	20%	10%	10%

Rubrics: Using rubrics allows students to know teachers' classroom expectations and requirements for individual assignments. A sample writing rubric follows.

Student Monitoring

Equally important is to allow students to record their subject grades for each marking period throughout the year to track their progress and needs. The following metacognitive sheet can be duplicated, stapled, and distributed in sets of four to students for each quarter.

MOVING FORWARD

There are a variety of ways to teach students. On a topic such as the French and Indian War, students can be shown a video or a slide presentation, read a textbook passage or historical novel, act out a play, complete cooperative assignments, or listen to a lecture with guided note taking—for example, they could fill in graphic organizers and outlines. Just as there are different modes of instruction, evaluations can also vary. The following offers different

Category	4—Excellent	3—Good	2—Fair	1—Needs Improvement
Introduction (Organization)	The introduction is inviting, states the main topic, and previews the structure of the paper.	The introduction clearly states the main topic and previews the structure of the paper, but is not particularly inviting to the reader.	The introduction states the main topic, but does not adequately preview the structure of the paper nor is it particularly inviting to the reader.	There is no clear introduction of the main topic or structure of the paper.
Transitions (Organization)	A variety of thoughtful transitions are used. They clearly show how ideas are connected.	Transitions clearly show how ideas are connected, but there is little variety.	Some transitions work well, but connections between other ideas are fuzzy.	The transitions between ideas are unclear or nonexistent.
Support for Topic (Content)	Relevant, telling, quality details give the reader important information that goes beyond the obvious or predictable.	Supporting details and information are relevant, but one key issue or portion of the story line is unsupported.	Supporting details and information are relevant, but several key issues or portions of the story line are unsupported.	Supporting details and information are typically unclear or not related to the topic.
Focus on Topic (Content)	There is one clear, well-focused topic. Main idea stands out and is supported by detailed information.	Main idea is clear but the supporting information is general.	Main idea is somewhat clear but there is a need for more supporting information.	The main idea is not clear. There is a seemingly random collection of information.
Sentence Length (Sentence Fluency)	Every paragraph has sentences that vary in length.	Almost all paragraphs have sentences that vary in length.	Some sentences vary in length.	Sentences rarely vary in length.
Grammar and Spelling (Conventions)	Writer makes no errors in grammar or spelling that distract the reader from the content.	Writer makes 1–2 errors in grammar or spelling that distract the reader from the content.	Writer makes 3–4 errors in grammar or spelling that distract the reader from the content.	Writer makes more than 4 errors in grammar or spelling that distract the reader from the content.
Word Choice	Writer uses vivid words and phrases that linger or draw pictures in the reader's mind, and the choice and placement of the words seems accurate, natural, and not forced.	Writer uses vivid words and phrases that linger or draw pictures in the reader's mind, but occasionally the words are used inaccurately or seem overdone.	Writer uses words that communicate clearly, but the writing lacks variety, punch, or flair.	Writer uses a limited vocabulary that does not communicate strongly or capture the reader's interest. Jargon or clichés may be present and detract from the meaning.
Conclusion (Organization)	The conclusion is strong and leaves readers with a feeling that they understand what the writer is "getting at."	The conclusion is recognizable and ties up almost all the loose ends.	The conclusion is recognizable, but does not tie up several loose ends.	There is no clear conclusion; the paper just ends.

SOURCE: Karten, T. (2005). *Inclusion strategies that work!* Thousand Oaks, CA: Corwin Press.

Table 2.3   How Am I Doing?

Circle marking period:

1   2   3   4

My Grades

Reading/Language									
Writing									
Spelling									
Math									
Science									
Social Studies									
Music									
Art									
Physical Education									
World Language									

presentations and four assessment options on the topic of the French and Indian War. First off, students are asked to list what they deem to be the main ideas concerning this conflict, to establish prior knowledge. Next, the students read a nonfiction selection about the incident and then write and act out their own play to learn more. This particular lesson addresses the NCSS (National Council for the Social Studies) standards by having students learn how human beings interacted in their environment with reference to power, authority, and governance.

Sample Lesson 1

French and Indian War: Prelude to the American Revolution

Before students receive any formal classroom instruction about this topic, they are asked, "Do you know what happened during the French and Indian War?" to establish prior knowledge. Students are then directed to list as many facts as they know. Afterward, they complete the readings to compare their prior knowledge with the facts from their texts, nonfiction books on the historical topic, and/or online research. To assess their knowledge and take it a step higher on Bloom's Taxonomy—beyond just knowledge and comprehension, to synthesis, analysis, application, and evaluation—the students then cooperatively write a play about the French and Indian War, including the verified facts from readings and instruction. A sample of such a play follows.

Remember that this is just one example of how instruction and evaluation options can be applied across the content areas. Notice the incredible amount of facts included. It's a viable alternative to boring textbook readings, yet students delve into texts anyway!

Background to American Revolution Play

<u>Narrator</u>: The year is 1740 and there are problems between the French fur traders and the British in the Ohio River Valley.

<u>French</u>: We have to protect our land and fur trade from the British. We will build forts to keep the British out.

<u>George Washington</u>: We tried to stop you by building Fort Necessity and had some fierce battles. Even though we lost to you French then, everyone recognized me as a great military leader. That's probably why I became a general and then president of our country.

<u>Ben Franklin</u>: I think we need to get the Native Americans on our side. Let's try to get the Iroquois to join the British and the colonists in our battle against the French. We met in Albany, but the colonists weren't ready to join together and the Iroquois still don't want to take sides. All in all, I'd rather be flying a kite!

<u>Iroquois and other Native Americans</u>: We are trying to stay neutral, and not side with the British and colonists against the French, but everyone keeps taking our land! Finally we decided to side with the French and become their allies.

British: That's it! We declare war on France!

Narrator: It is 1756 and it will be the beginning of what will later be known as the *French and Indian War.*

Pontiac: I am a great Ottawa chief and I want to stop the British from taking our land. I will organize my people to rise up and attack British forts.

British: Okay, we will respond with a proclamation. This is being issued in response to Pontiac's Rebellion. We declare that all land west of the Appalachian Mountains is owned by Native Americans, not the colonists.

American colonists: Who cares about the Proclamation of 1763? We are moving west. Let's ignore the proclamation!

French: We tried our best, but we surrender. We will sign this treaty.

Narrator: In 1763, the Treaty of Paris was signed and this war was over. France lost all of its land in North America and Britain gained a lot of land. Native Americans also kept losing land as colonists moved further westward. Now Britain has to send many more soldiers to protect all of this new land. Because of the French and Indian War, Great Britain was having money problems and asked the colonists to help pay for the soldiers who were protecting the colonists' land. The Parliament, which was the British government, issued the Stamp Act—a tax on all paper goods—to help pay for keeping soldiers here.

Colonists: We will ask Britain to repeal or cancel this tax law! How dare Britain tax us!

Britain: Okay, we will take the Stamp Act back but replace it with the Townsend Acts, which tax imported goods from England.

Colonists: We hate these also! We will not pay taxes on paint, paper, glass, lead, or tea!

Sons of Liberty: We refuse to purchase any paper goods! The Daughters of Liberty will now make their own tea and clothes. We protest these taxes. We will boycott or refuse to buy these goods! No taxation without representation!

Britain: We will not stand for this protest from you colonists. Parliament has allowed us to send British troops to Boston.

Narrator: This was the beginning of the trouble between Great Britain and the colonists, about 250 years ago. It eventually led to the American Revolutionary War.

Now, after writing and putting on the play, students are evaluated. Only, who says that the assessment on this topic must be one generic shape or form? Just as instruction may be varied, so too can students' learning achievements be determined in different ways. The following options illustrate this point.

Sample Assessments

Ways to Assess This Subject

Choose one of the 4 assignments below:

1. List 3 points you now understand about this conflict.

   a.

   b.

   c.

2. Draw a captioned picture about what you heard on the back of this page.

3. Fill in the blanks below.

> The _____ wanted more land in North America during the _____ century. The French had a large _____ trade here. The _____ declared war on France. _____ was a leader of the colonists at this time. Britain was having money problems and asked the colonists to pay _____. The Sons of Liberty declared, "No taxation without _____!" Parliament sent British _____ to Boston.

4. Research the French and Indian War online and write a paragraph describing what happened. Include information that addresses all 5 w's: what, where, when, who, and why.

The first assessment option might be chosen by the auditory learner, who has a good short-term memory. The second option asks students to draw a picture, visualizing the events, honoring the creative student who prefers to use his or her visual-spatial intelligence. The third choice wants the student to complete the cloze exercise by filling in missing key content-related words, thereby assessing the student's retention of the main concepts taught, focusing more on reading and writing skills. The last option respects the independent, more introspective learners who need more wait time and prefer to show what they know in their own setting, using online sources. This last option also allows a learner who may have been inattentive during instruction, not focused, or disinterested in the topic a chance to redeem him- or herself by conducting outside research. Maybe this student is also a logical thinker who prefers technology as his or her means of instruction. If the point is to determine what each student knows, then why not provide several options such as these to assess students' knowledge?

The following chart is an example of an informal type of assessment that monitors functional objectives throughout the school year. Keeping track of progress with quarterly checklists such as this one allows the teacher at a quick glance to note and rate progress. If it is then shared with families and students, the learning becomes an even more reflective and concrete tool for all. Sometimes it's not the academic content, but social issues, behaviors, or even the lack of motivation and necessary study skills that interferes with a student's progress. The *ABCD* chart that follows allows teachers a chance to monitor these objectives throughout the year.

ABCD* Quarterly Checklist of Functional Objectives *Student:*_____	*Sept.*	*Dec.*	*Mar.*	*June*
1. Establishes eye contact with teachers and peers				
2. Uses proper conversational tones				
3. Follows classroom and school rules				
4. Respects authority				
5. Exhibits social reciprocity				
6. Appropriately communicates needs				
7. Demonstrates consistent attention in classroom lessons				
8. Completes all classroom assignments				
9. Finishes all homework and long-range assignments				
10. Is able to independently takes class notes				
11. Writes legibly				
12. Has an organized work area				
13. Respects the property of others				
14. Works well with groups				
15. Adjusts to changes in routines				
16. Asks for clarification when needed				
17. Takes pride in achievements				
18. Displays enthusiasm about learning				
*Use these codes:				
A = Always				
B = Becoming better				
C = Can with reminders				
D = Doesn't display behavior				

Chapter Review Questions/Activities

Explain how grading, assessments, and analyzing data help the following people:

- Teachers
- Students
- Administration
- Parents
- Legislators

Cooperatively or individually think of an *instructional twist* to a topic or concept (use the French and Indian War as your model). Then give three different ways you plan on assessing students' knowledge/competencies.

Topic/Concept	Lesson Plan (with instructional twist)	3 Ways to Assess

3

How Students Learn

Brain Basics

The following research offers information on types of learners and ways that students learn. Gaining feedback and more metacognition is crucial for students and teachers. This chapter also stresses using multiple intelligences and project-based learning to motivate and focus on students' interests and strengths.

> *Research from the National Institutes of Health clearly indicates that good instruction actually improves how the student learns. New evidence-based instructional programs geared toward the needs of individual children are opening educational doors for students who never before had a chance to achieve academically.*
>
> —U.S. Department of Education, 2005b

> *If different methodologies are appropriate for addressing important questions in special education . . . we must be clear about the match between research findings and effective practices provided by methodology.*
>
> —Odom et al., 2005

How fortunate we are to live in an age of science in which research has taken us inside a human brain. Teachers' observations have always led to speculations, but now technologies such as positron emission tomography (PET) have confirmed the many existing pedagogical theories. Here's the dilemma though: all of this incredible research is wasted if, first off, teachers, students, and parents are not privy to this knowledge and, second, classroom lessons are not designed to include the best practices advocated.

Emotions also influence the way individuals learn. If a student is feeling fearful, angry, frustrated, or sad, how can that student attend to and understand a given lesson? Other students are highly motivated, yet have true academic issues, along with perceptual needs that interfere with their learning. Beyond understanding students' dis*abili*-*ties*, teachers must acknowledge and address how students learn, considering the whole child, not just the lesson objectives they've outlined. Vital organs such as the brain and heart must be nourished and duly honored, not ignored.

RESEARCH IMPLICATIONS

Research about the brain says the following:

> *We would be imprudent to ignore the brain research and say it has no implications for teaching and learning. . . . [T]he better we understand the brain, the better we will be able to educate it.*
>
> —Wolfe, 2001

> *No two brains are alike; from conception to puberty, students' brains weed out nearly 80% of their cells, keeping only the most useful 20% or so. The nerve cells they do keep form pathways of differing strengths based on frequency of use. So teachers must realize every brain—and student—is unique. Therefore, even the very best instructional strategy will not be best for everyone.*
>
> —Nunley, 2003

> *Diverse emotions such as sadness or joy, fear or excitement, surprise, disgust, contentment or anger, each have their own brain pathways and associated chemicals that if charged, can interfere with the delivery of even the best-designed lessons.*
>
> —www.projectcriss.com

> *Not all neuroscientists agree. Brain research doesn't prove things; it's up to us as educators to work in the laboratory called the classroom to take the research and interpret it for our use.*
>
> —Franklin, 2005

> *Neuroscientists have established that the storage and strength of memories can be increased if learning is done both at the emotional and at the cognitive level.*
>
> —LeDoux, 1997

> *Learning should feel good, and the student should become aware of those feelings.*
>
> —Zull, 2004

BASIC PRINCIPLES OF BRAIN-BASED LEARNING STRATEGY

- The brain changes and grows from repeated experiences and stimuli.
- Each child's brain is unique.
- Threat and fear responses activate responses in the amygdala, affecting how students think, feel, relate to others, and remember.
- Negative attention with bad emotional reactions decreases learning.
- There are links between movement and learning.
- Curricular areas are not remembered best with rote learning.
- The brain learns more when connections are made with prior knowledge.
- Repeating the context of learning helps students recall lessons.
- Students need wait time to recall facts.
- The brain likes when things make sense and form patterns.
- Activities such as simulations and role-playing provide real-life emotional connections.

LINK   REVIEW   REPEAT CONCEPTS   INCORPORATE INTO LIVES

Resources to Consult:

National Science Teacher's Association: www.nsta.org

National Council for the Social Studies: www.ncss.org

National Council of Teachers of Mathematics: www.nctm.org

National Council of Teachers of English: www.ncte.org

National Association for Music Education: www.menc.org

National Standards for Physical Education—American Alliance for Health, Physical Education, Recreation and Dance: www.aahperd.org/NASPE/publications-national standards.html

The Kennedy Center ArtsEdge: www.artsedge.kennedy-center.org/teach/standards. cfm

Franklin, J. (2005, June). Mental mileage: How teachers are putting brain research to use. *Education Update, 47(6),* Alexandria, VA: Association for Supervision and Curriculum Development.

Gregory, G., & Chapman, C. (2007). *Differentiated instructional strategies* (2nd ed.). Thousand Oaks, CA: Corwin Press.

Jensen. E. (1998). *Teaching with the brain in mind.* Alexandria, VA: Association for Supervision and Curriculum Development.

Nunley, K. (2003). Layered curriculum brings teachers to tiers. *Education Digest, 69,* 1.

Sousa, D. (2002). *How the special needs brain learns* (2nd ed.). Thousand Oaks, CA: Corwin Press.

Sylwester, R. (2005). *How to explain a brain.* Thousand Oaks, CA: Corwin Press.

Zull, J. (2004). The art of changing the brain. *Educational Leadership, 62,* 68–72.

Obviously, there are complex issues involved as the brain sends messages that students receive. Cognitive, academic, behavioral/social, learning, perceptual, communicative, and physical issues are all components that make up individual student responses and performances. Everybody's brain is wired differently. In addition, personalities are influenced by environments in which students are raised and taught. Genetics plays a role as does a lack of learning exposure in exclusive vs. inclusive settings. The chart that follows is meant to help educators and adults who come into contact with students to focus on an array of open-ended questions. Not all of these questions can be answered in the course of a day, but throughout the year, many of these questions can help teachers tailor lessons with curriculum-based objectives that match and focus on students' unique characteristics. It brings to mind that at times the weaknesses must be circumvented to allow students' strengths to flourish!

Connective Academic Issues:

Cognitive levels:

Is the student a concrete learner who has difficulties with abstract facts?

Is that learner operating at his or her frustration level, missing prior knowledge?

Learning concerns:

What value does education have in the student's home environment?

Have prior experiences soured this student to learning?

Is the student attending to classroom instruction and exhibiting appropriate study skills?

Behavioral/social issues:

Does the student care more about fitting in and being cool than about what is being taught?

Is the student quiet, shy, or overly withdrawn, keeping to him- or herself?

Does the student cooperate and socialize with peers in formal and informal assignments?

Perceptual issues:

Are visual or auditory confusions interfering with the understanding of reading, math, or other content areas?

Is the child lacking self-regulation or overwhelmed by internal or external distractions?

Communicative needs:

Can the student verbalize misunderstandings?

Does the student's command of the English language match the instruction given?

Physical difficulties:

What fine or gross motor issues must receive proper environmental/student accommodations?

Are some tasks too physically demanding?

MULTIPLE INTELLIGENCES HONORED

Just as the sounds of string, woodwind, and percussion instruments combine to create a symphony, the different intelligences intermix within a student to yield meaningful scholastic achievement and accomplishments. (Gardner, 2006)

In recognition of Howard Gardner, remember these multiply intelligent learning options. Touch upon ones that you as an educator might not prefer,

---

I can use_____

Visual-Spatial:

Clip art, Post-its, graphic organizers, illustrations, charts, technology programs such as interactive boards, online museum sites, digital storytelling, content-related art projects that sharpen perceptual needs, and observational skills

Bodily-Kinesthetic:

Manipulatives such as clay, pipe cleaners, toothpicks, salt, koosh balls, kneaded erasers, content-related movement exercises during classroom instruction, and brain breaks that stretch the body and mind

Interpersonal:

Cooperative learning, plays, role-playing, committees, stations

Intrapersonal:

Journals, self-directed learning, tape recorders, candid videos, mirrors, writer's notebooks, diaries, graphing progress, metacognitive reflections

Verbal-Linguistic:

Books, tapes, debates, poems, essays, videos, magazines, newspapers, weekly readers, illustrative charts and graphs

Logical-Mathematical:

Computers, thinking activities for deductive and inductive reasoning, life-related learning such as catalogue shopping sprees to improve computational skills or coupon clipping, classroom consistency with rules and structure outlined

Musical-Rhythmic:

Songs with content-related lyrics, environmental sounds, instruments, creative expressions and interpretations, background sounds or music while learning, tapping to the learning

Naturalist:

Organized school and home environments, classification projects, community connections such as beautification projects and more recycling efforts

Existential:

Questionnaires, surveys, quotes, infinite sources, those things beyond sensory data, reflective classroom

---

but are students' favorites. Encourage students to branch out as well in *intelligent* ways! Also, you might check out Gardner's Web site, www.infed.org/thinkers/gardner.htm.

PROJECT- AND STUDENT-BASED LEARNING STRATEGY

Much is to be gained when projects assigned are not just about the projects, but draw students into the learning with personalized connections. Yes, the theme can be generic; however, the skills infused are based upon students' needs, strengths, interests, and multiple intelligences, as well as specific content, state-mandated, and national standards. Teaching and learning can be fun, not just a rote delivery of assignments. Projects need not overwhelm either the students or the parents, but through their completion, they can teach students strategies and skills that will help them to feel a sense of accomplishment. Students can learn how to compensate for weaker areas, and then apply and generalize their learnings as exemplified through these sample month-by-month projects.

September Project

Now that you have returned to school, it's time to prepare lessons for the year. Make a wish list of what you'd like to learn about in each subject. Then pick one topic and prepare a lesson for the class. (Younger and more concrete learners will orally scribe thoughts, cut out magazine pictures, use clip art, or illustrate ideas and interests. Each month another student will teach his or her lesson.)

October Project

In some parts of the world, October is a time for changes. For example, leaves turn color, birds migrate to warmer climates, people wear different clothing, and pumpkins grow. The theme here is changes that exist in nature. Take a walk outside and observe and record what you see in your surroundings. Be as detailed as possible, squaring off an area and listing or illustrating what you see. Then make a predictive list or predictive illustrations of how you think the same area will look in 4 weeks. After the month has passed, review your area again and share your findings with the class. How close were your predictions? What changes actually took place? (Younger learners can also photograph pre and post pictures of their spaces in nature.)

This activity supports the NSTA (National Science Teacher's Association) recommendation to learn about interactions and changes among populations, resources, and environments.

November Project

Just what are you thankful for and what are you hoping for others? Research what children from another country might do on a typical day. Compare and contrast your typical day to theirs. Would you like to trade places with them? If you could change their day, what would you try to include? What do you think they are thankful for? What are you thankful for? What are your hopes for yourself, and for others? (Some students can verbally list their thoughts.)

This project supports the NCSS (National Council for the Social Studies) recommendation to learn about people, places, cultural diversity, individual development and identity, global connections, and interdependence.

January Project

Define a New Year's resolution (strong wish). Then interview 5 people, asking them their wish for the New Year and the steps or plan they are taking to make that resolution happen. Then interview yourself. Pick your favorite resolution and share it with the class. Act it out in a skit with you playing multiple characters; compose a song or poem or choreograph a dance that highlights the New Year's resolution. (Students could also draw wish pictures.)

This project values dramatization, song, and critical and creative thinking skills in dance as recommended by Kennedy Center ArtsEdge, www.artsedge.kennedy-center.org/teach/standards.cfm. It also encourages more understandings about individual development and how human beings view themselves, as recommended by the NCSS (National Council for the Social Studies).

February Project

Hearts are organs inside our bodies, but are often given more credence than other organs on Valentine's Day and other times. For example, we have chocolate candy "hearts" and we even say, "You broke my heart" or "That's a heartache!" With a few classmates, cooperatively choose another organ and design products that personify it. Some students in the class can trace, outline, or color pictures of organs if this assignment is too difficult. Others can also label the locations of organs within our bodies. Students with more time or advanced skills can investigate illnesses caused by organ dysfunctions and how to prevent them. The culmination of the lesson will be Valentine's Day cards, of course!

This project supports the NSTA (National Science Teacher's Association) recommendation to learn how organisms function.

March Project

March onward! The subject here is marching. With a group of classmates, pick a musical piece as your background and design a march to the song. Your lyrics (words to your song) need to be about something you have learned in language arts, math, science, or social studies. The key is to plan, sing, recite, step, and learn together in March and other months!

This activity supports the MENC (National Association of Music Education) recommendation to increase understanding of relationships between music, the other arts, and disciplines outside the arts. In addition, it supports the NCTM (National Council of Teachers of Mathematics) idea of applying mathematical principles to other contexts.

April Project

Look around you and discover things that are new and blooming. Find a favorite flower to sketch, press, or write about in a poem. Listen to and imitate the spring sounds. Look at the birds, squirrels, and other animals scurrying. Make an advertisement, song, or diorama about the seasonal changes and rebirth you see in your environment.

This project supports the NSTA (National Science Teacher's Association) recommendation to learn about organisms along with changes in populations and environments.

May Project

Complete this statement in a brief paragraph:
One day I may . . .

Then pair up with another classmate to combine your thoughts:
Together we may . . .

Illustrate both of your thoughts in a cartoon, storyboard, poem, song, or dance to share with classmates.

This project supports the NCTE (National Council of Teachers of English) standards to communicate effectively by using spoken, written, and visual language.

June Project

Summer, weddings, flowers, swimming, camps, no homework, and vacations may be some of the things that you are thinking about now. However, think about the past school year too. Pick a subject: Science, Social Studies, Math, Health, Language Arts, Art, or Music. Next, choose your favorite topic in that subject. Now teach a lesson to the class about a subject that you have learned about this year. Use the class texts or other research materials to help you. You can create a PowerPoint presentation, mural, storyboard, dance, or skit on that topic. Also, design an assessment for the class (now your students). Will your tests have essays, multiple-choice questions, true/false, or open-ended questions? Decide on the point value for your questions. Now, remember to find out more about some of these things over the summer!

This project supports the NCTM (National Council of Teachers of Mathematics) standards by applying number systems, making connections, and using computations outside mathematics. It also gives merit to the use of technology to communicate ideas. In addition, it connects the visual arts to other disciplines, values classroom dramatizations, and uses dance as a way to communicate meaning, with reference to the Kennedy Center ArtsEdge, http://artsedge .kennedy-center.org/teach/standards.cfm

The next activity focuses not only on matching standards with students' strengths, but also on the important concept of student motivation. Emotional intelligence greatly influences academic performances. The *possibilities* follow!

POS-*ABILITIES*: PLEDGE OF STUDENT ALLEGIANCE STRATEGY

Is it possible that some students just don't care about school? It's a rhetorical question, but a vital one to ask. Students need to be ready to learn, before subjects are differentiated. Just as we pledge our allegiance to the flag, which represents our country, students must pledge their allegiance to the concept of learning. I've had students repeat this pledge daily, reading from their individual copy, which can be kept in a folder, notebook, or loose-leaf binder. Aside from putting this motivation issue right on a child's lap or shoulders, it increases vocabulary and adds a touch of humor to those sleepy and disaffected learners who realize just how tenacious you are about getting them to commit to learning. Without their consistent motivation, no matter how much planning time goes into a given lesson, the best of instructional designs is a lesson with the theme of futility for educators and students.

Directions: Teachers ask students to recite the following pledge, substituting the word "morning" or "afternoon," depending upon the time of day. Another excellent activity is for students to cooperatively design a learning symbol. Just as the flag represents our country, what classroom signs might represent learning? Students can design one as a class or work in teams, and then vote on which one they like best, or even combine elements from different ones. Now they've taken ownership of their commitment to not only be physically present, but emotionally as well! This links to the NCSS standards by valuing individual identity and interactions with others. It also emphasizes collective principles and ideals.

Student Pledge (to be recited with enthusiasm!)

I know it's the *morning* (afternoon)

And we're *still yawning* (leaving soon)

But this is my promise for *today* (now)

When I will *say* (vow)

That I will do my best

And it's not said in jest

To really care

And be sincere

To listen and learn

And respect each in turn

We all have many a need

But we all can succeed

If we use our mind

And to each other be kind

So here I am in school

Where not only teachers rule

But it's each student

That needs to be prudent

If I have a positive attitude

I could master math, reading, and even latitude

The implications are great

I decide my own fate

So I'll give it my best try

And that's no lie

It's my promise, no fingers crossed

I'll ask questions when I'm lost

I'll care about this stuff

Even when the going gets tough

And I think I'll even smile

May as well, I'll be here awhile

—© 2005 by Toby J. Karten

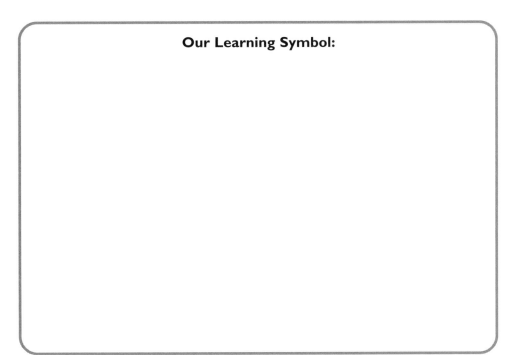

Our Learning Symbol:

Younger learners or students with lower vocabulary or reading levels can view digital movies of themselves during classroom learning and then be asked if they think they were paying attention. They can also be shown candid classroom pictures of themselves to increase metacognitive levels, and read or repeat a simpler pledge such as

I can

Plan

And say

Each day

Will be fine

I won't whine

I will always try

And that's no lie

There are a lot of facts I need

That will feed

My budding brain

And I won't complain

Because being smart

Is an art

So I promise to grow

To be a kid who'll know!

—© 2005 by Toby J. Karten

Chapter Review Questions/Activities

- How can teachers pragmatically develop a plan with other teachers, assistants, students, and parents to prevent cognitive, behavioral/social/ emotional, learning, physical, communicative, and perceptual issues from interfering with lessons?

- Cooperatively use the *brainy info* in this chapter to create a poem about how the principles of brain-based learning relate to education.

- Explain what is meant by the following quote: "I don't teach geometry. I teach students geometry."

4

How Teachers Teach

Good Practices for All

Special education research, because of its complexity, may be the hardest of the hardest-to-do science. One feature of special education research that makes it more complex is the variability of the participants.

—Odom et al., 2005

When classified students are included in classrooms, both special education and general education teachers are indeed challenged to figure out ways that students with special needs can learn skills and strategies in a whole-class environment as opposed to a small-group setting. Some teachers are under so much pressure, trying to do it all, while a few do not even try to adjust their way of teaching to reach a variety of learners. However, with the right attitude and support, all students can learn and be successful.

First off, educators must buy in, and know that students do not know. Some educators feverishly try to teach every aspect of a concept without intermittently stopping the learning and assessing the knowledge. Students need to practice, apply, and test out the *new stuff.* Teachers, assuming that the students *know the lesson,* often allow misconceptions to escalate! It may sound ridiculous, but some teachers need to do less. When teachers observe and listen to the verbal and body language of their students, they are more attuned to their students' needs, even before formal assessments are given. Classified students in inclusive classrooms are often quite good at *feigning* their understanding with the correct body language, such as direct eye contact or even nodding their head, without actually *getting the concept.* Frequent observation and assessment of their knowledge, such as asking students to paraphrase their understandings with informal questions, is a valuable and revealing strategy. Sometimes, educators, paraeducators, and even parents want to help, but they instead enable students by doing more than the students do on their own. Good practices also include letting students realize their levels and mistakes, before the learning is corrected by an

67

adult. This accurate self-reflection can then yield compensatory strategies for students to develop under teachers' and families' coordinated auspices.

Keeping this in mind, grade-level teachers sometimes get quite caught up in what can be dubbed as *speed teaching.* Here's an example: From Monday to Friday, we will learn all about igneous rocks. Next week's lesson will uncover sedimentary rocks, while the following week, we'll dig up facts about metamorphic rocks. After that, it's time to launch forward with astronomy. Okay, we all like to reach for the stars sometime in our lives, but where are the connections? By the time you deal with the next topic, most students have forgotten the prior learning, since they—forgive the pun—no longer have rocks in their head. Quite a classroom avalanche!

Next, here's a huge bonus of inclusion. Instead of singling out students within the room for specialized instruction, drill, redrill, or just about any needs governed by the *paper IEP* or the *commonsense IEP* (it's educationally prudent), why not teach the skill or strategy to the whole class? For example, my students, when formerly pulled out for instruction, recorded and graphed their test grades for all subjects during each marking period in a folder with their name on it, which was kept in a separate room. This metacognitive grading system helped them to stay on track and visually see which subjects and areas they needed to improve. I was then faced with a conundrum: How do I let them continue to record their grades when they are no longer pulled out, but, as their program currently states, included in the classroom full time, with two teachers supporting them? My answer was simple: Why not let entire classes record their grades too? Couldn't this metacognitive strategy benefit the general education students as well?

Another time, I was concerned with students completing long-range assignments on time. In this instance, I collaborated with my coteacher, and we decided that the entire class would be given monthly calendars to track upcoming school events, tests, assemblies, reports, and anything else. This general educator continues to use monthly calendars with all of his students, classified or not! The wonderful side effect of inclusion is that it benefits the "regular" kids too. Good practices are not exclusive to only those students with IEPs!

The appropriate delivery ensures the successful mastery of any set of teaching/learning objectives. So what constitutes appropriate learning objectives? They need to be spiraling, vertically and horizontally aligned, student-based, interdisciplinary, standards-based, content-driven, and challenging, thereby allowing students of all levels to reap successes. Consequently, well-designed instruction allows students to generalize, apply, and connect learning principles to their lives. Teachers not only teach, but also have the instructional power to create lifelong learners, instilled with the joy of knowledge, or the *joie de learning.* Teachers who give step-by-step explanations avoid the rushed instructional pace that sometimes leads to nowhere quickly! Modeling examples and frequently checking baseline knowledge is crucial. All students benefit from creative teachers whose delivery and communication systems advocate and propagate the idea that learning is meaningful, *including inclusive classrooms!*

Most important is that the classroom is not a teacher-centered one, but rather one that fosters long-term student learning and achievements leading toward mastery of the general education curriculum. When it's student-centered, individual needs are addressed, aiding curriculum connections. Connecting to real-world issues through problem-based learning infuses the classroom with

Table 4.1   ICES: Inclusion Communication Exchange System

	Inclusion	*Communication*	*Exchange*	*System*
Nouns	involvement infusion interactions	consistency concepts collaboration	expertise emotions equity	supports students strengths
Verbs	involve interact improve	communicate collaborate coteach	evolve empower educate	support spiral structure
Adjectives	inclusionary interdisciplinary interactive	consistent critical conceptual	evolutionary effective emotive	supportive successful specialized
Adverbs	infectiously interactively intelligently	collaboratively cognitively conceptually	eventually emphatically effectively	supportively systematically skillfully

knowledge that goes way beyond the textbook facts and concepts. In addition, the availability of multimedia equipment awakens learners with instant information in an interactive way by having the students partner with available technology. Classroom communications are vital, as shown with this ICES chart.

MATCHING CONTENT TO DELIVERY

Just compare the next two items. One is a pictorial chart titled *Inclusion Strategies That Work!* The other one is a numbered list titled *Valuable and Applicable Things to Do in All Classrooms on a Daily Basis.* Notice that the basic content is the same, but the presentation differs. Which one would you prefer to use to best deliver the information? How does your brain process each of these two items? Now think about how you instruct your students. Can the same concept be delivered differently? Was the learning material in any way sacrificed by the accompaniment of the visuals? Picture your own handouts!

COLLABORATION, COTEACHING, AND PREPARATION

> *Clearly there are many paths. . . . It is only through the combined efforts of general and special educators in collaboration with parents that schools move toward inclusive practices and ultimately strengthen teaching and learning for all students.*
>
> —Burstein, Sears, Wilcoxen, Cabello, & Spagna, 2004

> *Due to greater numbers of students with disabilities receiving instruction in general education classrooms, the need has increased to provide training for general educators to meet the needs of a diverse range of students.*
>
> —Harriott, 2004

Figure 4.1   Inclusion Strategies That Work!

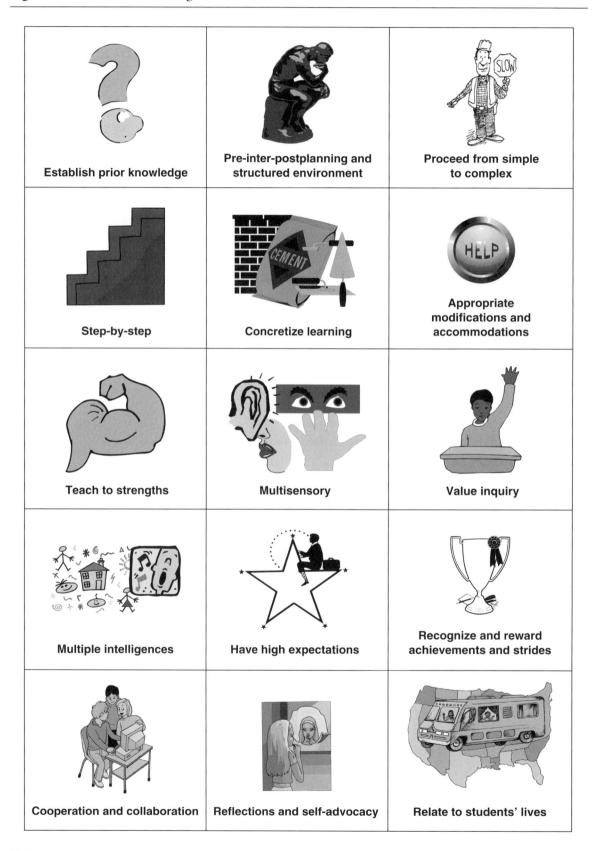

SOURCE: Adapted from Karten, T. (2005). *Inclusion strategies that work!* Thousand Oaks, CA: Corwin.

Figure 4.2   Valuable and Applicable Things to Do in All Classrooms on a Daily Basis

1. Establish prior knowledge.
2. Preplan lessons with structured objectives, allowing for inter-postplanning.
3. Proceed from the simple to the complex by using discrete task analysis, which breaks up the learning into its parts, yet still values the whole picture.
4. Use a step-by-step approach, teaching in small bites, with much practice and repetition for those who need it.
5. Reinforce abstract concepts with concrete examples, such as looking at a map while walking around a neighborhood or reading actual street signs.
6. Think about possible accommodations and modifications that might be needed, such as using a digital recorder for notes or reducing or enhancing an assignment.
7. Incorporate sensory elements: visual, auditory, and kinesthetic/tactile ones.
8. Teach to strengths to help students compensate for weaknesses, such as "hopping" to math facts, if a child loves to move about but hates numbers.
9. Concentrate on individual children, not syndromes, with a growth vs. deficit paradigm.
10. Provide opportunities for success to build self-esteem.
11. Give positives before negatives.
12. Use modeling with both teachers and peers.
13. Vary types of instruction and assessment, with multiple intelligences and cooperative learning.
14. Relate learning to children's lives using interest inventories.
15. Remember the basics such as teaching students proper hygiene, respecting others, effectively listening, or reading directions on a worksheet, in addition to the 3 R's: *Reading, 'Riting,* and *'Rithmetic.*
16. Establish a pleasant classroom environment that encourages students to ask questions and become actively involved in their learning.
17. Increase students' self-awareness of levels and progress.
18. Effectively communicate and collaborate with parents, students, and colleagues, while smiling—it's contagious!

SOURCE: Adapted from: Karten, T. (2005). *Inclusion strategies that work!* Thousand Oaks, CA: Corwin.

> *Special and general educators must work together to ensure that the highest possible number of students with exceptionalities successfully access the important concepts and skills in the general education curriculum.*
>
> —Kozleski, Mainzer, & Deshler, 2000

Some partnerships and corporations continue productively for years, while others dissolve as quickly as a rain puddle in the afternoon sun. The question here is, why? Compromises, ownership issues, effective division of work responsibilities, academic preparation, knowledge of appropriate instructional strategies, and degrees of flexibility influence collaborative relationships. Everyone needs to be involved in the planning, decisions, and training, including not only the teachers, but also administration; related staff such as educational assistants and speech pathologists; art, music, gym, and foreign language teachers; nurses, occupational therapists, mobility trainers, and physical therapists; and, of course, families and students too! Training needs to begin in preservice courses with proper instructional strategies and knowledge that is then applied in educational settings.

So, how can you describe the climate in a classroom that practices effective collaboration? That question is as easy to answer as comparing the climate of totally different countries, such as Vietnam, Switzerland, Tanzania, and Argentina. So many factors influence climate, such as topography, location in relation to the equator or poles, nearby bodies of water, and so on. Now, what influences classroom collaboration? Changing climates in school classrooms are influenced by some of these factors:

Teachers' preservice training: "I had no preparation for this in my Education 101 course" or "Oh, I remember learning about collaboration" or "I am proficient in this subject matter!"

Prior experiences in and out of education: "I firmly believe there's no *I* in the word *team*" or "I'd prefer to figure this out myself!"

Controlling vs. flexible (*Gumby-like*) personalities: "No need to be a Frank Sinatra here; we can do it *Our Way!*" or "It's my class, not yours!"

Self-confidence levels: "I'm a good teacher, and it's okay if someone else shares his or her knowledge with me so we can both learn from each other" or "Just who do they think they are, questioning what I do!"

Attitude toward students: "I know that they can succeed, if we . . ." or "This is just a waste of time. *Those kids* belong in a separate class, so I can really teach!"

Administrative support: "How can we plan together, if the only shared planning time we have are those casual, impromptu meetings in the restroom?"; "How do they expect us to teach when all they care about are standardized test grades?"; "What does it mean that we only have to provide an *appropriate* education vs. the best education?"; or "So much more is accomplished in an atmosphere of collegial respect when the central office and supervisors listen to, understand, respect, and support staff needs." "Let's listen to and respond to our teachers' everyday classroom concerns, aside from just evaluating their performances. We will provide ongoing training for all staff to help students with disabilities succeed in general education classrooms."

Defining roles: "Not sure what I should be doing here"; "How can that teacher treat me like his personal secretary? I can do more than make copies"; "There should be equality in the classroom, and that doesn't just go for students!"

Bridges can be built to do the following:

- Include children in general education classrooms, removing distinctions between general and special education students
- Collaborate between general and special education teachers and all staff to intermingle personalities and workloads
- Close the achievement gap and benefit all students
- Ensure that teachers are allotted time to conduct meetings to discuss past, present, and future lessons (including staff such as speech pathologists and occupational therapists)
- Connect the learning to the home environment, enlisting families and guardians as allies and partners in the education of their children

Today, special and general educators must collaborate to figure out ways that all students can and will be successful in school and in their futures by creating and instilling high expectations for all. Specific time needs to be spent on effective classroom designs, along with models of instruction that include collaboration and coteaching. Collaboration encompasses all school personnel, families as partners, and transitions between grades and schools.

The following highlights some coteaching issues that need to be addressed (to circumvent possible oil-and-water relationships between teachers):

Figure 4.3   Collaborative Survey to Promote Productive Relationships

Write some brief thoughts about ....

Classroom Modifications and Accommodations:

(Varying learning objectives, requirements, instructional materials):

Curriculum Concerns:

Teacher Knowledge of Subject Matter:

Instructional Style:

Methods of Testing/Grading:

Varying Classroom Rules/Organization Preferred:

SOURCE: Adapted from Karten, T. (2005). *Inclusion strategies that work!* Thousand Oaks, CA: Corwin.

Figure 4.4

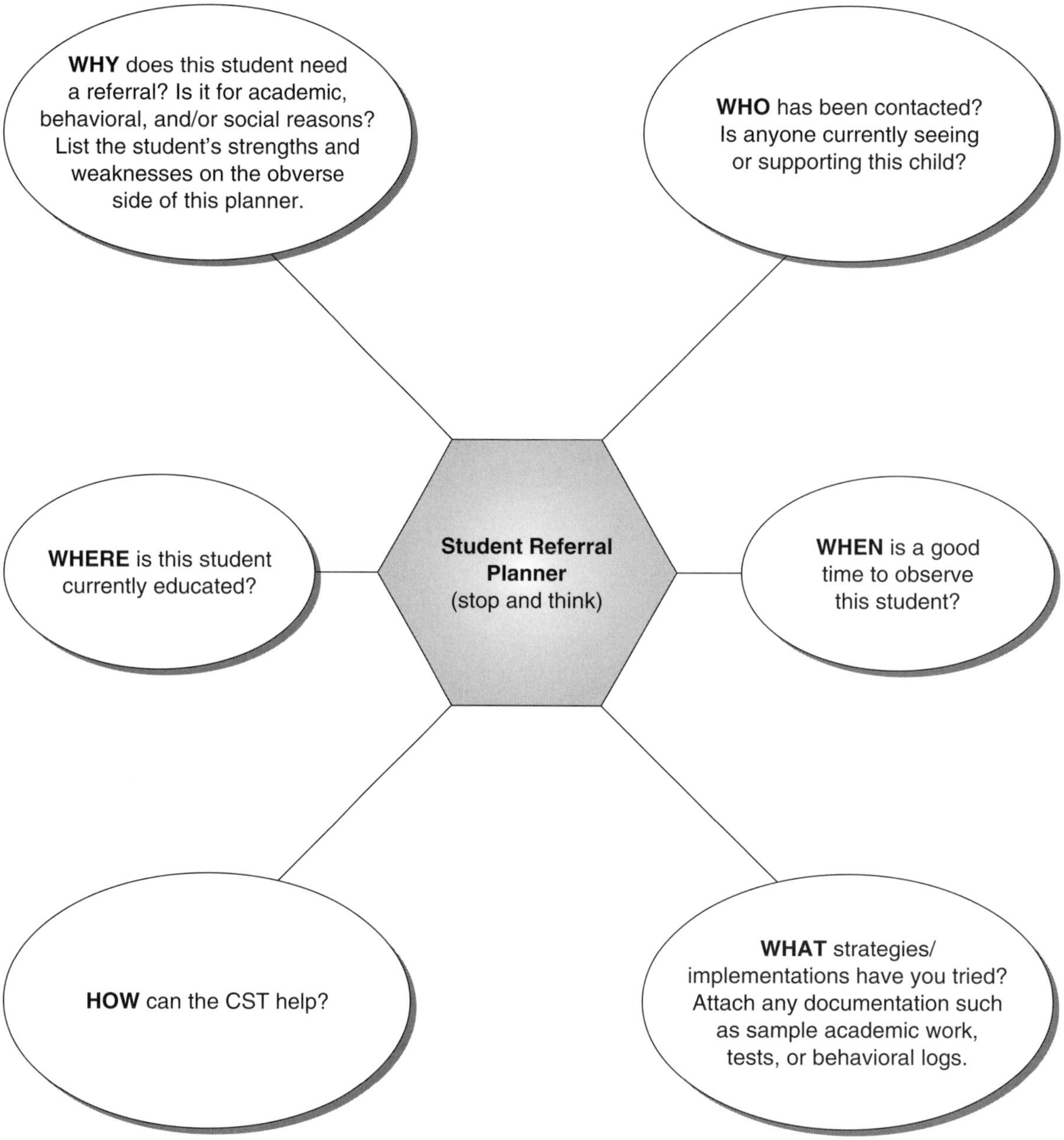

WHY does this student need a referral? Is it for academic, behavioral, and/or social reasons? List the student's strengths and weaknesses on the obverse side of this planner.

WHO has been contacted? Is anyone currently seeing or supporting this child?

Student Referral Planner (stop and think)

WHERE is this student currently educated?

WHEN is a good time to observe this student?

HOW can the CST help?

WHAT strategies/implementations have you tried? Attach any documentation such as sample academic work, tests, or behavioral logs.

Teacher: _____

School: _____

Student's Name: _____

Primary Language: _____

Teacher Contacts: E-Mail: _____

Phone: _____

Date: _____

Increasing Communications

Teamwork with instructional support teams (ISTs), student study teams (SSTs), child study teams (CSTs), and related services reduces miscommunication and includes all staff and teachers in the planning stages.

Joie de Learning

Structured lessons are necessary for students to understand the standards-based curriculum, since many learnings follow a sequence. Yet holding on to the teacher's manual as if it is the educational bible omits the spontaneity in the learning process. Just like rote memorization of facts negates application of learning and the generalization of concepts, *rote teaching* negates students' understandings and thwarts instructional passion. Doing the same lessons, year after year, is boring for the students if the teacher cannot exhibit enthusiasm about the subject matter as if it was his or her first time teaching it. When you walk into classrooms with excited learners, the following things happen:

The first question they ask as you hand out a paper is *not*

"Is this for homework?" but "Wow! What's this about?"

When you ask students to write, they *don't* say

"How long should it be?" but "Could I write more?"

When you assign only one novel chapter to read, the students voraciously forge ahead because they are enjoying the book.

Okay, maybe I am being overly melodramatic here, but the point is that many students do not care about the learning because they think it's just *stuff* they need to know for the test. To many students, school is not fun; it's a chore, and to some it's even a necessary evil that they are compelled to attend. Anticipation sets the classroom stage for a classroom audience that is ready and excited to learn. Teachers in some cases need to be educational performers, who can convince students that this *stuff* is not only worth knowing, but downright interesting!

Joy

Of

Involvement in

Education

Does

Equal

LEARNING

Nothing Taken for Granted

Some teachers work in a linear manner: "After Math Lesson 1.3, we'll move ahead to 1.4, then 1.5, 1.6, 1.7, 1.8, 1.9, and then comes the Chapter Test." If the schedule is not followed, some teachers are fearful that the class will fall behind in their learning. There are valid arguments for such a regimented pace; however, this type of teacher is assuming that no regression or *learning amnesia* has occurred and that the whole class has the exact same prior knowledge on every given topic. Before moving on to the next lesson, taking a few minutes to review prior learning and allow for student connections is time well spent. Teachers teach, students listen; teachers teach, students forget; teachers test, students fail. Nothing can be taken for granted with today's classroom of diverse learners if a successful outcome is the ultimate goal!

Here are some examples of this *forgettable* scenario:

- Having students identify the location of continents on maps without determining if they know the difference between a continent and a country
- Adding, subtracting, multiplying, and dividing decimals without making the connection to how and when decimals appear in our daily lives
- Giving weekly spelling tests that do not define the words and failing to review them at a later date to maintain competencies
- Teaching about patterns without identifying patterns around us—e.g., nature, clothing, foods—or making real-life connections
- Giving instruction on the Linnean classification system, without teaching about how to classify common objects that surround us
- Teaching about the crisis in the Middle East without addressing past economic, political, and religious issues, or explaining the difference between these terms

These scenarios are given for teachers to realize that it is wise to

- Never assume students know the answers you think they should know
- Review prior learnings; it assists students in preparing for tests and high-stakes exams
- Ask varied questions and give frequent formal and informal evaluations to determine students' levels and to gauge pacing of your own lessons

Spiraling Objectives

So often, teachers are frustrated because it seems that some students with learning issues who are included in their classes are just not *getting it!* I use these words because I am actually paraphrasing the answer some students give when you ask if there are any questions: "I don't *get it.*" Well, what don't they get? If they cannot even define the *it*, then where do you proceed from there? Now, how do you as a teacher help them *get it*? And, if the curriculum spirals, won't these gaps hinder their future exposure to the same material? How will they *get it*?

Check yes or no to these *pedagocially ponderable* questions:

QUESTIONS	YES	NO
1. Was this student's prior knowledge increased?		
2. Even though this student did not receive a passing grade—e.g., 50% on an evaluation or test—did he or she master 50% of the material?		
3. Do you think this student will be more proficient when he or she learns about this topic, content area, or skill again?		
4. Is there a way to repeat this learning and somehow individualize instruction within the classroom—e.g., alternative assignment on the same topic—if appropriate support is given, such as a parent, peer coach, or paraeducator?		
5. Would assigning a peer coach be beneficial to both this child and his or her student mentor?		
6. Can the student chart his or her progress to take more ownership and responsibility for the learning?		
7. Is the student experiencing more accomplishments than frustrations with his or her inclusion experience in your class?		
8. Has physical inclusion allowed this child to develop a more positive self-image, which has translated to increased self-confidence and motivation?		
9. Are you experiencing personal or professional growth by having this child included in your class?		

The major point here is that inclusion has academic and social merits. The spiraling curriculum adds on to each student's differing prior knowledge, when they see the same topic with broadening concepts in future years. The curriculum exposure that they receive within the general education classroom, although not always geared to individual levels, allows for increased instruction on subject matter that in the past was very often deleted from specialized programs conducted in separate classrooms. Spiraling curriculums set the stage for spiraling brains that shelve or file the information or facts for a while. If the initial instruction included research-based strategies, such as kinesthetic learning with meaningful engagement, then *déjà learning* occurs. Now the prior learning is more apt to be retrieved from or added to the child's file of *stuff I heard before!* Equally important here are the social benefits of inclusion. Even though there are no standardized tests for social improvements, these gains are truly immeasurable. The spiraling curriculum also includes spiraling life skills that lead to independent living decisions, fostered by increased social interactions with peers. Students develop, observe, and model emotions. The *hidden curriculuum* develops character education with rewarding extrinsic and intrinsic behavioral choices! Social and academic growth are utterly compatible classroom objectives.

VERTICAL AND HORIZONTAL ALIGNMENTS

Picture an apartment building with an elevator or stairs. Well, that's comparable to the vertical alignment of objectives from one grade to the next. Now picture a house with a wraparound porch, and you have a scenario of horizontal alignment. Students, like apartment or home dwellers, are school residents who strive to master grade-level standards and objectives. Seeing what preceded or follows that grade in a fund of knowledge, or on the prior or next learning level, allows teachers to review facts and concepts if gaps are evident. Educators can now easily shift gears and accelerate to more challenging levels when different grade-level competencies are displayed. Elevators have a menu of floor choices!

Baseline, Advancing, and Challenging Assignments

Now think about a large apartment building with many families living together on different floors under the same roof. Well, today's classrooms are inhabited by *learning tenants* who are classmates instructed by the same teacher, but they too reside on different *learning floors.* Production of student clones who have identical knowledge negates the nature of what we know about learning. Teachers may have a baseline of knowledge that they want students to learn, but all students will not master these objectives at the same time, since they all did not begin on the same level, nor do they all achieve understandings at the same pace. Some students need more repetitive learnings, while others thrive when given challenging assignments. So, how does a teacher handle these differences in a classroom of diverse learners? Well, when I coteach in a math class, I deliberately introduce a difficult topic and expose even the lower learners to the more challenging assignments, not to frustrate them, but to include them in the learning. Surprisingly successful results often follow!

Never assume that a student with learning needs is not capable of achieving bigger strides on different topics. Each child displays varying achievements based on complexities of assignments, interest levels, instructional presentations, and sometimes just their moods, mind-sets, or even the weather on that particular day! How teachers teach is affected by the content, objectives, and skills they hope students will understand and gain, as well as their own proficiency with the content. In addition, who is in the class most definitely affects the pace, instructional delivery, classroom design, modifications, assessments, and varied activities required for the students to master that megalist of skills and objectives. Delivering this knowledge to students with different abilities becomes a rewarding experience when you as the teacher help those children increase their baseline knowledge and then move on to more advanced and challenging levels. It's quite a view from the school's penthouse!

The following chart, which is to be used as a planner, points out that teachers are not only instructing topics, but students as well. Fill in the skills and objectives as well as the students instructed, then look back at the accommodations chart in Chapter 1 and see which learning, behavioral/social/emotional, perceptual, and physical suggestions apply.

Grades	Skills and Objectives	Students with ...							
K–2									
3–5									
6–8									
9–12									

Skills and Objectives:

A. Word Decoding
B. Word Encoding
C. Reading Comprehension
D. Writing Skills
E. Literacy
F. Language Skills
G. Listening Comprehension
H. Math Computations
I. Problem Solving
J. Perceptual Activities
K. Everyday Math
L. Consumer Education
M. Measurement
N. Pattern-Based Thinking
O. Critical-Thinking Skills
P. Biology
Q. Chemistry
R. Physics
S. Earth Science

T. Map Skills
U. World Cultures
V. Ancient Civilizations
W. Citizenship
X. Environment and Society
Y. Geography
Z. Economic Literacy
AA. Understanding Government
BB. Cultural Awareness
CC. Media
DD. Music/Art Education
EE. Visual Information
FF. Physical Education
GG. Family Life
HH. Technology
II. Career Education
JJ. Self-Management
KK. Study Skills
LL. Other Skills/Topics

Delivered to students with

1. Above Average Skills
2. Asperger's Disorder
3. Attention Deficit/Hyperactivity Disorder
4. Auditory Processing
5. Autism
6. Cerebral Palsy
7. Communication Disorder
8. Conduct Disorder
9. Deafness/Hearing Loss
10. Depression
11. Developmental Disorder
12. Dyscalculia

13. Dysgraphia
14. Dyslexia
15. Obsessive Compulsive Disorder
16. Oppositional Defiant Disorder
17. Physical Impairments
18. Specific Learning Disability
19. Tourette's Syndrome
20. Traumatic Brain injury
21. Twice-Exceptionality
22. Visual Impairment
23. Other Needs

These two lists must be collated for classroom learning achievements to occur. Teachers teach subjects, but the first consideration must be teaching the students.

Figure 4.5

FIRST:

WHOLE

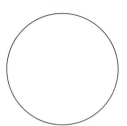

Everyone in the class could

- listen to the same speech, lecture, story, poem, or mathematical word problem
- look at the same picture prompt related to the content
- chorally read or write a story together on chart paper
- have a group discussion about . . .
- be introduced to science and social studies vocabulary or unfamiliar reading/language words or terms
- preview and discuss what skill(s) the lesson will focus on (e.g., scientific method, time lines, decimals, finding the main idea, how to improve writing by substituting words)
- be involved in a teacher demonstration or experiment, while handling concrete objects or appropriate lesson-related manipulatives

---

NEXT:

PART

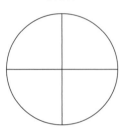

Students can work with smaller groups, partners, or individually,

- completing an assigned reading or writing task
- creating a product based upon what was learned (e.g., poem, story, short skit, illustrating captioned pictures, crossword puzzle, word search, solving given problems, reenacting an experiment, researching on the computer, reading and learning more about . . .)

Learning under teacher's auspices now exists for all students. During this time, the teacher walks around supervising or instructing smaller groups or individual students while recording observations and individual needs evidenced.

THEN:

WHOLE

again ☺

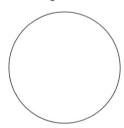

Together, the class becomes a whole unit again, while individual students, teachers, partners, and groups share

- what else they learned or discovered about the topic from a book, computer, other student, teacher, self
- a finished product created
- what they now know, giving specific details
- what they still wonder about
- questions about the material presented

It's basically a time for all learners to celebrate their discoveries and progress with each other, while validating and reflecting upon their own learning.

SOURCE: Karten, T. (2005). *Inclusion strategies that work!* Thousand Oaks, CA: Corwin.

Yes, there are curriculum mandates, but without individual student consideration, lessons become meaningless rather than beneficial academic experiences for both teachers and students of all levels. In inclusionary classrooms, this becomes a more challenging task, but a feasible one, when the learning needs of individual students are known and addressed before standards are applied.

Classroom Structure

So how can educators simultaneously address different objectives?

INTERDISCIPLINARY LESSONS

Learning must address students' interests, curriculum objectives, classroom structure, and the changing legislative dictates. Interdisciplinary lessons are certainly a way to meaningfully relate to different students' strengths, motivation, and the standards. Not every lesson needs to include every subject, but equally true is that every subject does not exist on its own. For example, if math is a student's least favorite subject, then this student might be turned off by anything that deals with numbers or problem solving. However, suppose this particular student loved to write short stories. Couldn't you somehow tap into this student's preferred intelligence, and couple the math instruction with writing strategies?

> *A growing body of research in the fields of mathematics education and literacy supports the inclusion of children's literature into the teaching and learning of mathematics.*
>
> —Ward, 2005

> *Words and images have the power to communicate analytical reasoning and insight and at the same time connect math to a world of things— nature, science, art, and stories—that matter to kids.*
>
> —Tang, 2003

	Writing/Art	Reading	Science	Social Studies
M A T H	Choose words from the glossary in the back of the math textbook to create a *math story* each month. For example, October's story could be about patterned pumpkins exponentially increasing. Then draw pictures that illustrate your math stories! In 3–5 sentences, explain the steps you used to solve the word problem. Can you draw a sequence of pictures that accompany each step? Exchange problems with a classmate and see if you could solve each other's problems.	Cut out or highlight mathematical words and pictures from articles and ads in magazines and newspapers. Design your own shopping coupons with words and pictures that offer consumer discounts. Create a bound classroom math collage or scrapbook with mathematical captions that refer to characters in recent stories read.	Find math in nature; e.g., symmetry, shapes, angles, trees, and other *environmental math.* Design an experiment that uses math; e.g., charts, graphs, probabillity, decimals, measurements. Be certain that the experiment includes the scientific process.	Investigate mathematical operations across cultures. Do they have different ways of adding, subtracting, dividing, or multiplying? What was math like in past civilizations across the world? Identify the currency, values, economy, and trade rules in different countries.

	Reading/Writing	Technology	Math	Cultures
S C I E N C E	After conducting research on your favorite scientific topic in biology, earth science, physics, or chemistry, write a play with this scientific theme. Write out the alphabet from A–Z in a column on lined paper and try to think of as many science words as possible that begin with each letter.	Create a Web search for your classmates on your favorite topic. First ask the teacher to approve your chosen sites, then gather information and compose 10 questions, which your peers will answer. View the site www.brainpop.com to see if there's a science-related movie about the concept you are now learning.	Choose some math formulas and plug them in to solve some everyday scientific situations. Think of how math and science go hand in hand in scientific experiments. Research how many mathematicians were also scientists.	How do some cultures view science vs. religions? Create a time line of different scientific discoveries and inventions. Then list the country in the world where the discovery or invention began. Explore how scientists from different cultures communicate and share ideas.

This chart offers some interdisciplinary connections with standards addressed, using math as an example. Remember, not every lesson needs to include every subject, but if the connections are feasible, then crossing over to another discipline does not dilute the present one. Interdisciplinary lessons strengthen concepts, beyond relying on the textbook as the only means of instruction. Here's an ongoing example with math. More interdisciplinary lesson ideas follow here and in a later chapter.

National standards addressed: *NCSS:* Understand global connections and interdependence, cultural diversity, and how human beings view themselves in and over time. *NCTE and IRA:* Adjust use of spoken, written, and visual language for communication while participating in literacy communities.

National standards addressed: *NRC:* Increase ability to conduct scientific inquiry and understandings of the environment. *NCTM:* Monitor and reflect upon problem solving, spatial relationships, connections, representation, and communication.

National standards addressed: *NCSS:* Understand individual identity and development along with interactions among groups and institutions. *NCTE and IRA:* Read, interpret, and comprehend a wide range of materials. Use techological resources. Employ sound-letter corresopondence and sentence structure. *NRC:* Understand relationships between science, technology, and society. *NCTM:* Connect mathematics to other contexts and understand the language of math.

National standards addressed: *NCSS:* Understand how human beings view themselves in and over time. *NCTE and IRA:* Accomplish a purpose with written language to exchange information. *NRC:* Increase ability to conduct scientific inquiry and understanding of science as a human endeavor. *NCTM:* Apply spatial reasoning and visualization.

	Science	Music	Physical Education	Art
R E A D I N G	Dissect the story you read, pretending one of the main characters is a scientist conducting an experiment. Cooperatively decide what experiment the character would conduct if he or she was a scientist. Plug in all of the details of the scientific method steps of your *fictional scientific character*. Identify the following: hypothesis materials procedure observation/results conclusion	Pretend that the book or story you just read is being made into a movie. You are in charge of deciding the musical score for the movie. Pick what songs or musical pieces will be the chosen. Decide when the pieces will be played. Be certain that the songs and music reflect the book's mood.	Create a dance or team game your book's characters could play. Decide the rules and steps for the dance or noncompetitive (fun) game.	Design a storyboard for the novel you have just read. You can use clip art or draw your own pictures. Other classmates can sequence your pictures or retell the story using your pictures as their prompts. If you prefer, you can sculpt your characters using clay or whatever other medium you desire.

Chapter Review Questions/Activities

1. What additional points would you add to the list of 18 Valuable and Applicable Things to Do in All Classrooms on a Daily Basis?

2. Cooperatively design an interdisciplinary lesson similar to the reading, science, and math ones modeled in this chapter. Vertically place your main topic or concept in the first column, and then list the headings of subjects you'd like to include and touch upon in the following four. Then make the connective multisubject lesson happen!

3. Use these words in an *educationally instructive* paragraph:
   a. baseline knowledge
   b. advancing knowledge
   c. challenging assignment
   d. vertical alignment
   e. horizontal alignment

PART II

Standards-Based Inclusion Strategies That Work

Standards-Based Reading Objectives

As shown with the following research implications, objectives, and worksheets, reading is a complex, yet step-by-step process! Knowledgeable teachers can help all learners decode and comprehend. Reading accommodations allow students' strengths to be addressed through guided and systematic instruction that honors the mastery of standards.

RESEARCH IMPLICATIONS

Reading research says the following:

> *There is growing evidence that with meaningful and systematic instruction, many students with developmental and multiple disabilities can develop literacy abilities and benefit in many ways from shared interactions around texts.*
>
> —Schnorr & Davern, 2005

> *Current research indicates that organized, direct instruction in linguistic understanding, phonetic rules and word attack strategies are essential components of a successful reading program.*
>
> —Orton Gillingham, n.d.

> *A team of American scientists says that misfired neurons leave the brain unable to pick out visual and auditory cues from surrounding sounds. Students with dyslexia struggle to both spell and read because of a difficulty interpreting different sounds within words.*
>
> —"Dyslexia Theory," 2005

> *Kids with reading problems need reading programs that are scientifically proven to work; they also need intensive intervention—not just*

15 minutes or a half hour a week. . . . Reading needs to be taught, and it needs to be taught in ways that are effective.

—Shaywitz, 2005

Providing students with time for independent reading during content-area classes increases their motivation, background knowledge, and vocabulary.

—Ivey & Broaddus, 2001

You build upon what they know and what they care about. You also give them books to choose from so they can extend what they know.

—Ivey & Fisher, 2005

Direct, explicit instruction in such strategies as summarizing, identifying text structure and visual clues, calling on prior knowledge, and using graphic organizers improves students' reading comprehension.

—National Reading Panel, 2000

Effective reading instruction for adolescents should integrate writing as a measure of comprehension and as a tool for learning across content areas.

—Biancarosa, 2005

SAMPLE LESSONS/CONNECTIONS FOR K–12

READING AND UNDERSTANDING WORDS

Teachers' familiarity with their students' backgrounds, interests, and socio-cultural identities is at least as important in identifying appropriate books for students as are lists based on book, print, language, and literary uniformity.

—Dzaldov & Peterson, 2005

Connective Academic Issues

> Teacher request/question: What is a ratio?
>
> Student response: "A ratio means that you are against something."

A few scenarios could be possible here. First off, this student might have auditory processing issues, being unable to tell the difference between similar sounding words (*racist* and *ratio*). Obviously, this child attached meaning to the word *racist*, and it was therefore within his realm of prior learning. Yet the word *ratio* was never anchored or understood. Maybe this child dislikes math and automatically avoids related learning! Or perhaps this student was never instructed about the meaning of a ratio. Either way, when reading this word incorrectly in the context of a sentence, the wrong meaning confuses the comprehension, and alters both vocabulary and math development. Investigation and practice listening to similar-sounding words along with auditory discrimination strengthening and math instruction about ratios would be most beneficial here.

Figure 5.1

Grades: Students With . . .	Content Area/Skills: Reading and Understanding Words: Decoding, Encoding, Word Recognition, Vocabulary, Phonological Awareness, Print Concepts
K–2	Distinguish letters from nonletters. Read and write basic sight words, including own first and last names. Know the sound–symbol relationship and apply it to spellings. Understand directionality. Follow printed words. Realize that letters form words. Match all sounds with symbols. Blend sounds to decode; e.g., c-v-c (consonant-vowel-consonant). Identify, delete, and substitute phonemes and blends. Develop knowledge of how to spell high-frequency words. Understand that context clues can help identify words. Read and write both nonsense and real words with different syllable types. Introduce rhyming words and word families. Sort vocabulary into categories or headings. Identify basic relationships of words; e.g., whisper or shout.
3–5	Sort words into word families; e.g., define, confine. Apply structural analysis; e.g. prefixes, root words, suffixes; and syllabication rules to readings. Reinforce knowledge of phonemes, including diphthongs, digraphs, and various syllable types. Use a table of contents, index, and glossary. Use pronunciation keys in dictionaries. Apply context clues to identify words. Infer word meanings. Use a dictionary, thesaurus, and computer language tools to define unfamiliar words. Build personal vocabulary "fund" with other word choices such as synonyms, antonyms, and homophones. Identify common idioms.
6–8	Continue building grade-level vocabulary through a variety of genre. Know different spellings of homophones and homonyms. Apply phonetic principles in readings and writings, with student automaticity. Critique different print formats; e.g. magazines, newspapers, poems. Self-correct and reread to clarify. Infer word meanings by understanding word derivations of root words, prefixes, and suffixes from Latin and Greek origins. Continue increasing vocabulary bank through a variety of genres, understanding word relationships, idioms, and analogies. Substitute vocabulary learned in writings.
9–12	Reinforce all skills through a variety of genres in readings and writings. Continuation of all phonetic knowledge using higher-order thinking skills. Compare and contrast organizational structures of fictional and nonfiction texts. Contrast word relationships with different connotations and denotations in readings and then writings.

Sample Primary Reading/Decoding Lesson

Baseline Knowledge Standards

Students demonstrate the sounds of consonants and long and short vowels by listening to or reading words in simple picture books. Some students who cannot yet read will point to pictures of words beginning with studied consonants as the book is read to them. Others might listen to the book on tape and turn the page as directed by auditory cues.

Advancing Level

Students sort words into their families, identifying consonant blends, diphthongs, digraphs, and r-controlled vowels in readings above current grade levels. Students here could also make flash cards by writing words on index cards, finding clip art and downloaded images that match the word's meaning.

More Challenging Assignments/Accommodations

Students write poems and short stories with rhyming words and varying syllable types. Some students will use a rhyming dictionary or refer to teacher- or student-constructed lists of rhyming words. Other students will play a rhyming game, where they raise their hand or tally the number of rhyming words heard in a story that is read to them by a peer coach or teacher. If rhyming words are still too difficult, then the goal here might be for a student to verbalize his or her favorite-sounding words and copy the letters that spell those words in a salt tray, match a prompt with the illustrated word, or trace the letters.

Possible accommodations for a child with *visual, perceptual, or learning* needs:

- Pocket charts set up to neatly compartmentalize types of syllables or word prefixes, suffixes, and root words written on differently colored index cards
- Salt tray to feel letters or raised bumpy letters
- Magnification page
- Peer coach
- Taped, guided, repeated, or rephrased instructions
- Books on tape
- Words written on individual index cards, or inside a *tachistoscope* (a cardboard holder with a cutout slit to view one word at a time)

Possible accommodations for a child with *behavioral/attention* needs:

- Personalizing picture books relating to child's interests
- Frequent monitoring
- Praise or individual rewards/certificates for achievements
- Behavioral plan that charts time on task
- Additional time in class or at home to complete assignments
- Choices in vocabulary lists to give student empowerment and stake in learning (e.g., choice to define any 6 of these 10 words)

Possible accommodations for a child with *cognitive/developmental* needs:

- Sort and match a list of functional color-coded words with graphics that pictorially define them
- More graphics for words and for sound–symbol association, such as video clips (see, for example, www.unitedstreaming.com)
- Concrete learning examples to have the letters jump off the page, such as touching their nose for words that begin with the letter *n* or touching their toes for words that begin with the letter *t*
- Practice writing and identifying the individual and combined sounds of letters in their own name and street address
- Modified assessments that ask students to identify rather than write words

Teachers can use the following ungraded reproducible charts in their lessons to accommodate individual students' decoding, encoding, and vocabulary needs. The purpose here is consistent, direct skill instruction to increase phonemic awareness.

It's important that students learn to actually break the reading code to associate the correct sounds with their letters and not just rotely memorize words. One way to ensure this is to have students read individual nonordered syllables and then write the correct word, with properly sequenced syllables. Later on, students choose words from texts and novels and create their own unsequenced boxed words. Some examples follow.

Figure 5.2   Unsequenced Syllables

Unsequenced Syllables

sion	clu	in

Correct word_____

cing	bal	an

Correct word_____

tent	ment	con

Correct word_____

Figure 5.3a   Silly Syllable Student Sheet

Silly Syllable Student Sheet

Directions: Place scrambled syllables in the boxes, then exchange papers with a partner to see if they can sequence (order) the syllables to correctly form a word. You can use a dictionary to check if you have correctly divided the words before you pass on your paper to a peer. If you have time, try to create more boxed syllables on the reverse side of the paper.

Correct word _____

Correct word _____

Correct word _____

Correct word _____

Figure 5.3b   Scrambled Continents

Student directions: say each syilabie individually, and then identify the scrambled continents. Use an atlas to see if your answer are correct. Next locate 2 countries on some of these countries. Note the difference between a continent and a country.

OPE EUR _____

Countries on this continent:

1.

2.

ER CA A I SOUTH _____

Countries on this continent:

1.

2.

FRI A CA _____

Countries on this continent:

1.

2.

ARC TI ANT CA _____

A CA I NORTH MER _____

Countries on this continent:

1.

2.

SIA A _____

Countries on this continent:

1.

2.

STRAL IA AU _____

Figure 5.4

Some Phonetic (fo-net-ick) Facts:

1. There are 26 letters in the alphabet that make up 44 different sounds or phonemes.

2. Every word must have a vowel that speaks.

3. Words have vowels and consonants.

4. Some vowels can be short, long (say their own name), or contolled by the letter r.

5. Syllables are parts of words.

6. Digraph sounds include th, ch, wh, sh

7. Diphthongs include -oi, -oy, -aw, -au, -oo, -ew, -ui, -ue, -ow, -ou

8. The letter y can have a vowel or consonant sound, depending on where it is placed in a word. The y at the end of a one syllable word usually says "i" (try) and when y is at the end of a multisyllabic word, it says "e" (happy).

9. Words are not always spelled how they sound.

10. Phonics is a key that can unlock the mystery of words.

Directions: Write words from your readings in the correct columns below.

One-Syllable Words	Multisyllabic Words

READING COMPREHENSION SKILLS

Connective Academic Issues

Evaluate this student response, considering the classroom/individual learning implications.

Teacher request/question: Use the word *handful* in a sentence.

Student response: "I ate a *handful* of Eminems."

This student spells well and understands the dynamics of sentence structure. However, this student is also a concrete thinker who understands more about things and people that interest her, such as the music of Eminem. She was quite surprised to find out that the candy was spelled differently than the singer. If asked to write the lyrics of an Eminem song, she could do so with ease, but she experiences difficulties when asked to answer questions from nonfiction reading-comprehension passages. Before learning occurs, this student must be focused and attentive. During most classroom instruction, she is not disruptive, but while she is physically present, she is emotionally somewhere else. Her brain hears the words, but does not connect it with her prior knowledge or consider the information important. It's as if she has an internal *delete button* that unconsciously filters out the knowledge before her neurons can relate or associate it with other learning. Teachers need to somehow first reach her, and then teach her!

Reading Comprehension: Baseline Knowledge Standard

Students understand the main idea of short reading passages and information/plot development in fiction and nonfiction books after listening to teacher's oral reading. Students identify the main idea, details, plot and information from books read on their instructional reading level vs. grade level.

Advancing Level

Students demonstrate higher-level reading skills by answering inferential-type questions, understanding what the text or prose hints at but does not specifically state; e.g., drawing conclusions, cause/effect, characterization.

More Challenging Assignments

Independent and individual/cooperative reading assignments geared to classroom or research projects that synthesize and apply readings and understandings from fiction and nonfiction texts.

Possible accommodations a child with *lower cognitive skills* might need:

- An assignment that has students identify, match, or highlight functional sight words in texts rather than reading word for word, if reading level is too difficult
- Increased teacher monitoring of texts assigned to avoid the frustration of stumbling through readings that are above skill level
- Practice reading everyday text such as menus, maps, recipes, job applications, instructional manuals, and how-to books
- Accompanying visual dictionaries
- Lower reading-level texts that illustrate concepts
- Real photographs of concrete items and situations
- Frequent checks of prior knowledge and comprehension with teachers or peer coaches, so faulty reasoning or misunderstandings do not escalate or interfere with lessons

Figure 5.5

closed vowel is closed in by a consonant and does not end a syllable	open vowel is left open at the end of a syllable long vowel sound	consonant —le No vowel sound is heard in this syllable	vowel—e e at the end of the word is silent, very quiet, but lets the other vowel do the talking	Vowel Digraphs (2 vowels with 1 sound) *ai, ay, ea, ee, ei, ey, ie, oa, oe, ow (bow)*	r-controlled vowels **ar, er, ir, or, ur**	Vowel Diphthongs (2 vowels with a different sound) *aw, au, ew, oi, oo (moon), oo (cook), ou, ow (how), oy, ui*
gap	**a** ble	scrab **ble**	gap**e**	w**ai**t	st**ar**k	ap pl**au**se
bet	**be** yond	med **dle**	ex cr**ete**	br**ea**d	st**er**n	fl**ew**
pil grim	**hi**	twin **kle**	p**i**l**e**	el b**ow**	m**ir**th	fl**aw**
cod dle	**o** pen	cod **dle**	n**ote**	c**oa**l	d**or**m	p**ow**er
un til	**mu** sic	cud **dle**	dif f**use**	rev en **ue**	spl**ur**ge	re cr**ui**t er
Except: -ind, -old, -ost, -ild -olt	schwa sound, com**pli** ment **A** las ka	When s is followed by the letter t: whis tle (silent t)	Long vowel sounds, except for a word like dis tinc **tive**	Usually long, except for the the **ea** team (b**ea**d vs. br**ea**d)	r is a stronger letter than the vowels	Vowels are not short or long

Figure 5.6   Word Exploration

Knowing about prefixes is important because _____

_____

_____

Words can often _____.

Circle the subject chosen for the essay:

Science	Math	Social Studies	Language Arts
Physical Education	Music	Technology	Other

Ten words I used in the essay:

1.   6.

2.   7.

3.   8.

4.   9.

5.   10.

alt- high			
amphib- both			
anthro-homo- **hum-** man			
arch- ruler			
arth- joints			
astr- star			
bar- pressure, weight			
bi/du two			
bio- life			

(Continued)

Figure 5.6 (Continued)

carn- meat				
chlor- green				
chron/temp- time				
circ- around				
curr- run				
de- opposite of				
dict- say				
end- inside				
ep- over				
equ- equal				
exo- outside				
flam- fire				
flect- bend, back				
fract- break				
gen- birth				
geo- earth				
graph- write				
gravi- heavy				
hemi- half				

herb- plant				
hydro- water				
im-in- **non-un-** **dis** not				
man- hand				
mini- small				
mono-uni- one				
ped-pod- foot				
phon- sound				
photo- light				
pre- before				
prim- first				
sed- settle, sit				
rota/volv- turn				
sol- sun				
strat- sheet, layer				
syn- put together				
tele- distance				
therm- heat				
trop- turn				
vor- eat				

Figure 5.7

Grades: Students With . . .	Content Area/Skills: Reading: Comprehension Skills
K–2	Develop tracking skills by following a line of print. Scan texts for clues from pictures. Introduce graphic organizers to help sort reading details. Actively participate in classroom reading discussions, sharing thoughts, relevant insights, and/or predictions. Identify main characters, settings, and retell events. Teachers can read or help students sound out more difficult words to aid with comprehension of the story. Students can dictate understandings of classroom stories read to them.
3–5	Apply prior knowledge to readings. Scan nonfiction material to gain understanding of book's format, italicized words, and how main ideas are portrayed. Self-correct reading errors. Proficiencies with a variety of visual organizers to map out story elements and facts. Introduce underlying themes, humor, sarcasm, imagery, and authors' viewpoints. Independently summarize readings into paragraphs. Ask for help when readings are misunderstood. Exposure to a variety of fiction and nonfiction books to both read for enjoyment and to research content-related topics.
6–8	Paraphrase what was read. Draw conclusions from readings. Develop note-taking skills to organize thoughts. Translate fiction and nonfiction readings into writings of 3–5 paragraphs or essays. Self-select readings to complete assigned tasks across content. Demonstrate research skills with books and electronic media.
9–12	Conduct literature studies to compare and contrast authors' styles. Apply inquiry skills to complete a computer-written research project with text citations. Continue exploration of readings in a variety of genres, while analyzing and reflecting on passages, texts, and writings from all sources.

Possible accommodations a child with *visual/perceptual issues* might need:

- Extra time to complete readings
- Blocking out other text on pages to concentrate on line-by-line readings, such as a slide (e.g., folded paper) to place under a line of text to block out other words; magnification page; or handheld magnifier to enlarge smaller print
- More frequent oral reading to monitor whether student is omitting words or letters, substituting letters or words, or skipping lines
- Electronic/digital books that speak words
- Handheld scanners
- Visual tracking exercises to strengthen eye coordination

For example, circle the letters in the correct order for the word *against*:

amrcadugreiuatrufzixcewponyhgnmsrcxjyrt

Figure 5.8

SOARing into Reading

S can-

Look at all of the titles, pictures, **bold** letters, highlighted words, charts, graphs, and other *cool things* in print that you see in your textbook.

O utline-

Read only the title headings of each section or chapter to determine the main idea. Place the main idea inside the **M section** of your **M**/D/Y chart.

Main Idea	Details	You

A nalyze-

You are not ready to read yet. *Think* about what you wrote as the main idea and how the pictures, charts, vocabulary, and other things you saw on the pages relate to that main idea. Get a general **understanding** of your topic.

R ead-

Now you are finally ready to *read* because you have previewed your topic. After you finish reading, fill in the **D**(details) and **Y**(you) **sections** on your M/**D/Y** paper. The You section tells about how you relate to the topic or if it reminds you of something you may have read or heard about before. The readings will now make a lot more sense.

Main Idea	Details	You

After you have filled out the **M/D/Y** sheet, you will further explore the textbook pages by cooperatively completing outlined requirements at chosen stations below:

Research Station

Performance Station

Word Station

Picture This Station

Teacher Station

SOURCE: Karten, T. (2005). *Inclusion strategies that work.* Thousand Oaks, CA: Corwin Press

LITERATURE THEMES: MAN VERSUS MAN, MAN VERSUS NATURE, MAN VERSUS SELF, MAN VERSUS SOCIETY

When students reach higher grades, they are expected to identify themes in literature. All of a sudden the word *theme* appears, but this concept can be introduced in younger grades to set up a *thematic foundation* as shown by the following selection of literature.

Figure 5.9

	Man vs. Man (one person against another)	Man vs. Nature (will to live or survive)	Man vs. Self (inner feelings)	Man vs. Society (values, customs)
K–2	*Are You My Mother?* by Dr. Seuss *Alexander and the Terrible Horrible, No Good, Very Bad Day* by Judith Viorst *The Brand New Kid* by Katie Couric	*The Biggest Bear* by Lynd Ward *The Snowy Day* by Ezra Jack Keats *The Day Dizzy Duckling Got Lost* by Maggie	*Amazing Grace* by Mary Hoffman *Where the Wild Things Are* by Maurice Sendak	*Follow the Drinking Gourd* by Jeanette Winter *The Terrible Things* by Eve Bunting
3–5	*In the Year of the Boar and Jackie Robinson* by Bette Bao *Freak the Mighty* by Rodman Philbrick	*The Big Wave* by Pearl S. Buck *Little House in the Big Woods* by Laura Ingalls Wilder *The Incredible Journey* by Sheila Burnford *Hatchet* by Gary Paulsen	*From the Mixed-Up Files of Mrs. Basil E. Frankweiler* by E.L. Konigsburg *Are You There G-d? It's Me Margaret* by Judy Blume *Sees Behind Trees* by Michael Dorris	*Roll of Thunder, Hear My Cry* by Mildred Taylor *Letters from Rifka* by Karen Hesse *Snow Treasure* by Marie McSwigan *Who Was That Masked Man?* by Avi
6–8	*Maniac Magee* by Jerry Spinelli *Lord of the Flies* by William Golding	*The Old Man and the Sea* by Ernest Hemmingway *My Side of the Mountain* by Jean Craighead George	*My Side of the Mountain* by Jean Craighead George *Going Solo* by Roald Dahl	*The Witch of Blackbird Pond* by Elizabeth George Speare *The Giver* by Lois Lowery
9–12	*To Kill a Mockingbird* by Harper Lee *Of Mice and Men* by John Steinbach *Cat's Cradle* by Kurt Vonnegut	*Robinson Crusoe* by Daniel Defoe *Into the Wild or Into Thin Air* by Jon Krakauer	*Of Human Bondage* by Somerset Maughn *The Tell Tale Heart* by Edgar Alan Poe *Catcher in the Rye* by J.D. Salinger	*The Scarlet Letter* by Nathaniel Hawthorne *The Color Purple* by Alice Walker *The Color of Water* by James McBride

Possible accommodations a child with *autism* might need:

- Consistent and structured behavior modification to reinforce time on task
- Teacher–student private signal to increase student's self-awareness if he or she is displaying inappropriate motoric behavior (e.g., flapping hands)
- Establishment of eye contact with teachers and peers
- Coordination/communication with parents for student to complete unfinished tasks at home and to reinforce and maintain school learning
- Social rules explained during cooperative learning activities/classroom discussions of readings
- Explanation of higher-level vocabulary or the giving of simpler texts
- Help understanding pronominal references (phrases that function as pronouns)
- Choosing books on topics that parallel students' interests
- Explanation of figurative and nonliteral language such as irony, sarcasm, and dual meanings
- Modeling of proper inflection in readings
- Storyboards or picture clues to identify main idea, setting, characters, and plot to visually sequence supporting details in textbook readings

---

Resources to Consult for Reading Strategies & Standards:

Academy of Orton-Gillingham Practioners & Educators www.ortonacademy.org

International Reading Association www.reading.org

The International Dyslexia Association www.interdys.org

National Council of Teachers of English www.ncte.org/

Wilson Language Training http://www.wilsonlanguage.com/

Novel Resource Guide and Literacy Analysis www.novelguide.com

Fry, E., Kress, J., & Fountoukidis, D. (2000). *Reading teacher's book of lists.* Hoboken, NJ: John Wiley & Sons/Jossey-Bass.

Harvey, S. A. & Goudvis, (2000). *Strategies that work: Teaching comprehension to enhance understanding.* Marham, Ontario, Canada: Stenhouse Publishers/Pembroke Publishers

Karten, T. (2005). *Inclusion strategies that work! Research-based methods for the classroom.* Thousand Oaks, CA: Corwin Press.

Reutzel, D., Cooter, R. (2006). *Strategies for reading assessment and instruction: Helping every child succeed* (3rd ed.) Indianapolis, IN: Prentice Hall/Allyn & Bacon.

Sejnost, R., & Thiese, S. (2007). *Reading and writing across content areas* (2nd ed.). Thousand Oaks, CA: Corwin Press.

Trelease, J. (2006). *The read-aloud handbook* (5th ed.). New York, NY: Penguin Books.

Young, S. (1997). *Scholastic rhyming dictionary.* New York: Scholastic Press.

Zimmerman, S., & Hutchins, C. (2003). *7 keys to comprehension: How to help your kids read it and get it!* New York: Three Rivers Press.

6

Standards-Based Writing, Listening, and Speaking Objectives

The communication umbrella covers the three topics of writing, listening, and speaking, since they are all ways of relating information using the tools of the brain, hands, fingers, mouth, and ears. Pencils, paper, pens, computers, and text messaging are just some instruments that spur the communication process! Writing and speech are like close cousins, since writing is actually talking on paper, with some editing. Sometimes teachers form opinions of students' thought processes based upon what they see on paper or what is articulated. Communication basically needs to be legible and intelligible. Research purports that writing is a process that can be developed and strengthened when educators use structured lessons with specific objectives and accommodations for students to successfully maximize their strengths. The worksheets, graphic organizers, and guided teacher lessons that follow are tools and models to help learners improve their writing.

RESEARCH IMPLICATIONS

Writing research says the following:

> Students with disabilities are more likely to have incomplete understanding of, limited perspective on, or even lack of access to daily information affecting their lives, thereby giving them less fodder for written

communications. . . . [S]ince computers are used to write for a variety of audiences and purposes, students will need to learn acceptable conventions and pragmatics of each situation.

—Strassman & D'Amore, 2002

A critical aspect of functional communication is that it emphasizes skill actualization, where teachers give students the opportunity to use their already developed communication skills across multiple everyday situations . . . requiring a careful analysis of the child's abilities and the communication expectations of teachers and peers, as well as class activities, materials, and natural opportunities for communication.

—Cascella & McNamara, 2005

Helping students understand figures of speech takes more than a book— it takes a creative teacher and interested students.

—Meagher, 2005

Teachers up and down the grades and all across the curriculum need to teach their students to write. Writing is important in every subject, because it is through writing that students learn to grapple with understanding difficult problems.

—Barlow, 2005

SAMPLE LESSONS/CONNECTIONS FOR K–12

HANDWRITING AND NOTE TAKING

Baseline Knowledge Standards

All students legibly write their name and address in manuscript and cursive. They write their telephone number; emergency contacts of parents, family, or friends as well as local emergency numbers for police and fire departments; and list important e-mail contacts. In addition, all students will legibly copy and write numbers to correctly solve simple computation problems. To help more concrete learners, illustrate or include a picture or photograph for each contact with an appropriate caption. Try to include graphics, or if possible concrete objects to accompany learning.

Advancing Level

Some students keep an alphabetic directory of important names and numbers for personal use—e.g., classmates' phone numbers and e-mails; names of other friends or relatives; local businesses such as pizza delivery, movies, and

Figure 6.1

Grades	Content Area/Skills and Standards: Handwriting/Note Taking
K–2	Increase proper pencil grip control. Copy shapes, patterns, and lines. Legibly write all lower- and uppercase letters from both a teacher's model and memory within given parameters. Follow manuscript design, while exhibiting proper size and slant of the letters. Copy numbers correctly from model and auditory memory with increasing complexity; e.g., gradually adding more words to write.
3–5	Learn and practice cursive writing with lower- and uppercase letters. Continue design copying on more intricate levels, varying sizes and directions. Properly copy numbers and letters from the chalkboard and teacher's statements for independent assignments. Learn ways the computer can organize notes.
6–8	Legibly take notes from class lectures. Transcribe written works into legible handwritten and typed communications as a reference for self and others.
9–12	Continue note-taking strategies. Use computer programs to organize written notes, assignments, reports, and essays.

more. These children will also take notes on class lectures, listing basic points made by teachers. Some students might need to highlight photocopied pages from the textbook of points said, if they cannot keep pace with the writing demands.

More Challenging Assignments

Some students write detailed personal directories or keep journals that include all vital information, using proper grammatical sentence structure. Some students will be able to accurately paraphrase statements from the teacher's lecturette in oral and then written form.

Possible accommodations a child with *learning differences or dysgraphia* might need:

- Ruled paper to ensure proper size and direction of letters and numbers
- Tracing paper to outline letters or numbers
- Desk copy of manuscript and cursive alphabet to imitate
- Slantboard for writing
- Prewritten words or phrases
- Model of a completed directory to establish written expectations
- Number line
- Larger-sized pencils, pens, or crayons to ease tensions with writing implements, along with pencil grips
- Salt trays to practice letter formation
- Tactile numbers and letters to manipulate
- Repetition of statements
- Frequent monitoring
- Initial eye contact established to ensure listening posture before lecturette begins
- Manipulatives that concretize concepts
- Computer printouts of lectures; e.g., outline of major points

- Voice recognition software
- Word processing with spell checker and language tools
- Written copy of lecture to check spelling and ease copying requirements

Possible accommodations a child with *traumatic brain injury* might need:

- Repeated directions with step-by-step instructions
- Communication board with photographs that match names and contacts
- Illustrated word cards, classroom wall of words, labeled items in room
- More time to practice
- Additional graphic organizers to help with class notes
- Classification exercises with word categories
- Increased technology with word prediction program
- Laptop or portable word processing program
- A volunteer peer or assistant to take and share notes
- Emphasis on functional communication for daily schedule and needs

Possible accommodations a child with *oppositional defiant disorder* might need:

- Choices in some assignments to avoid classroom power struggles; e.g., "Which names would you like to include in your directory?"
- Closer monitoring of behaviors with a home–school connection; e.g., same expectations of written work in class and assignments completed at home
- Reward system to recognize written handwriting/note-taking strides
- Personalized and individualized comments on writings
- Frequent teacher proximity to reinforce positive classroom note taking
- Learning stations that allow students some control and guided choices

Handwriting and note taking, like other disciplines, requires an approach that begins with easier assignments, and then advances and spirals toward more complex assignments. This step-by-step approach should be applied in all handwritten papers, whether evidenced in composition books, ringed loose leafs, tests, letter writing, reports, or essays. The following sheet asks students to copy some shapes, keeping the size and direction the same, to thereby increase observational skills, along with fine motor control.

CREATIVE AND EXPOSITORY WRITING

Baseline Knowledge Standards

Summarize texts read across content areas by producing a written report with multiple paragraphs. Some students will need a web planner to help sort their ideas, focusing on extracting details that answer *what, where, when, why, how, and who* questions. Other students will be guided to answer teacher-directed questions, and then asked to turn those notes into cohesive sentences and paragraphs.

Figure 6.2

Copy these shapes and lines in the boxes below each one, trying to keep the size, direction, and details the same.

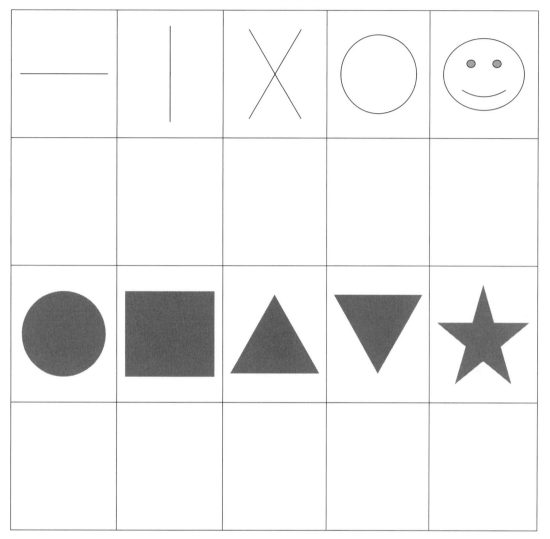

Advancing Level

Write and cooperatively perform curriculum-related plays. To honor individual intelligences, students could type scripts on the computer, choreograph dances, compose songs, construct props, design costumes, or create background scenery.

More Challenging Assignments

Leadership role in cooperative groups, such as being assigned the position of newspaper editor. Using an actual newspaper, students first learn about the individual sections of a paper. Then they choose interest-driven pieces, writing diversified articles; e.g., travel section, food column, crossword puzzle, cartoons, horoscope, weather report, fashion article, local news, international news, sports article, real estate section, classified ads, and more!

Figure 6.3

Grades	Content Area/Skills and Standards: Creative and Expository Writing
K–2	Write about illustrations. Write captions about pictures to express ideas. Notice authors' patterns and style in writings.
	Learn how to sequence events using pictures, words, and numbers. Write simple sentences on given topics. Use teacher modeling to write initial drafts. Cooperatively write stories with peers. Use graphic organizers to organize writing thoughts. Write a paragraph tied to one idea.
3–5	Reflect upon and edit writing, using checklists and rubrics. Write sequential stories and narratives with multiple paragraphs that engage the reader with a good opening, detailed body, appropriate transitions, and conclusion. Write nonfiction texts such as reports and letters. Connect curriculum with writing products to reflect on learning Write and revise drafts, editing under direction of teacher, self, and peers to entertain, inform, and persuade readers. Learn about manual and computer writing tools such as spelling dictionaries and thesauruses. Support and develop a main idea with detailed facts and examples from multiple sources. Insert appropriate graphics and other illustrative material in writings, such as maps, tables, and charts. Learn how to use dialogue with quotations in writings. Explore figurative language in writings. Learn about open-ended writing responses. Identify patterns in poetry and other writings. Imitate style of authors and poets.
6–8	Write logical stories with a specific audience in mind using a variety of genres. Demonstrate writing skills with descriptive, personal, persuasive, and issue-based essays. Write expository pieces on math, science, and social studies lessons. Learn how to paraphrase writings in written reports.
	Use appropriate quotations in nonfiction writing pieces.
	Attach a bibliography to well-written research reports.
	Write diversified genre pieces with a well-developed personal voice and style. Write essays to answer open-ended questions showing knowledge of higher-order thinking skills.
9–12	Draft and defend a thesis statement. Critique journal articles.
	Write multipage research reports, correctly citing primary and secondary sources. Continue demonstration of sophisticated, organized, and well-thought-out writing, evidencing planning, revising, and editing skills.
	Write a position paper with supportive details. Use headings and subtitles in writings. Apply all copyright laws, correctly quoting, crediting, or paraphrasing sources. Write informative, purposeful pieces such as friendly and business letters, resumes, and job applications.

Possible accommodations a child with *dysgraphia* might need:

- Computer voice recognition or word prediction software programs
- Digital recorder to remember thoughts
- Writing templates
- Variety of pencils or pens with differently sized grips
- Portable word processor
- Classroom environment with interactive Smart Boards
- Peer coach that could help transcribe verbal thoughts into written form
- Extra time in class or at home to complete assignments
- Grading on content of work, not appearance

Possible accommodations a child with a *learning difference* might need:

- Organized lists of transitional words to connect thoughts
- Rubric outlining requirements for the written assignments

Figure 6.4

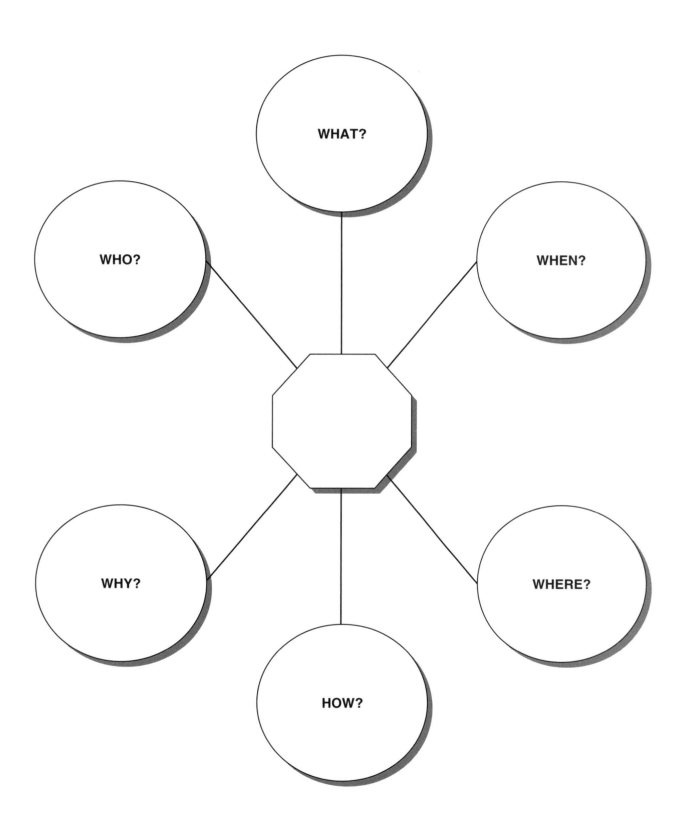

Figure 6.5

Editing and Illustrating Sentences

1. I like cookies.

   I like different kinds of sugary cookies.

   This sentence now expands the thought to include more
   details and lets the reader know more about the cookie types.

   I like to eat different kinds of sugary cookies.

   Was the cookie a friend? How could you like a cookie? The verb *to eat* is included.

   I like to eat different kinds of sugary cookies after my meal.

   When are the cookies eaten? Now the concept of time is added.

   After my meal, I like to eat different kinds of delicious sugary cookies! Don't com-
   pete for the, *I Award!* That's the one given for beginning every sentence with the
   word *I.* Just move some words around for a refreshing sound and a more *tasteful*
   sentence! The adjective *delicious* also lets the reader know that it's a quality
   cookie.

   After my meal, I like to devour different kinds of delicious sugary cookies! You don't
   just *eat* the cookies, you *devour* them! Replacing *eat* with this more emphatic word,
   devour, adds an image of a cookie fiend! Reread the original sentence, and note how
   it's changed and most certainly expanded from your first thoughts.

   Directions: Try illustrating and expanding these sentences:

2. The students learn.

3. Computers are fun.

Figure 6.6

Fill in the Tenses and Write More!

Tenses (when)						My picture:
Past (then)	Yesterday, the children stood in a line.		The boy ran.		They sat on the chairs.	
Present (now)	The children are standing in a line today.	The woman is eating.				
Future (later)	The children will stand in a line tomorrow.			She will ride the camel.		

Directions for *Picture Writing*:

1. Fill in complete sentences in the blank boxes above that correctly describe and match the pictures and tenses.

2. Next, choose a picture you like best. It can also be the one you drew.

3. Expand upon that picture by thinking about a setting for your picture. You can use some of the ones below, or think of your own.

4. Then think of some characters, a plot, a theme, and an ending. Again, you can use some of the choices given below, or think of your own.

5. Write a paragraph with at least 5–8 sentences about the picture.

Settings	Characters	Plot Themes	Endings
Beach	Happy	Friendship	Happiness
Desert	Sad	Love	Satisfaction
Forest	Anxious	Thriller	Marriage
School	Excited	Sports	Divorce
Park	Creative	Cooperation	Partnerships
Shopping Mall	Funny	Adventure	Decisions
House	Pleasant	Confidence	Safe returns
Restaurant	Angry	Intelligence	Winning
My choice	My choice	My choice	My choice

Turning Facts into Expository Writing

Directions: Choose 1 of the topics below and use many of the words from the transitional (connecting) words and phrases to create an essay about the important points of either the Crusades or the Magna Carta. Then research more facts using online sources, your text, and other books. Include information about the governments, commerce, art, music, scientists, technology, and architecture. Name your sources and paraphrase what you have read. In other words, *use other words!*

Crusades Facts

- Series of wars
- 1095–1271 AD
- Europeans wanted to take the Holy Land from the Moslems
- Led to the end of feudalism
- Serfs escaped
- Nobles were killed
- Led to much travel and trade

Magna Carta Facts

- Document
- 1215
- English knights forced King John to sign
- Gave rights to nobles
- King had to obey certain laws
- Raised taxes
- Trial by jury for people
- Beginning of democracy

Words to Connect Thoughts:

First,	Instead,	Undoubtedly,
Elsewhere,	Likewise,	Yet,
As a result,	However,	In spite of,
For instance,	Formerly,	Nevertheless,
Moreover,	At that time,	In this way,
Without,	Frequently,	Still,
To be specific,	During this time,	In addition,
Occasionally,	Before,	Close by,
Consequently,	After,	Ultimately,
		To sum up,

- Breaking up of more complex assignments with step-by-step editing instruction
- Timetable with completion dates for long-range assignments
- Multisensory approaches such as videos that further explain more abstract text concepts in content areas
- Metacognitive writing strategies for revision techniques
- Lists of frequently misspelled words and appropriate content vocabulary
- Alphabetized lists of vocabulary words

Possible accommodations a child with *deafness/hearing loss* might need:

- More content-related visuals; e.g., visual dictionaries, illustrated sentences
- Lectures accompanied by written instructions
- Direct skill instruction with grammar rules; e.g., past, present, and future tenses
- Preferential seating during lessons
- Elimination of unnecessary background noises

Stop and Think Sheet

Graphic organizers help writers *stop* and *think* about what to say on and off the paper, while they stay on the topic!

SPEAKING AND LISTENING

Baseline Knowledge Standards

Students speak about their favorite person, researching facts about living or historical figures. Categories include famous artists, sports figures, government leaders, authors, scientists, mathematicians, explorers, dancers, singers, musicians, and more. Some students will recite facts about that person, while others will deliver a soliloquy, pretending to be that person. If this is too abstract for more concrete learners, they can make it autobiographical, telling about themselves, including present and past experiences, along with future aspirations. Students also choose and include props in their speeches.

Advancing Level

Write and cooperatively perform curriculum-related plays about given time periods on content-related lessons learned in science, social studies, literature, math, and more. If the reading is too difficult for some students, they can help with the typing of the script, costumes, scenery, directing, choreography, or sound effects.

More Challenging Assignments

Leadership role in a debating team, assigning research to team members to support a controversial topic, such as involving armed forces in another

Figure 6.7

Grades	Content Area/Skills and Standards: Communication: Speaking and Listening
K–2	Listen to instructions and read alouds. Follow directions.
	Contribute to conversations. Stay focused on one topic.
	Speak in complete sentences. Share opinions and thoughts with and without prompting. Wait and take turns to speak with peers and adults. Rephrase what is heard in their own words. Explore a topic with questions. Chorally recite, sing, read poems, and talk about stories. Use proper expression and pacing in conversations with peers and adults.
3–5	Listen for meaning and take notes. Clarify ideas by adding appropriate details and vocabulary related to a topic. Respond respectfully to others. Orally present a speech to peers using guided notes, pictures, and prompts. Use proper expression, volume, and eye contact. Revise speeches based on feedback from student and adult audiences. Use speech-scoring rubrics. Converse with peers, teachers, and adults in academic and social situations. Interpret information from books and stories read aloud.
6–8	Communicate effectively with peers in cooperative assigned projects. Ask questions and use research to gain more information. Paraphrase speakers. Value merits of differing opinions and points of view. Participate in debates and formal discussions. Continue oral presentations on curriculum-related topics. Accept and give constructive comments.
9–12	Develop interview skills. Participate in formal and informal discussions; e.g., debates, roundtable discussions.
	Determine speaker's purpose, arguments, and credibility.
	Select readings that support points of view. Understand perspectives of others. Edit speeches in response to differing audiences. Use appropriate rhetorical devices; e.g., parallelism, onomatopoeia, alliteration, and more.

country's affairs. Team members will support their points from research, while respecting other classmates' viewpoints. All students will be aware of their audience, demonstrating appropriate gestures, eye contact, timing, expressions, and changes in voice. Some students will practice with a *speaking coach partner* or in front of a mirror.

Possible accommodations a child with *visual needs* might need:

- Magnification page to enlarge writings for speeches
- Computer or handheld voice/technology programs to read, write, predict, and rehearse printed words for research with speeches
- Braille-transcribed writings of teacher's worksheets and graphic organizers
- Braille texts transposed way ahead of time with publishers providing format in advance to avoid delays
- Additional auditory cues
- Tracking devices to follow line of print
- Enlarged font size on the computer or copier for easier reads
- Tactile stage directions on where to stand
- Repeated practice on audience cues
- More auditory or kinesthetic tools and props to concretize concepts (e.g., raised relief map, digital recorder to ease eye strain with readings)
- Appropriate lighting adjustments, removing extra glare from window lights or other interfering visual distractions

Possible accommodations a child with *Down syndrome* might need:

- Peer coach to help with more difficult reading assignments
- High-interest, lower reading-level books on same topics that include pictorial explanations for more difficult vocabulary
- Social directions and modeling on how to interact with peers
- Additional time on task and repetition of main ideas and details
- Rephrased and simplified directions
- Praise for partial accomplishments
- Functional academic assignments on speech topics that relate to daily living skills; e.g., how to speak to a waiter or waitress in a restaurant, interacting with a customer on a job, asking a store employee for directions, proper volume in a crowded venue
- Demonstrate and assist with communications as needed

Possible accommodations a child with *cerebral palsy* might need:

- Microphone to project voice
- Speech therapist to help practice the speech
- Chair to sit, if standing is too physically taxing
- Mirror to monitor facial expressions and body movements
- Auditory or visual playback of speech for self-reflection
- Lessening of physical requirements upon student request

Figure 6.8   *ABC*ing Your Thoughts

	Use the alphabet to organize your thoughts. Your thoughts can then be expanded into longer speeches and stories. Writing begins with these simple letters, which then become words, sentences, paragraphs, and stories. Remember it all begins with the ABCs!
A	
B	
C	
D	
E	
F	
G	
H	
I	
J	
K	
L	
M	
N	
O	
P	
Q	
R	
S	
T	
U	
V	
W	
X	
Y	
Z	

E   xpansion

D   eletion

S   ubstitution

C   ombine

A   nd

R   earrange

Ask these questions to expand your sentences: Who? What? When? Why? Where? How?

Figure 6.9   Functional Words to Speak and Understand

make	look	take	give	show
like	ask	find	tell	write
help	need	thank	want	point
I me	he him	she her	you	we us
they them	our	everyone	teacher	mom dad parent
sister brother	family	dog cat pet	friend	neighbor
classroom	bathroom	store	outside	inside
games	television	movies	car	music
pencil	crayon	computer	toys	food

Figure 6.10

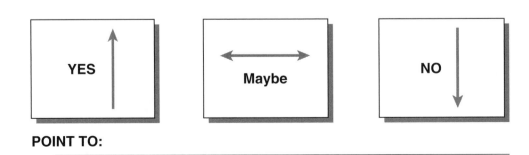

POINT TO:

Baseline Knowledge Standards

Students will name familiar objects in their surroundings. Preschoolers and some more concrete or less expressive learners will be required to master and appropriately respond with answers: *yes, no*, and *maybe*. Students will also identify functional everyday words used, people in their lives; e.g., peers in the classroom, teachers, family members, favorite activities/subjects, toys, and foods. Basic verbs and proper tenses will also be applied in communications.

Advancing Level

Students will understand the similarity and differences between the connotations of words such as the verbs *say, shout, whisper*, or *promise*. Students will explore word choices in conversations between friends vs. adults. Learners complete assignments that associate the spoken with the written word.

More Challenging Assignments

These students will categorize words from content areas as well. Everyday spoken words will trigger auditory memory skills that show the student's ability to successfully follow multistep spoken directions.

Possible accommodations a child with *communication issues* might need:

- Articulation exercises for remediation of difficult sounds
- Step-by-step language instruction to improve categorization of words
- Conversational practice with peers and adults
- Picture AAC (Augmentative and Alternative Communication) device
- Structured listening exercises to strengthen auditory memory
- Visual dictionary
- Repetition of learning in a variety of environments
- Explanation of sarcasm, irony, and words with dual meanings

Possible accommodations a child with *lower cognitive needs* might need:

- Picture schedule for directions
- Memory-strengthening activities
- Illustrations for written words
- Concrete objects in environment to accompany abstract words
- Explanation of body language in communication
- Direct social-skills training
- Help reading printed material or directions
- Charts to organize thoughts and ideas, which are later sequenced into short speeches around a central topic
- Topics relevant to life functioning; e.g., how to listen during a conversation, steps needed to prepare for a job interview

Figure 6.11

Sample of Teacher-Given Oral Directions Using Visuals to Increase Communication:

1. Point to things you like to do.
2. Point to something that scares you.
3. Point to something that you eat.
4. Point to a place.

5. Point to a person.
6. Place a chip on something that begins with the letter *m*.
7. Place chips on animals you like.
8. Place a chip on the picture that makes you smile a lot!

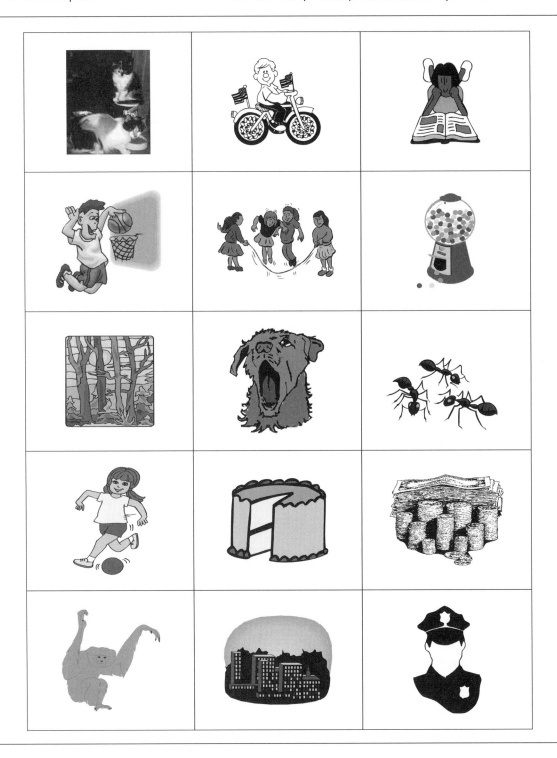

Figure 6.12

Figuratively Speaking:

Words are sometimes *food for thought*! Illustrate these idioms.

It's a piece of cake!	That's a pie in the sky!	It's easy as pie!
Don't spill the beans!	He's working for peanuts!	She eats like a bird!

Possible accommodations a child with *hearing loss* might need:

- Printout of spoken material to get information
- Visual prompts for spoken directions
- Establishing of more eye contact to read lips
- Practice saying and articulating words
- Increased grammar instruction
- Environments that eliminate background noises
- Individualized educational programs
- Accompanying gestures or signs
- Explanation of pronominal phrases
- Concrete explanation of higher-level vocabulary

Figure 6.13

Fill in these sentences, then find pictures or clip art to illustrate the words.

I'm as hungry as a _____!	Don't sugar-coat the _____!	I could eat a _____!
You are the apple of my _____!	Take it with a grain of _____!	That's a half-baked _____!

Word choices for fill-ins:

truth	eye	idea
horse	bear	salt

Check out these idiom resources: www.english-zone.com/idioms/food, and *Scholastic Book of Idioms* by Marvin Terban.

Resources to Consult for Writing Strategies and Standards:

National Council of Teachers of English: www.ncte.org

Calkins, L. (1994). *The art of teaching writing.* Portsmouth, NH: Heinemann.

Fountas, I., & Pinnel, G. (2006). *Teaching for comprehending and fluency: Thinking, talking and writing about reading, K–8.* Portsmouth, NH: Heinemann.

The Write Track: www.thewritetrack.com

Gess, D. (2005). *Teaching writing: Strategies for improving literacy across the curriculum.* Suffern, NY: The Write Track.

Gess, D. (2003). *The writer's book of synonyms.* Suffern, NY: The Write Track.

Karten, T. (2005). *Inclusion strategies that work! Research-based methods for the classroom.* Thousand Oaks, CA: Corwin Press.

Handwriting Without Tears: www.hwtears.com

Sebranek, P., Kemper, D., & Meyer, V. (2001). *Writers INC: A student handbook for writing and learning.* Wilmington, MA: Great Source Education Group.

Tate, M. (2006). *Reading and language arts worksheets don't grow dendrites: 20 literacy strategies that engage the brain.* Thousand Oaks, CA: Corwin Press.

7

Standards-Based Mathematics Objectives

Mathematics involves task analysis, step-by-step approaches, and meaningfully connecting to students' lives. Developing logical thinking and problem-solving skills can be applied across the curriculum to help students achieve academic successes with all subjects. The following research, objectives, worksheets, lessons, and strategies acknowledge the standards while focusing on individual appropriate accommodations for students with varying prior knowledge, abilities, and strengths.

RESEARCH IMPLICATIONS

Mathematics instruction in special education, particularly, has been characterized to a large extent by its emphasis on rote memorization of facts and computational skills, rather than on developing important concepts and applying mathematics to real-world situations.

—Asha, DiPipi, & Perron-Jones, 2002

In areas of curriculum and in mathematics in particular, data support the academic effects of accelerated or advanced curricula for high-ability learners . . . [and] using increased pace and less repetition for advanced learners.

—Kettler & Curliss, 2003

Individuals with dyscalculia need help in organizing and processing information related to quantity and space. . . . [Dyscalculia] can be defined as the dysfunction in the reception, comprehension, or production of quantitative and spatial information. . . .[Teachers can] improve learners' self-esteem by giving them real-life exposure to mathematics as a part of everyday life.

—Sharma, 2003

Students with dyscalculia can usually learn the sequence of counting words, but may have difficulty navigating back and forth, especially in twos, threes or more. . . . [In addition,] difficulty in estimating numbers is impaired in comparison to that of their peers. . . . Children's ability to understand the language found in word problems greatly influences their proficiency at solving them.

—Vaidya, 2004

In this high-tech and globally competitive society, it is becoming more and more important that all citizens be confident in their ability to do mathematics. Knowledge of mathematics is an important skill necessary to succeed in today's world. All students deserve equal access to learning math, and teachers must make the effort to ensure this happens.

—Furner, Vahya, & Duffy, 2005

Excellence in mathematics education requires—high expectations and strong support for all students. . . . Equity requires accommodating differences to help everyone learn mathematics. . . . All students have the right to learn math and feel confident in their ability to do math. . . . Developing a positive attitude toward learning mathematics is an important aspect of a student's learning experience.

—National Council of
Teachers of Mathematics, 2000

A mathematics lesson should begin with the incorporation of the perspective and knowledge that children bring to school. . . . [M]ajor components include . . . manipulatives and representations, variety of strategies . . . [and helping students to] see relationships and connections between different concepts and procedures.

—Sharma, 2003

Teaching mathematics to include the needs of low achievers and students with learning difficulties is a challenging task. However, it is also rewarding and will make anyone who successfully teaches these children a better teacher, one who can justly be proud of supporting the learning and promoting the success of our most challenged children.

—Silva, 2004

SAMPLE LESSONS/CONNECTIONS FOR K–12

PRACTICAL MATH APPLICATIONS

Too often, mathematics is viewed as an isolated subject, only taught through the dictated pages of math textbooks. When the numbers and concepts *jump off the pages and enter students' lives*, then the understandings and skills become concretized through animated and relevant applications. Basically, math does not exist within a vacuum. The following examples illustrate these practical mathematical life connections, while valuing the best ways that students learn.

Proportions and Ratios

Ask five students to stand in front of the class, while the class answers proportional questions such as

- What is the ratio of students wearing sneakers to those not wearing sneakers?
- What's the ratio of boys to girls? Girls to boys?
- What's the ratio of students standing to those not standing? Those seated to those not seated?

Question: Is this an effective way to teach about proportions and ratios?

Answer: Yes! Students are actively involved in their learning. It's a change from the omniscient teacher expelling the knowledge, since students are learning by watching their peers instead, with improved attention and focus on the lesson. It also allows fidgety learners a structured opportunity to get out of their seats. It appeals to visual, kinesthetic, and auditory modalities, while literally and physically relating to students.

Calculating Rate

Ask students if they've ever been on a long car ride. Call on one student and use his response as a *model* for how to calculate rate (speed). Ask the student where he and his family traveled to and how long it took them to get there. For example, if a student knew his destination, but wasn't sure of the distance in miles, together the class could use a map with a scale of miles, look up the distance, or find it out on a computer map program such as Mapquest or Google

Maps. Once the miles and time are now known, the following formula is introduced to the class:

$$R = \frac{D}{T}$$

- Tell students to box this formula since it will *take us places*, while we figure out rates, or in this case the average speed the car was traveling. Before even plugging in the known variables, have students write what each letter represents in the formula, such as R = speed (how fast the car was traveling), T = time (students draw a circle with the numbers 12, 3, 6, and 9 to represent a clock), and D = distance or how far the car was traveling for each unit or in this case, hour. Let's suppose the student said that his family traveled 5 hours to go 340 miles, $\frac{R}{1} = \frac{340}{5}$. Then students would cross multiply to see that 5R = 340. The next step is to divide both sides of the equal sign by 5 to have R stand alone to calculate that the car was traveling an average of 68 mph.

Question: Is this an effective way to teach about rate?

Answer: Yes! Students connect the math to their lives through real-life problems that relate to personal experiences. Now, it's not just about math, but about them!

Another example would be to ask the class what their favorite candy was and take the response of the majority. For example, if most students liked jawbreakers, then you would ask them a question such as, Would it be cheaper to buy a dozen jawbreakers for $1.50 or buy 12 at $0.15 each? The basic point here is that, instead of doing many textbook problems, students internalize and apply the learning better when given skills that relate to their own personal experiences. After figuring out a similar *jawbreaking* problem, one student's only concern was what size the jawbreakers were. She related to this math problem and actually wanted to know more specifics about the jawbreakers! It's an excellent way to have students *taste the learning* by making it so real that they can apply it to their own lives.

How about figuring out a tip amount that's 15%–20% of your restaurant check, or being able to walk into a store and figure out what the cost of a sweater is after a 25%-off discount? These are real-life skills that students will need whether they become electricians, plumbers, teachers, doctors, parents, artists, or bus drivers. This is not an automatic inborn skill, but one that needs to be taught incrementally throughout the grades. To understand more about percentages, students can be given grades on tests that are fractions. For example, 18 out of 20 correct, or $\frac{18}{20}$, is equal to 90%, which students need to calculate themselves by making an equivalent fraction out of 100 or dividing 18 by 20. Students need increased familiarity and practice with these skills, not the deletion of skills from the mathematics program.

The following chart is a helpful one that breaks this concept down into columns, where students can see the percentages side by side. The first step here is to understand what 10% of a number is, and to continually practice that before moving on to higher percentages. Then find 5%, or half of 10%. To find 20%, you double 10%. To find 25%, you would then double 10% and add half of the 10% to that amount. So 50% can be 25% times 2, 5% times 10, or 10% times 5. To find 60%, you multiply 10% by 6, and so on. The chart makes it easier to understand because students see computations next to each other and realize the percentage patterns and procedures. Charts are an effective visual tool!

Estimating Tips and Discounts

Use Figure 7.1 to *estimate* percentages, and then answer questions below to calculate restaurant tips and store discounts. Remember to do the 10% column first, by moving the decimal one place to the left. Some numbers have been filled in to get you started.

Connections to life are essential for students who may have had past failures with math concepts. If they can *see* the math, understanding that it is all around them, then they will exponentially erase their historical *numerical discomforts* and *calculate the benefits with much interest!* How boring math would be if teachers just stuck to instruction with papers and pencils! For example, what's geometry? Where is geometry in the classroom? Is it shown with windows, bulletin boards, clocks, pencils? Of course, parallel and perpendicular lines, spheres, rectangles, squares, and more are all around us. Students can be asked to kinesthetically demonstrate intersecting lines, rays, and triangles, as well as acute, obtuse, and right angles. Placing Post-its on students allows them to represent different points. For example, one student can wear a Post-it representing point A, while another student wears one that is labeled with a dot that represents point B. If they spread their hands out and connect them, but keep their exterior arms by their sides they can be a line segment. If their exterior arms stretch straight out, then they can be lines (like arrows) that continue on and on. If one student places their exterior hand by her side, but holds hands with another student or representative point that stretches out, she can represent a ray. Four students with different points can arrange themselves to create a rectangle or square, or parallel, intersecting, or perpendicular lines. Forgive the pun, but the geometric points here are *endless.* This type of kinesthetic learning *comple(i)ments* not only right angles, but learning styles as well! Specific math objectives, along with possible accommodations, follow.

NUMBER SENSE, OPERATIONS/ COMPUTATIONS, AND MEASUREMENT

The following charts and programs address mathematical objectives and ways for students to better achieve standards. Varying mathematical approaches, manipulatives, and strategies ensures better understandings for

Figure 7.1

Estimate Actual Amounts	5%	10%	15%	20%	25%	40%	50%	65%	70%
Actual: $11.75 Think: $12.00	.60	$1.20	$1.80	$2.40	$3.00	$4.80	$6.00	$7.80	$8.40
Actual: $23.99 Think: $24.00		$2.40							
Actual: $48.99 Think:									
Actual: $74.50 Think:									
Actual: $98.99 Think:									
Actual: $120.50 Think:									
Actual: $147.99 Think:									
Actual: $196.35 Think:									

Tipping Questions: Use the range of 15%–20% as an average tip.

1. a. What tip should your family leave on a restaurant bill that was about $75.00?

   b. What would the total cost of the bill be, including the tip?

2. a. How much of a tip should you and your 4 friends spend, if the food bill was about $50?

   b. What is the total cost of the food, including the tip?

   c. How much would each of you spend, if you divided the bill equally?

It's a Good Deal Questions:

3. a. What's the price of 3 sweaters that are now on sale for 60% off, if they originally cost $20 each?

   b. What is the cost if there was 7% tax added after the discount?

   c. What change would be received if someone paid with a $100 bill?

4. Would you prefer spending $200 for items with a 70% discount or $100 for the same items with a 20% discount?

Figure 7.2

Grades	Content Area/Skills and Standards: Math: Number Sense, Operations/Computations, Measurements
K–2	Order both objects and numbers in decreasing and increasing amounts and sizes. Perform basic computations involving addition and subtraction. Know that with addition, items are combined and become bigger, while subtraction separates objects to make things smaller. Learn and practice basic facts with multiplication and division. Pictorially review and demonstrate representations of all operations. Create problems that can be solved with addition and subtraction. Understand basic place value. Compare sizes of physical objects (e.g., longer, shorter, heavier, lighter). Learn about standard units of measurement.
3–5	Represent, order, and compare numbers. Solve simple word problems involving everyday situations. Use addition and subtraction and multiplication and division as inverse operations. Estimate and round numbers to determine if a word problem answer makes sense. Use skip counting in operations. Know all number facts with automaticity. Perform complex operations with multidigit numbers. Represent fractions and compute problems with fractions. Use concrete objects to represent fraction parts and decimals. Know decimal values to the thousandths place. Perform investigations with number properties. Learn about ratios and proportion. Apply standard units of measurement.
6–8	Solve problems involving negative numbers. Know the relationship between fractions, decimals, and percentages. Find squares and cubes of numbers. Apply order of operations. Solve problems with proportions. Explain methods for solving problems. Compare and order rational and irrational numbers. Know meanings of irrational numbers; e.g., pi. Apply units of measurement with greater accuracy. Convert units of measurement. Apply logical reasoning skills in algebraic equations.
9–12	Develop proofs for number system properties. Continue to expand applications to real numbers and algebraic expressions. Demonstrate operations on matrices. Simplify expressions. Use logic and reasoning for solving word problems. Utilize estimation to judge reasonableness of answers. Cooperatively solve given group assignments involving math applications and measurements across the curriculum.

eclectic students in inclusive classrooms.

The *hundreds' chart* can be used across the grades to visually highlight principles in addition, subtraction, multiplication, and division. Students can skip count with this chart, highlighting multiples, or place chips on numbers to visually solve computations. Initially a blank chart is horizontally filled out by students. In addition, this chart can be used to find all sorts of number patterns.

Figure 7.3

1	2	3	4	5	6	7	8	9	10
11	12	13	14	15	16	17	18	19	20
21	22	23	24	25	26	27	28	29	30
31	32	33	34	35	36	37	38	39	40
41	42	43	44	45	46	47	48	49	50
51	52	53	54	55	56	57	58	59	60
61	62	63	64	65	66	67	68	69	70
71	72	73	74	75	76	77	78	79	80
81	82	83	84	85	86	87	88	89	90
91	92	93	94	95	96	97	98	99	100

Baseline Knowledge Standards

Sequencing, seriation, and ordering are skills to practice and develop. Students will horizontally write seriated numbers from 1–100 on multiple 10×10 tables. If this is too difficult for some learners, they can copy from a written desk model or work with a partner. Upon verbal or written prompting, students will also highlight numbers as they skip count from 2–20, 3–30, 4–40, 5–50, 6–60, 7–70, 8–80, 9–90, and 10–100 on individual duplicated hundreds' charts. For example, if learning the multiples of 3, the numbers 3, 6, 9, 12, 15, 18, 21, 24, 27, and 30 would be highlighted on the *I Can Count by 3s* page.

Advancing Level

It is important to recognize the relationships between numbers. Some students will find nontraditional patterns on their hundreds' charts and highlight vertical, horizontal, and diagonal ones; e.g., 21, 32, 43, 54, 65, 76, 87, and 98 (pattern of +11).

More Challenging Assignments

Learners can use the hundreds' chart to cooperatively create their own word problems and solve computations involving the four operations of addition, subtraction, multiplication, and division.

Figure 7.4

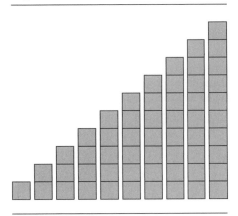

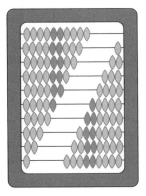

Cuisenaire rods or attachable cubes seriate number values and concretize ordering from 1–10. Some students need to mentally see this *mathematical staircase!* Operations of addition, subtraction, multiplication, and division can be concretely shown with rods such as these.

There are tactile ways for students to concretize math facts, instead of counting on their fingers and toes! Unifex cubes, Cuisenaire rods, and even abacuses ask students to seriate and understand number and place values, associating the abstract with the concrete. Students can learn to point to dots on numbers; develop sequencing and pattern skills; and kinesthetically add, subtract, multiply, and divide. TouchMath is a specific program that asks students to kinesthetically associate numbers with their values while performing computations (see www.touchmath.com).

Learners can refer to the next chart to solve more difficult multiplication and division problems, so that the inability to remember basic facts will not interfere with learning of harder computations such as multiplying two digits by three digits. It also helps with multiple-digit divisors and dividends when students estimate to find compatible numbers; e.g., $826 \div 93$ (think $810 \div 90 = 9$ as a reasonable answer).

Figure 7.5 Multiples Chart

Multiples Chart

1	2	3	4	5	6	7	8	9	10
2	4	6	8	10	12	14	16	18	20
3	6	9	12	15	18	21	24	27	30
4	8	12	16	20	24	28	32	36	40
5	10	15	20	25	30	35	40	45	50
6	12	18	24	30	36	42	48	54	60
7	14	21	28	35	42	49	56	63	70
8	16	24	32	40	48	56	64	72	80
9	18	27	36	45	54	63	72	81	90
10	20	30	40	50	60	70	80	90	100

PROBLEM SOLVING

Baseline Knowledge Standards

Multiplication is like repeated addition, while division involves sharing and repeated subtraction. Check reasonableness of answers in computations involving addition, subtraction, multiplication, and division with whole numbers. Understand how computations can be applied to solve word problems.

Advancing Level

Develop mental math sense performing operations involving money and counting, such as solving problems related to everyday living; e.g., shopping discounts, tipping, interest on a bank account, keeping a checkbook balance, taxes, estimation of prices of a collection of store items, and so on.

More Challenging Assignments

Have students keep a math journal that budgets their own daily expenses. Some students can research and budget expenses for their families, hypothetical careers, and employers—e.g., building supplies and construction costs, school district budgets, advertising agencies, movie theaters, department stores, and other small businesses.

Possible accommodations a child with *cognitive/developmental disabilities* might need:

- Parallel assignments such as meaningful counting exercises (e.g., keeping track of scores in games or sequencing seriation); left–right tracking activities involving concrete manipulatives (e.g., Cuisenaire rods, keeping temperature logs)
- More praise for achievements

Figure 7.6

Directions: Place your finger or a chip on your starting point (meters, grams, liters), then move the chip or your finger (decimal) the correct number of spaces, either to the left or right, to convert numbers. Either multiply or divide by 10 for each box. For example, 3 meters = 300cm = 3000mm = .003km.

⟵─────────────────────   ─────────────────────⟶

divide by 10 for each box   **METRIC SYSTEM**   multiply by 10 for each box

King kilometers	**Henry** hectometers	**died** decameters	**Monday** meters grams liters	**drinking** decimeters	**chocolate** centimeters	**milk** millimeters

King kilometers	**Henry** hectometers	**died** decameters	**Monday** meters grams liters	**drinking** decimeters	**chocolate** centimeters	**milk** millimeters

King kilometers	**Henry** hectometers	**died** decameters	**Monday** meters grams liters	**drinking** decimeters	**chocolate** centimeters	**milk** millimeters

King kilometers	**Henry** hectometers	**died** decameters	**Monday** meters grams liters	**drinking** decimeters	**chocolate** centimeters	**milk** millimeters

King kilometers	**Henry** hectometers	**died** decameters	**Monday** meters grams liters	**drinking** decimeters	**chocolate** centimeters	**milk** millimeters

King kilometers	**Henry** hectometers	**died** decameters	**Monday** meters grams liters	**drinking** decimeters	**chocolate** centimeters	**milk** millimeters

King kilometers	**Henry** hectometers	**died** decameters	**Monday** meters grams liters	**drinking** decimeters	**chocolate** centimeters	**milk** millimeters

Figure 7.7

Gades	Content Area/Skills and Standards: Math: Problem Solving
K–2	Realize that math is a way of thinking about the world. Use concrete and semiabstract representations to discuss and collectively solve simple word problems. Be introduced to word problems involving one operation, and gradually add complexities as understandings increase.
3–5	Compare strategies chosen to solve word problems. Solve word problems with two and three steps, choosing correct operations. Demonstrate accuracy with computations used to solve problems. Check answers with calculators. Realize that word problems may have multiple solutions. Connect word problems to everyday situations. Verify all answers with reasoning and estimation. Understand the difference between relevant and irrelevant information.
6–8	Evaluate and analyze different ways to solve the same problems. Solve word problems with increasing difficulties and multiple steps, demonstrating accurate computations with whole and rational numbers. Increase reasoning skills with algebra, geometry, and measurement.
9–12	Continue to evaluate math thinking and reasoning skills chosen to solve word problems. Work cooperatively in group situations, demonstrating accuracy and higher-order thinking skills in mathematics. Achieve mastery of all computational skills, algebra, geometric principles, and mathematical number sense while solving given word problems that incorporate math principles, reasoning, and connections.

- Calculator instruction for more difficult computations
- Number line or abacus
- Visual demonstration of abstract concepts
- Modeling of word problems
- Step-by-step repetitive approach
- Emphasis upon functional math; e.g., paying for lunch in the school cafeteria, measuring quantities of food along with sizes for portion control, as well as solving problems that relate to their own experiences, such as bus or train fare, paying for a movie, or figuring a restaurant tip
- Additional time to complete tasks
- Math software to reinforce concepts and computations
- Teaching that is concrete, explicit, and constructive

Possible accommodations a child with *more advanced skills* might need:

- Problems that build upon curiosity
- Opportunities to formulate their own questions and problems to share and solve
- Meaningful, ongoing, self-directed math projects/centers
- Mind plexers and logical reasoning activities and problems; e.g., *Soduko*
- Less time to complete activities
- Computer programs with challenging assignments

Possible accommodations a child with *emotional issues* might need:

- Increased praise to build self-confidence
- Monitoring of frustration levels
- More opportunities for success
- Explanation of procedures for cooperative learning activities
- Structure and consistency
- Trusting adults who develop a rapport with the student

Figure 7.8   Problem-Solving Strategy Chart

Data Box: Information from the problem	*What's the Question?* Answer:

Estimate It's about _____	**Guess and Check**	**Draw a Picture**
Make a List 1. 2. 3.	**Break It Into Parts**	**Create a Chart or Table**
Look for a Pattern 2, 4, 6, 8, 10 . . . 3, 5, 8, 12, 17, . . .	**Work Backward**	**Act It Out**
Use Logical Reasoning	**Solve a Simpler Problem** How can I make this easier?	**Set Up an Equation** $A + B = C$ $C - B = A$

SOURCE: Karten, T. (2005). *Inclusion strategies that work!* Thousand Oaks, CA: Corwin Press.

- Understanding peer coaches
- Help/encouragement to develop a positive attitude about math advances and overall school progress and accomplishments
- Guided empowerment in assignments; e.g., have them choose 3 out of the next 5 questions to answer, allowing students to have a stake in their learning to avoid other power struggles, since they can somewhat control the lesson's dynamics
- The addition of personal elements to word problems; e.g., include students' names, same name of city where they live, topic redirected to relate to things students like such as music, television shows, video games, sports, fashion, pets, and more

GEOMETRY

Figure 7.9

Grades	Content Area/Skills and Standards: Math: Geometry
K–2	Compare sizes and shapes of objects. Create patterns and collages with shapes. Combine or break up shapes. Describe and classify different concrete 2-D and 3-D shapes. Learn about grids as a way to locate places. Identify position of shapes in space. Count the number of sides in shapes. Put shapes together and take them apart.
3–5	Create shapes on grids. Describe translations, rotations, and reflections. Know properties and relationships of lines, line segments, polygons, angles, circles; e.g., parallel, perpendicular, intersecting. Know basic geometric formulas. Measure angles with protractors. Learn about symmetry and congruency.
6–8	Compare properties of shapes. More practice with tessellations. Continue study of angles, lines, circles, and polygons. Graph points and their coordinates. Match 3-dimensional and 2-dimensional objects (nets). Explore proofs of the Pythagorean theorem. Investigate and apply formulas to determine areas, perimeter, and circumferences of 2-D and 3-D shapes. Graph inequalities. Apply slope formula.
9–12	Apply geometric principles to everyday situations. Use reasoning with theorems. Solve or refute proofs. Use principles of perspective to draw 3-D objects. Utilize more intricate computer programs and software.

Connective Academic Issues

Teacher request/question: What is the surface area of this solid figure?

Figure 7.10

4 ft.

3 ft.

10 ft.

Student Responses:

"120 ft."

"17 ft."

"164 ft. □"

"164 ft.²"

These are interesting responses that need to be analyzed. The first and second answers, although conceptually incorrect, indicate that the students know how to compute accurately. The first one indicates correct multiplication skills, and the second one shows a correct addition answer. Now the third answer is too bizarre for me to have concocted, but is what actually happened. The student was able to go through the tough process of making separate problems, specifically: $2(4 \times 10) + 2(10 \times 3) + 2(4 \times 3) = 80 + 60 + 24 = 164$. I was so impressed that this student knew how to conceptually see the front, back, top, bottom, left, and right sides of the object and then apply the instruction after repeated practice. I was stunned that when I told the student that the answer must have the tag of squared, he drew a square. Again, back to basics, and never assume anything about prior knowledge. Exposure here to proper mathematical nomenclature is crucial!

Baseline Knowledge Standards

Students will identify basic shapes and place objects beside, inside, next to, close to, above, and below other objects. Some students will sort and compare 3-D shapes according to size, color, and type. Some students will also list real-life situations in which geometric principles can be applied.

Advancing Level

Students create collages of overlapping shapes to demonstrate understanding of both positive and negative space. If there are perceptual, fine motor, or interfering visual issues, some students can use precut congruent and similar figures, templates, stencils, and computer-generated ones. Students will also visually identify rotations, reflections, and translations.

More Challenging Assignments

Students create an art tessellation project with rotations that turn, reflections that flip, and translations that slide, using free-form shapes with and without computer art tools.

Possible accommodations a child with *dysgraphia* might need:

- Larger sized pencils or other writing implements
- Safety scissors
- Pencils with adaptive grips
- Tracing paper
- Stencils or templates of shapes
- Modification of project, using drawing tools and shapes on the computer
- More time to complete project in class or at home

Possible accommodations a child with *visual/perceptual needs* might need:

- Braille ruler
- More verbal directions
- Raised outline of shapes for easier cutting
- Peer/teacher model to follow
- More guided step-by-step instructions
- Tessellation project that just concentrates on one skill; e.g., reflection only

Possible accommodations a child with *autism* might need:

- Repetition of instructions
- Establishment of eye contact before oral directions
- Accommodation to complete project with a peer to also develop social skills
- Headphones to increase focus; e.g., with soothing music
- Personalized pictures of favorite objects cut up into different shapes as a puzzle
- Visual sequencing of steps to accompany written words or directions
- Tactile concrete objects with different shapes to sort
- More frequent monitoring to ensure time on task
- Peer coach to assist and focus on geometric assignment
- Parallel assignment, such as finding all circular, rectangular, or square shapes of objects in the room or on a picture
- Alternative grading system, based upon efforts and advances achieved from assessed baseline point

Figure 7.11   Where Do I See These Shapes?

Rectangle	Triangle	Oval	Octagon	Sphere	Cylinder

ALGEBRA, PATTERNS, AND RELATIONSHIPS

Baseline Knowledge Standards

Students will understand that a variable is synonymous with an unknown number. Some students will solve simple equations filling in missing elements.

Advancing Level

Students will solve equations with two variables and coefficients.

More Challenging Assignments

Students will solve equations involving negative numbers. Others will develop and connect skills with algebra tiles and blocks.

Figure 7.12

Grades	Content Area/Skills and Standards: Math: Algebra, Patterns, Relationships
K–2	Identify, repeat, and create simple patterns with concrete objects and pictures. Solve simple open sentences with addition and subtraction. Identity zero property. Understand commutative and associative properties with addition.
3–5	Extend patterns by repeating formulas. Identify applicable arithmetic properties for all operations. Solve simple equations with whole-number coefficients and answers. Relate algebra to everyday situations; e.g., gaining and losing yards in a football game.
6–8	Solve equations with whole and rational numbers. Apply properties for all operations. Solve multistep linear equations with variables on both sides. Evaluate inequalities. Demonstrate graphing knowledge on a number line. Use additive and multiplicative inverses. Understand absolute value. Describe and graph functions. Substitute values for variables. Describe, complete, and extend patterns. Learn more about how tables, graphs, and equations represent relationships in math. Identify linear and nonlinear functions.
9–12	Reinforce and extend practice of all algebraic skills. Demonstrate knowledge of all properties with equalities and inequalities. Analyze functional relationships with equations, tables, and graphs.

Possible accommodations a child with a *lower cognitive/intellectual level or more concrete learners* might need:

- Students demonstrate understandings by acting out equations.

Example: $2X + 4 = 10$. Two students will each wear a Post-it with an X on themselves to represent 2X. Another student will wear a plus (+) sign Post-it. Then another student will represent an equal sign (=). Four students will be put on the left of the = sign and 10 on the right. The next step will be to subtract 4 students from one side and take away 4 students from the 10 standing on the right of the = sign. This concretely shows students that whatever you do to one side of the = sign you must even out with the other side, like balancing a seesaw. Students will see a human equation that says $2X = 6$. Now there is no need for the + sign anymore. Each side will be divided by 2, to have X stand alone. This will mean that the left side loses its coefficient and remains x while the 6 is divided into two groups of 3 each. *Aha!* Visual insight is now achieved, since $X = 3$. Then the answer is substituted into the original equation to see that $2(3) + 4 = 10$.

GRAPHING, DISCRETE MATHEMATICS, PROBABILITY, AND DATA INTERPRETATION

Baseline Knowledge Standards

Students will understand the difference between problems or situations that have exact answers and those problems that can have variable outcomes. Students will interpret basic picture, line, bar, and pie graphs.

Figure 7.13

Grades	Content Area/Skills and Standards: Math: Graphing, Discrete Mathematics, Probability, and Data Interpretation
K–2	Read and interpret pictures, charts, and graphs. Use everyday experiences to collect and record data; e.g., class heights. Understand chance happenings such as tossing a coin. Identify, sort, and order data in proper size and sequence.
3–5	Sort and organize information into lists, charts, and graphs. Draw conclusions from data collected. List different possible or probable outcomes. Identify terms: mean, median, mode, and range.
6–8	Predict and estimate probability. Explore compound events and relationships between different combinations of data. Use Venn diagrams to list multiple attributes in different contexts. Increase knowledge of measurements of central tendency. Understand sampling; e.g., everyone vs. random.
9–12	Evaluate and interpret data and probability in experiments and complex situations. Apply data to varying content areas; e.g., inserting a graph into a written report. Synthesize probability of events. Identify and apply Pascal's triangle. Justify choices made to represent data collected. Use algorithmic thinking and vertex-edge graphs. Use computer programs with databases and spreadsheets to further analyze data. Make predictions; analyze discrepancies and outcomes of experiments.

Advancing Level

Students will gather information from surveys and other collected data to create their own graphs that accurately portray varying results.

More Challenging Assignments

Students will compare and contrast a variety of data and predict probability of outcomes.

Possible accommodations a child with *attention/behavioral issues* might need:

- Frequent monitoring and supervision
- Establishment of personal signal for increased attention during independent activities
- Kinesthetic instruction; e.g., *human* graphing
- Graphing information that relates and connects to own lives
- Directions in both written and oral form
- Praise for partial achievement of task, if best observed efforts were given; e.g., praise for input, not just output

Possible accommodations a child with *lower cognitive levels* might need:

- Graph template to color or fill in; e.g., bar/circle graph
- More visuals or concrete objects to represent abstract information
- Explanation of the word *probability* by making personal/functional connections; e.g., if you regularly brush your teeth you will probably have healthier teeth

Figure 7.14

Do I Have Enough Money for These Items?	Cost	Money I Have to Spend	Circle Yes or No and fill in blanks
Laptop Computer	$1,000.00	11 of these $100 bills	Yes, I'll have this much money left over: _____ No, I need _____ more
Sweater	$36.00	3 $10.00 bills 1 $5.00 bill 5 quarters	Yes, I'll have this much money left over: _____ No, I need _____ more
Bicycle	$99.00	3 $20.00 bills 2 $10.00 bills 1 $5.00 bill 4 $1.00 bills	Yes, I'll have this much money left over: _____ No, I need _____ more
Video Game	$50.00	3 $20.00 bills	Yes, I'll have this much money left over: _____ No, I need _____ more
CD	$17.00	60 dimes 12 $1.00 bills	Yes , I'll have this much money left over: _____ No, I need _____ more

- Help translating and organizing information from verbal responses to charts and graphs, using a step-by-step instructional and repetitive approach
- Direct instruction on how to *tally* votes

Possible accommodations a child with *communication disorders* might need:

- Rewording of more difficult vocabulary
- Illustrated/visual dictionary as a reference to consult
- Collaboration with speech teacher, giving her or him an advance copy of your lesson plans so vocabulary can be pretaught in smaller setting or at home
- PECS (Picture Exchange Communication System) to communicate needs if speech is impaired
- Appropriate level of technology support necessary to maximize communication with teachers and peers
- Customized communication board or key ring with shapes and individual math assignments; e.g., laminated folder with Velcro pictures or graphs
- Yes or no chart to point to or color-coded questions and answers

Eye-Opening Lesson

Problem posed: What is the probability that two parents with brown eyes would have a child with blue eyes?

Figure 7.15

Objective: To accurately apply knowledge on probability and genetics

Procedure: After learning about recessive and dominant genes, students are asked to create Punnet squares to answer this question.

Realistic results: Some students with more advanced skills will apply the learning and create the appropriate T-squares. Other students might stare at you with blank looks or not make *eye contact*, literally and figuratively!

Accommodations: You, as the teacher, need to observe, assess, and *jump-start* some students in the right direction, with such assistance as the following:

- Preprinted empty T-squares as templates for them to fill in genetic information
- Review of directions, task requirements, and possibly reteaching of probability and genetic concepts; e.g., each parent has two genes for eye color in different dominant (stronger) and recessive (weaker) combinations
- T-squares with some or all of the genetic possibilities of brown-eyed parents clearly labeled or filled in with a key that explains the coding

Lettering code: B = dominant, b = recessive

Figure 7.16

A

	B	B
B		
B		

B

	B	B
B		
b		

C

	B	b
B		
b		

- Both parents have brown eyes, each with 2 dominant genes (BB, BB)
- One parent has brown eyes with 2 dominant genes (BB), and the other parent has one dominant, and one recessive gene (Bb)
- Each parent has mixed genes, one dominant and one recessive (Bb + Bb)
  - Modeling of how to fill in one square, before students complete squares on their own, if there is weak prior anchoring knowledge, perceptual issues, or confusion
  - Frequent checking to ensure that students complete one box correctly, and do not repeat errors that imprint learning incorrect information
  - Asking the student to paraphrase and explain what each box means
  - Review of skills with fractions and percentages
  - Allowing the use of a calculator for final percentage totals

---

**Resources to Consult for
Mathematics Strategies and Standards:**

National Council of Teachers of Mathematics: www.nctm.org/

Touch Math: www.touchmath.com

Everyday Mathematics: www.everydaymath.uchicago.edu/

A+ Math: www.aplusmath.com

Keymath: www.keymath.com

The Math Forum Internet Mathematics Library: www.mathforum.org/library/

Karten, T. (2005). *Inclusion strategies that work! Research-based methods for the classroom.* Thousand Oaks, CA: Corwin Press.

McNamara, T. (2006). *Key concepts in mathematics: Strengthening practice in Grades 6–12* (2nd ed.). Thousand Oaks, CA: Corwin Press.

Solomon, P. (2006). *The math we need to know and do in Grades PreK–5: Concepts, skills, standards, and assessments* (2nd ed.). Thousand Oaks, CA: Corwin Press.

Tang, G. (2001). *The grapes of math.* New York: Scholastic Press.

8

Standards-Based Science and Technology Objectives

Science was never my favorite subject. When I was in elementary school in the 1960s, my *scientific knowledge* was basically memorized facts and being able to define vocabulary words. Our science lessons were really reading lessons using science as the subject. The benefits of inquiry and discovery through observation and experimentation were missing. The following research, sample lessons, and worksheets value both the science standards and individual strengths. The accommodations listed can strengthen scientific thought and transfer this inferential and deductive thinking and reasoning to other curriculum areas to help students better understand logical principles across various disciplines.

RESEARCH IMPLICATIONS

Activities that foster and encourage the use of science process skills, such as those that involve the use of Venn diagrams, sorting hoops, and attribute blocks, provide children with the skills they need to understand how scientists work. . . . A sorting activity is concrete in nature and promotes the use of manipulatives; group work; class discussion; and hands-on, minds-on instruction.

—Moore, 2003

143

Students who learn to think creatively, while engaging in scientific endeavors, hone skills applicable to other contents. . . . Teachers need to facilitate learning episodes through which students have sufficient opportunities to develop true scientific understanding, science process skills, and corresponding creative thinking skills.

—Meador, 2003

Instructors should utilize multiple constructivist teaching strategies and combine a variety of instructional activities to promote learners' cognitive structure development and knowledge construction in science classrooms. . . . [They should] help learners develop more integrated cognitive structures by paying more attention to making the connections between students' prior knowledge and instructional materials.

—Kelly & Ying-Tien, 2005

If we want more young people to become mathematicians, scientists, and engineers, then we need to find ways to awaken and nourish a passion for those subjects well before high school.

—Wolk, 2006

The following pictorial books *illustrate* science with concrete examples and analogies that connect the vocabulary with the process. These Web sites also offer further elaborations.

Science Sources to Help Implement
Strategies That Connect With the Standards:

National Science Teacher's Association: www2.nsta.org/sciencesites/

Usborne books: www.theusbornebookstore.com

> Bramwell, M., & Mostyn, D. *How Things Work.*

> Craig, A., & Rosney, C. *The Usborne Science Encyclopedia.*

> Chisolm, J., & Johnson, M. *An Usborne Introduction: Chemistry.*

> Oxlade, C., Stockley, C., & Wertheim, J. *The Usborne Illustrated Dictionary of Physics.*

ScienceLynx: www.curriculum.edu.au/science

www.sciencenewsforkids.org/

Chemistry Web site: www.thecatalyst.org

Physics Web site: Association of Physics Teachers (AAPT), www.aapt.org

National Institute of Environmental Health Sciences for Kids: www.niehs.nih.gov/kids

Biology Lesson Plans: www.biology.about.com/od/biologylessonplans

Science Sources by Earth Enterprises: http://kids.earth.nasa.gov/

Animated curriculum movies: www.brainpop.com

SAMPLE LESSONS/CONNECTIONS FOR K–12

INQUIRY SKILLS

Baseline Knowledge Standards

Students will understand that the way a scientist thinks, works, and studies problems is called a process, which includes observation, recording data, classification, prediction, experimentation, interpreting data, and drawing conclusions.

Figure 8.1

Grades	Content Area/Skills and Standards: Science: Inquiry Skills
K–2	Develop observational and questioning skills. Learn to gather appropriate information and materials. Identify patterns in nature. Think about scientific happenings in their community; e.g., weather, plants. Introduce students to basic logical skills; e.g., If . . . then. Categorize similar objects under larger headings.
3–5	Explore contributions of worldwide scientists and inventors. Understand and practice safety rules. Know the attributes of good scientists such as curiosity, organization, and open-mindedness. Compare and classify objects. Understand basics behind scientific experiments. Define a *variable*.
6–8	Plan experiments with hypotheses. Interpret, analyze, predict, and evaluate results. Realize that experimental results may vary. Describe how science correlates with different cultures.
9–12	Safely conduct scientific experiments. Hypothesize, define, and control variables. Understand how sometimes scientific theories may develop and change over time. Investigate how world scientists communicate. Evaluate role of technology in scientific study.

Advancing Level

Through the inquiry method of learning, students develop more curiosity, skepticism, and open-mindedness.

More Challenging Assignments

Increase directions, complexity; e.g., amount of variables, along with more detailed analysis of experiments.

Possible accommodations a child with *auditory processing concerns* might need:

- More visual instructions; e.g., step-by-step written directions with graphics or realistic photographs vs. just lecturing or oral instructions
- Appropriate rate and style of presentation
- Assistance to go beyond memorization of science facts to see connections, make generalizations, and achieve relevance using inquiry skills in their own lives
- Help processing questions if vocabulary is not within their realm of prior knowledge
- Lessons that are narrower in scope and of shorter duration
- The building of inquiry skills upon stronger perceptual foundations; e.g., using smell, sight, touch to identify the contents of a box of things found in nature or identifying how different gadgets work by taking them apart to add a tactile component
- Asking student to paraphrase steps to ensure understandings

Possible accommodations a child with *behavioral issues* might need:

- Appropriate *peer pairing* to encourage and model time on task
- Structured, predictable, and positive environment
- Detailed procedures, with both academic and behavioral expectations outlined
- Preview of lesson topic before class experiment to sensitize student and circumvent possible inappropriate reactions to unexpected results
- Encouragement and praise to participate in discussions if student is shy or withdrawn

CHEMISTRY

Baseline Knowledge Standards

Students will know that physical changes create mixtures that can usually be separated, but chemical changes form new substances. Students will explore fast and slow reactions (e.g., heating something vs. diluting an acid with water). Students will understand patterns in chemistry by identifying similar properties of elements arranged in the periodic table by groups and periods.

Advancing Level

Increased learning about how an atom's structure helps it react with other atoms. Some students will write balanced chemical equations, indicating knowledge of valencies (number of electrons that an atom needs to gain or lose in a chemical reaction). Students will learn more about chemical changes in the body caused by energy from food and oxygen, understanding the roles of different enzymes and catalysts.

More Challenging Assignments

Students will learn about organic compounds such as alkanes, isomers, alkenes, polymers, alkynes, and cyclic hydrocarbons. Students will expand

Figure 8.2

Grades	Content Area/Skills and Standards: Science: Chemistry
K–2	Sort objects according to their physical properties. Realize that some materials can change when combined with different ones; e.g., water and sand
3–5	Identify 3 states of water and its properties. Know that materials respond differently to similar conditions. Understand that when two or more materials are combined, the final product may have totally different properties; e.g., chemical and physical changes.
6–8	Realize that all matter is made up of atoms, which then form molecules. Distinguish between chemical and physical changes. Understand that atoms can be rearranged, but the mass and number of atoms remains the same as original substances.
9–12	Identify requirements for changes in chemical bonds. Know that the number of protons in the nucleus determines the element and that the positive nucleus is surrounded by negative electrons. Know that energy is transferred in most chemical reactions. Check out relevant chemistry info for secondary education/high school–level teachers at www.thecatalyst.org.

knowledge of role of catalysts, nature of reactants, concentration, pressure, and temperature.

Possible accommodations a child with *dyslexia or visual impairments* might need:

- Chemistry textbooks on tape (www.rfbd.org)
- Braille periodic table (www.tsbvi.edu/braille/index.htm)
- Talking calculators for computations in experiments
- Modified testing that allows student to orally answer questions, so reading difficulties do not interfere with their demonstration of chemistry knowledge
- More illustrations and visuals that accompany text and all written materials
- Enlarged, uncluttered worksheets or tables to compartmentalize information to ease perceptual difficulties
- More kinesthetic and auditory activities
- Breaking up larger words into their syllables to help with decoding; e.g., hy-dro-car-bons, i-so-mers

Possible accommodations a child with *attention issues* might need:

- Behavior modification program with increased praise
- Self-reflective strategies to increase level of awareness of time on task and positive strides gained, even though task may not be completed
- Extended time to complete work at home or in another setting
- Structured directions and consistent routines
- Increased parent communication to ensure task completion at home; e.g., parent signing off on a homework assignment pad, e-mailing

assignments, posting weekly classroom and homework assignments on a Web site
- Keeping a calendar for time management of long-range assignments

Possible accommodations a child with *physical differences* might need:

- Modified laboratory equipment; e.g., using a turkey baster instead of an eye dropper, if student has fine motor needs
- Environment that allows student in a wheelchair the same physical access as peers
- Scribe to copy notes if handwriting is illegible
- Peer education about appropriate assistance and sensitivities required
- Knowledge of medications taken or other health conditions
- Computer assistance; e.g., speech recognition or word prediction programs
- Adaptive mouse; e.g., head pointer, voice activation

LIVING ORGANISMS

The following study guides and tables examine how students with different needs and levels may require varying accommodations and modifications to better understand more about kingdoms, cells, and the Linnaean classification system. To no one's surprise, these classroom accommodations end up benefiting those students with and without individual learning, social/behavioral, or physical issues!

Figure 8.3

Grades	Content Area/Skills and Standards: Science: Living Organisms
K–2	Compare and contrast human characteristics such as walking, holding, seeing, talking. Know the needs of living and nonliving organisms; e.g., air, water, nutrients, light. Know that different types of organisms are found in different environments. Understand how plants and animals are similar to their parents. Explore life cycle process; e.g., born, live, grow, die. Investigate some humans, animals, and insects.
3–5	Determine roles of organisms in a food chain. Realize that organisms can be grouped according to different characteristics. Compare and contrast the needs and characteristics of plants and animals. Know different stages of some organisms. Identify human body systems of organisms. Realize that some traits and characteristics are inherited, while others are learned by interacting with the environment (e.g., riding a bicycle). Understand that some organisms are now extinct and the reasons why.
6–8	Learn about cells and cell parts. Identify major classifications of organisms. Compare and contrast organisms and their niches. Understand various human body systems. Investigate genetics and variations in offspring. Realize the positive and negative impacts the environment has on organisms.
9–12	Know how chemical energy is converted to light energy by plants. Understand the role of natural selection and the impact of technology on human characteristics. Identify how molecules relate to cellular structure and metabolism. Understand the relationships between diseases and system failures. Explore positive health choices on organs and systems.

Understanding the Five Kingdoms

Baseline Knowledge Standards

Students should know the difference between living and nonliving organisms. Students will also be able to match pictures of organisms with their correct kingdom.

Advancing Level

Some students will be able to chart these differences, noticing similarities and differences between kingdoms.

More Challenging Assignments

Students will compare and contrast different organisms.
Possible accommodations a child with *learning/perceptual needs* might need:

- A chart to visually differentiate and organize the information
- Visuals of organisms as examples
- Explanation of written directions
- Uncluttered worksheets
- Paraphrasing of more difficult multisyllabic words

Possible accommodations a child with *blindness* might need:

- Clay to make models of organisms; e.g., bacteria (monerans) in the shapes of spirals, rods, or spheres
- Textbook on tape and more auditory direction
- Peer coach to consult and assist
- Structured and predictable classroom setup
- Mobility training
- Raised pictures with tactile outlines

Possible accommodations a child with *deafness* might need:

- A copy of teacher's notes or teacher's manual
- Preferential seating
- More visuals of organisms
- Peers and teachers establishing eye contact with the student for lip reading
- Paraeducator, coteacher, or parent preteaching vocabulary
- Modified grading that does not penalize student for hearing loss, but allows a valid assessment that grades knowledge of content, not possible written or communicative language weaknesses

The following charts and tables organize information, concepts, and principles into a *student-friendly format*. The next one, "Be the King of the Kingdoms," emphasizes the concept that students need to memorize facts, but at the same time they need to see relationships and comparisons between the whole idea and its components. It has a self-monitoring element built into it. The study guide on kingdoms also values studying over time, rather than cramming learning into the night before the test.

Answer key

	one-cell	multicellular	cell wall	no cell wall	make/take in own food	don't make food	nucleus	no nucleus	move	don't move	Types: Answers can vary.
Monera	√		√		√			√	some		bacteria
Protista like	most	some	some	some	√		√		many		plant/animal
Plantae		√	√		√make		√				moss, trees
Animalia backbones		√		√	eat food	can cook-hunt	√		most		with/no
Fungi		√most	√		√		√			√	yeast, mushrooms

150

Be the King of the Kingdoms

Directions: Cover up the answer key and test yourself until you can fill in the entire chart correctly. Then wait an hour or two, or a day or two, and try it again.

Cells for Sale

Objective: To understand more about cell parts. Remember cells cannot be seen, but they are the basic units of life. Cells grow and divide and make more cells, taking in nutrients that give us energy. They have different shapes and sizes—e.g., nerve cells, brain cells, skin cells—and now in this lesson there's even going to be a *candylike cell!*

Materials: Lots of candy, such as mini chocolate chips, peanuts, snowcaps, M&Ms, fruit rollups, marshmallows, and more, along with differently sized paper plates, ziplock bags, and/or cupcake holders. Alternatives to food materials can include Legos, pipe cleaners, boxes, and so on.

Procedure (What to do!): Create an animal cell, telling what each food part represents. List its function (job) in the third column. Use the paper plate as your cell membrane. When you have completed this chart, draw your candy cell on a separate piece of paper.

Create your edible cell cooperatively, with your *cellmates!*

Figure 8.4

Food/Item	Cell Part	Function (how it helps the cell)
Paper Plate	Cell membrane	Gives the cell structure, protects it, and keeps everything inside the cell, controlling what enters and leaves
	nucleus	
	chromosomes	
	vacuoles	
	DNA	
	ribosomes	
	cytoplasm	
	mitochondria	
	nuclear membrane	
	genes	

Completed by *cellmates* (write names below):

_____

_____

_____

Bonus question: What cell parts would you need to add if this was a plant cell?

_____

Classification Lesson

Baseline Knowledge Standards

All things can be classified or put into groups with similar characteristics. Students choose an everyday object and subdivide it by observing similarities and differences, explaining their reasoning behind chosen classifications; e.g., classifying video games into violent/nonviolent ones or stores into food/clothing/other merchandise.

Advancing Level

The Linnaean classification system orders and divides organisms with specific names. The order of division from largest to smallest is kingdom, phylum, class, order, family, genus, and species. Students will be able to describe the scientific two-part names of several assigned organisms.

More Challenging Assignments

Students investigate and diagram classifications of organisms in all of the five kingdoms: plantae, animalia, monera, protista, and fungi.

Knowing Beyond

Students investigate the meanings of Latin names in the Linnaean system (e.g., *felis domesticus* means house cat).

Possible accommodations for a child with *reading difficulties:*

- Place divisions on differently sized and colored cards that have a self-checking visual aspect to them.

Possible accommodations for a child with *memory difficulties:*

- Use a mnemonic such as *King Phillip Came Over for Green Soup* to help students remember descending order.

Possible accommodations for a child with *developmental difficulties:*

- Use concrete objects involving functional academics to help them make subdivisions to understand how to classify objects; e.g., items used for hygiene: comb, shampoo, conditioner, toothbrush, dental floss, toothpaste, soap, wash cloth, towel. Categories under the topic of hygiene might include hair, teeth, body.

Figure 8.5

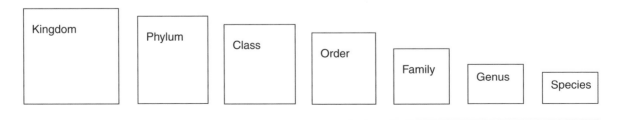

Possible accommodations for a child with *autism:*

- Modeling of lesson and allowing them to cooperatively work with assigned peers
- Focus on social skills

Possible accommodations for a child with *learning disabilities:*

- More visuals, with repetition, and frequent checking of understanding
- Give students a rubric to see expectations required for grades.

Possible accommodations for a child with *more advanced skills:*

- Allow students to creatively design and present their own classification project; e.g., book, newsletter, scientific article in a journal, song, dance, video, and more. This allows them to cooperatively continue learning under your auspices.

Vertebrates and Invertebrates

Concepts can be taught with frameworks or *backbones,* in some of these cases! The first thing is for students to concretely understand that there are two distinct types of animals, those with backbones (vertebrates) and those without backbones (invertebrates).

This information can be given through note-taking charts:

Another way to deliver this information is to for students to sort names of different animals, written on index cards, and then place them in correspondingly sized envelopes. For example, the arachnid would fit into the arthropod envelope, which would then fit into the invertebrate envelope, and then all of those would be placed into the largest envelope, in the category of animals.

PHYSICS/PHYSICAL SCIENCE

Baseline Knowledge Standards

Students will know that the sun is a source of light and heat and provides almost all of the energy we need. Students will also understand how some things do or do not allow light to pass through them; e.g., the difference between opaque and transparent objects. They will have the realization that when light hits opaque objects, it no longer travels in a straight line, but bounces off the object in its way, and makes shadows. Students will know that light travels fastest in air but slower in water, and even slower in glass.

Advancing Level

Some students will compare waves by measuring wavelengths (length from the top of one wave to the top of the next), amplitude (height of the wave), and frequency (number of waves that enter through a given point each second).

Figure 8.6

A: Vertebrates ⟶	Specific Types	B: Invertebrates ⟶	Specific Types
Birds	albatross, bluebird, cardinal, chickadee, ostrich	Mollusks	snails, lobsters, clams, octopus
Fish	Bony— lungfish, lobefin Cartilaginous— sharks, rays, skates Jawless— lampreys, hagfish	Arthropods	Crustaceans; e.g., lobster Insects; e.g., bees Arachnid; e.g., spider
Amphibians	**Frogs, Salamanders**	**Echinoderms**	**Starfish, Sea Urchin**
Reptiles	**Lizards, Turtles, Snakes, Crocodiles, Alligators**	**Worms**	**Flat, Round, Segmented, Parasitic**
Mammals	**Humans, Dogs, Pigs, Horses, Monkeys**	**Cnidarians**	**Coral, Jellyfish, Hydra**

Figure 8.7

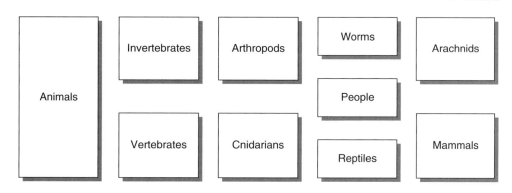

Figure 8.8

Grades	Content Area/Skills and Standards: Science: Physics/Physical Science
K–2	Understand that objects can move differently and are made up of different materials; e.g., wood, plastic, paper. Realize that objects produce sound through vibration. Explore the properties of light; e.g., traveling in a straight line until it hits an object. Understand reflection. Know that heat can move from one object to another. Understand the different ways to produce heat (e.g., rubbing, burning) or cool objects (e.g., freezing).
3–5	Know that the speed and direction of a force affects moving objects. Identify sources of heat and light. Learn basic principles of balanced and unbalanced forces. Understand properties of friction, magnetism, and gravity. Design an electric circuit. Know that electricity moves in circuits and can produce heat, light, sound, and magnetic effects. Know that there are many ways to transfer energy. Realize that the sun is a major force of energy and can lose energy by emitting light. Understand light properties (transmission-refraction), absorption, or scattering (reflection).
6–8	Explore influences of gravitational forces. Show how forces reinforce or cancel each other and can change speed or direction. Explore properties of radiation. Recognize types of solar energy.
9–12	Understand how electromagnetic, gravitational, and nuclear forces produce energy. Know about the mathematical relationship between the mass of an object, the net force, and the acceleration that results. Learn about the transformation of energy.
	Check out the Association of Physics Teachers (AAPT) at www.aapt.org.

More Challenging Assignments

Students will make a sundial and measure the sun's shadow each hour. Some students will also investigate how eyes and cameras work, where the lens bends light as it reaches a point on the retina or camera film. Some students will demonstrate an understanding of the law of reflection, where the angle of incidence = the angle of reflection, such as the *enlightening* principle of lighthouses.

Possible accommodations a child with *learning differences* might need:

- Concrete demonstrations and kinesthetic presentations that impact learning, such as playing tug-of-war to demonstrate forces, angling flashlights on objects to understand shadows and transparency of objects, using a shoebox with rubber bands stretched across for creating sound vibrations, or tapping on differently filled bottles to demonstrate sound

- Alternative assessments that value individual strengths, instead of relying on paper/pencil tests; e.g., pantomiming or creating a model of a concept
- Frequent monitoring and informal assessments to gauge understandings and avoid misconceptions or faulty reasoning
- Praise and encouragement for advancements
- Valuing of strengths and interests through a variety of classroom instruction honoring multiple intelligences, such as bodily-kinesthetic, musical-rhythmic, naturalistic, or visual-spatial preferences

Possible accommodations a child with *depression/mood swings* might need:

- Development of trusting relationships with peers and adults
- Increased attention and praise
- Motivating anticipatory sets
- Connections on how physics relates to their own lives; e.g., a rollercoaster
- Teacher awareness of types and schedules of medications taken by maintaining ongoing communication with school nurse, home environment, and all staff who come in contact with the student
- Other expressive and cathartic outlets; e.g., listening to soothing background music, allowing student to doodle during lectures
- Behavioral self-monitoring by rating feelings/moods on an hourly or daily basis
- Encouragement to share concerns with guidance counselor, chat/support groups

Possible accommodations a child with *above average skills* might need:

- Opportunities to expand upon classroom lessons with individual or cooperative research assignments
- Monitoring to ensure that along with mastering academics, appropriate social/behavioral skills are also developed
- Extension of knowledge through peer teaching and demonstration of additional concepts in physics through guided experiments
- Self-awareness/advocacy of individual goals and academic needs
- Encouragement to continually express and communicate knowledge
- Nonthreatening receptive classroom environment
- Valuing student's increased inquiry by having appropriate topic/concept-related creative outlets, centers, and ongoing projects

A *Hot* Lesson

Instead of listening to lectures, students establish understandings of concepts by self-discovery of answers to teacher-generated questions. They can use the class text, easier reading-level but high-interest books, appropriate teacher-directed online sites, and guided experimentation. Students can work individually or cooperatively, but all need to document answers. This type of *Q/A* setup allows students to delve into the learning!

Some Hot Questions

1. Explain how birds soar upward. How does this relate to *wind?*
2. What do electric fires, hot plates, electric grills, and lightbulbs have in common?
3. What car or clothing colors would reflect more heat? Which ones would absorb more heat? Which car color would be cooler to drive during the hot summer months? What color clothing is best to wear in the winter or summer?
4. Are heat waves themselves hot?
5. Which color panels would be the best choice to solar-heat a greenhouse?
6. What's the difference between radiation, conduction, and convection?
7. Compare and contrast conductors and insulators.
8. Explain the similarities in the two meanings of the word *current* in relation to both water and electricity.

Some Hot Answers

1. Birds soar up because of convection currents, which occur when the land is warmer than the air above it. The land warms the air and rises in the form of convection currents and is consequently *uplifting* to the birds. The birds do not even have to flap their wings, and they just soar upward! Wind is moving air that is also produced by convection currents.
2. They all radiate (give off and spread out) heat.
3. Lighter-colored cars or clothes reflect heat and darker-colored ones absorb more heat. It would be cooler to drive in a lighter-colored car such as a white or tan one that has the heat bounce off, instead of a darker-colored car that keeps or absorbs the heat. This is the same principle as the fact that lighter-colored clothing absorbs less heat in the summer than in the winter.
4. No, but when the heat waves are stopped and absorbed by something, then that object becomes hot.
5. Probably dark panels would be the best choice to heat a greenhouse; e.g., black, because they would absorb more heat and light for plants to grow.
6. Radiation happens when heat waves travel and move at the speed of light; e.g., hot plates, lightbulbs. Conduction happens when molecules are heated and move about, bumping into other molecules (kinetic energy). Convection happens when heat is transferred and carried by liquids and gases.
7. Conductors are objects that offer a small amount of resistance to an electric current or heat, while insulators are just the opposite, offering a greater amount of resistance to heat or an electric current.
8. Both an electric current and water current have strength that flows. An electric current is when electricity moves and is measured in amperes (amount of electricity every second). It is a constant flow of electrons through a conductor. Water currents also move, such as a river of water that moves through an ocean. Water currents can make a day at the beach a hairy one, if the currents are too strong. Never mix electric and water currents; e.g., if water was on an electric outlet, or an electric hair blower.

EARTH SCIENCE

Baseline Knowledge Standards

Students will recognize that water can disappear on hot surfaces (evaporate) and collect on cold surfaces (condense). Identification of world examples and locations of erosion, weathering, earthquakes, and volcanoes (many are underwater). Students will understand that weathering, erosion, and deposition change landforms. Students will be able to define the word *atmosphere* as a layer of insulation between the Earth and the sun (protecting us from extreme heat in the daytime and keeping us warm at night from absorbed heat). Students will also understand that the Earth is divided into seven continents that slowly move *(continental drift).* They will understand about how early plant and animal fossils help scientists learn about life millions of years before now. Students will also know that the Earth consists of three main layers—the *crust, mantle,* and *core.*

Advancing Level

Some students will learn additional facts about the Earth's layers: *crust* (outermost layer*), lithosphere* (crust and upper mantle), *asthenosphere* (melted rock in upper mantle), *lower mantle* (layer of rock above outer core, which is softer), *outer core* (liquid iron), *inner core* (innermost layer of Earth, made of solid iron).

Students will understand about short-term weather and long-term climate, which involves transfer of energy in and out of the atmosphere. They will understand frontal effects (the area between two air masses that collide):

Figure 8.9

Grades	Content Area/Skills and Standards: Science: Earth Science
K–2	Identify patterns found in nature. Understand more about rocks and soil. Describe and observe daily weather conditions. Observe and note the changes in the local environment. Learn more about characteristics of water.
3–5	Know that rocks and soil are composed of several substances. Understand how fossils tell us information about past plants and animals. Learn about erosion, weathering, earthquakes, and volcanoes. Explore the rock cycle. Understand about the properties of water. Illustrate the water cycle. Learn about the Earth's layers.
6–8	Learn more about marine environments. Relate atmospheric conditions and systems to weather maps. Evaluate how constructive and destructive processes affect Earth's landforms. Describe how Earth's geology is formed by sedimentary layers. Investigate characteristics of fossils. Learn how scientists use technology to study the Earth. Begin to learn about plate tectonics.
9–12	Investigate further how the plate tectonics theory explains volcanoes, earthquakes, mid-ocean ridges, and deep-sea trenches. Understand how the Earth's changes over time affect topography. Compare and contrast effects of climate and weather in different areas.

warm front—persistent rain, cold front—drenching rain, stationary front—cloudy, occluded front—cloudy/rainy. They will increase understandings about the terms *atmosphere, thermosphere, mesosphere, stratosphere,* and *troposphere.* Students will learn about how the Earth's crust consists of separate parts or plates that fit together like a jigsaw puzzle and that constantly move.

More Challenging Assignments

Deeper understandings about plate tectonics:

- Earthquakes are sudden movements in the Earth's crust caused when plates move against each other.
- Mountains are created over long periods of time when plates squeeze together and fold over each other.
- Volcanic activity is caused when plates move over hot spots so that the lava (hot liquid), ashes, and dust erupt through the crust. Students will know that mountains are created when the lava and cinders cool, harden, and build up.
  o Ridges happen when molten rock is pushed up at the edges of plates.
  o Deep ocean trenches occur when old crust is pushed down into the mantle.

Possible accommodations a child with *learning/perceptual issues* might need:

- Uncluttered, compartmentalized worksheets
- Using a concrete object such as a hard-boiled egg to visually demonstrate the layers of the Earth: shell (crust), white part (mantle), yolk (core)
- Layered lessons that coincide with varying prior knowledge of students
- Teaching at instructional, not frustration level
- Increased videos and graphics
- Acting out of concepts; e.g., pantomime birth of a mountain
- Supplemental low reading-level, but high-interest texts
- Breaking up of more difficult vocabulary words into their syllables
- Same opportunities to advance their knowledge as peers

Study Guides/Worksheets

Clutter-free, *down-to-earth* worksheets can display the same information as expository text, but increase the comprehension for some students whose primary way of understanding requires smaller bites of information without the interference of reading more difficult vocabulary. If the goal is to increase understandings about a given topic, then it is wiser to focus on the content, and not increase difficulties presented by *unfriendly* student formats. Notice that as with the 18 inclusion strategies in Chapter 4, the same information is pictorially more pleasing to the eye, less overwhelming, and an appropriate accommodation. Informational guides with this type of setup can help focus students with perceptual, attention, behavioral, reading, auditory, and visual issues on scientific concepts.

Examples follow on the water cycle, plate boundaries, and weather fronts.

The Water Cycle

First, the sun *e-vap-or-ates* water from the ocean's *sur-face*.

Then, water *con-den-ses* into tiny *drop-lets* to form clouds.

After that, winds sweep clouds over land.

Next, water falls as *pre-cip-i-ta-tion*.

Finally, precipitation runs off the land and returns to the oceans or lakes.

 Fact: All living or-gan-isms need _____.

Types of boundaries:

Figure 8.10

Figure 8.11

A. convergent boundary   B. divergent boundary   C. transform fault boundary

    A. plates collide into each other

    B. plates move away from each other

    C. plates grind past each other

Figure 8.12

Fronts = area between 2 colliding air masses	
warm front	persistent rain
cold front	drenching rain
stationary front	cloudy
occluded front	cloudy/rainy

ASTRONOMY

Baseline Knowledge Standards

The sun can only be seen during the day, but the moon can sometimes be seen in the day or the night. Students will understand that the way the moon looks depends upon its location in relation to the sun and the Earth. They will know that the sun's gravitational pull holds the planets in their orbits and that the planets' gravitational pull holds the moons in their orbits. The universe consists of billions of galaxies, and these have many billions of stars.

Figure 8.13

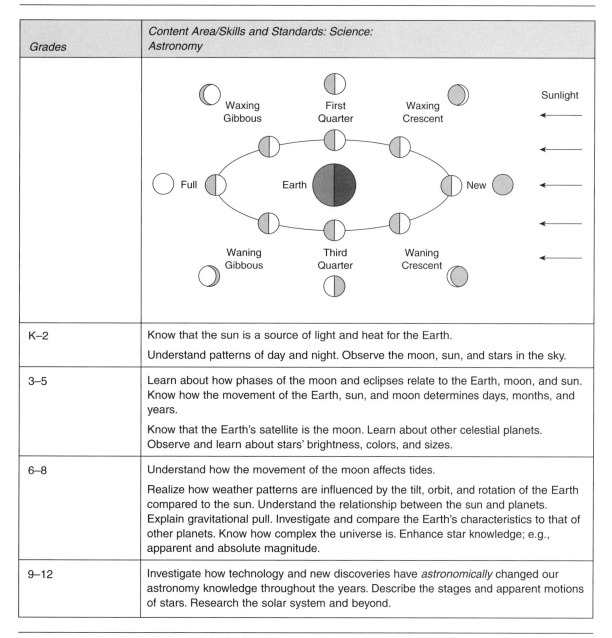

Grades	Content Area/Skills and Standards: Science: Astronomy
K–2	Know that the sun is a source of light and heat for the Earth. Understand patterns of day and night. Observe the moon, sun, and stars in the sky.
3–5	Learn about how phases of the moon and eclipses relate to the Earth, moon, and sun. Know how the movement of the Earth, sun, and moon determines days, months, and years. Know that the Earth's satellite is the moon. Learn about other celestial planets. Observe and learn about stars' brightness, colors, and sizes.
6–8	Understand how the movement of the moon affects tides. Realize how weather patterns are influenced by the tilt, orbit, and rotation of the Earth compared to the sun. Understand the relationship between the sun and planets. Explain gravitational pull. Investigate and compare the Earth's characteristics to that of other planets. Know how complex the universe is. Enhance star knowledge; e.g., apparent and absolute magnitude.
9–12	Investigate how technology and new discoveries have *astronomically* changed our astronomy knowledge throughout the years. Describe the stages and apparent motions of stars. Research the solar system and beyond.

SOURCE: Image courtesy of NASA's Space Place, spaceplace.nasa.gov

Students will pictorially identify these 4 phases of the moon:

New Moon

First Quarter

Full Moon

Last Quarter

Figure 8.14

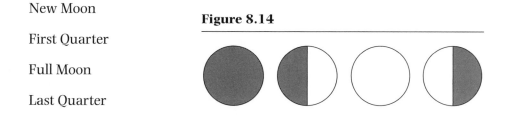

Advancing/Challenging Levels

Students will pictorially identify 8 phases of the moon:

New Moon

Waxing Crescent Moon

Quarter Moon

Waxing Gibbous Moon

Full Moon

Waning Gibbous Moon

Last Quarter Moon

Waning Crescent Moon

Figure 8.15

Possible accommodations a child with *obsessive-compulsive disorder* might need:

- Reassurance, praise, and monitoring to let student know that work is properly completed and to stop unnecessary frequent erasures and counterproductive rechecking behaviors
- Hand signals and increased eye contact if student has attention issues
- Self-monitoring system or rubric for student to review to match completed work with criteria. Then student can add or change elements only if warranted when compared to a sample model or written answer.
- Strategies to properly channel compulsions; e.g., allowed computer time when finished with work or ongoing stellar astronomy centers

Possible accommodations a child with *dysgraphia* might need:

- Templates of spheres to trace, color, or shade for different moon phases
- Computer access to replace handwritten assignments if student has difficulty keeping pace with note taking in *astronomical* lectures
- Pencil grips or larger sized writing tools
- Frequent breaks
- Allowances to tape record classroom lectures and lessons
- Copy of teacher's or peer's outlines/notes
- Parallel worksheet to circle moon choices instead of drawing phases

Possible accommodations a child with *traumatic brain injury* might need:

- Repetition of prior learning concepts before new material is introduced
- Structured and predictable environment
- Easier reading material on same concepts
- Semiconcrete/abstract levels of presentation
- Patience if concepts are misunderstood
- Practice to apply concepts and make generalizations
- Individual modifications based upon perceptual requirements and student's stamina
- Parental communication; e.g., e-mail homework or follow up on incomplete/misunderstood classroom assignments
- Additional videos or online sites that further explain astronomy concepts

ENVIRONMENTAL STUDIES

Baseline Knowledge Standards

Students will understand the difference between renewable (e.g., air, water, soil) and nonrenewable resources (e.g., minerals, fossil fuels).

Advancing Level

Students will understand that the physical and chemical properties of soil are related to its weathered rock particles and humus (decaying organic matter, such as insects, rotting plants).

Figure 8.16

Grades	Content Area/Skills and Standards: Science: Environmental Studies
K–2	Understand how different organisms have basic needs. Associate relationships humans, animals, and plants have with their surroundings and each other. Identify basic characteristics of different environments; e.g., beach, forest, mountains.
3–5	Identify how organisms interact within different ecosystems. Understand differences between renewable and nonrenewable natural resources. Learn about how animals and plants adapt to their environment.
6–8	Compare and contrast how the environment can be positively and negatively impacted. Identify environmental influences by humans and natural occurrences. Investigate endangered species and necessary measures to help alleviate their plight.
9–12	Research further how societal activity impacts ecosystems. Set up a plan to modify negative human interactions. Explain how humans can collectively design practices that manage the conservation of natural resources.

More Challenging Assignments

Students will identify characteristics and conditions for erosion and deposition over time. They will study effects of forest fires, floods, hurricanes, climate change, and ozone production.

Possible accommodations a child with *reading difficulties* might need:

- Assistance reading more difficult vocabulary
- Visuals to accompany written words and textbook passages
- Lower grade-level readability, but same content in textual information
- Breaking up of more difficult words into syllables
- Handheld speaking word dictionary
- Text recorded on tape
- More verbal cues with written directions in experiments
- Videos or visual scientific dictionary to concretize written text
- Experiments that let concepts be concretely demonstrated

Possible accommodations a child with *visual differences* might need:

- Graphic organizers with uncluttered formats
- Handheld magnifiers to enlarge written words
- Closer seating to chalkboards
- Kinesthetic reinforcement of written words with concrete curriculum-related items
- Peer coach or assistant to help with mobility and safety issues
- Additional auditory cues
- Braille texts and online speaking sites

ORGANIZED LESSONS FOR RESEARCH AND OBSERVATION

Students with learning, behavioral, perceptual, physical, cognitive, and sensory differences need organized lessons with structured questions and accompanying manipulatives that further concretize somewhat abstract concepts that may not be within their prior knowledge. These types of questions offer elements of self-discovery and can be completed cooperatively as well to develop social skills. More attention on task is evidenced, rather than sitting in classroom lectures to gain the same information. This partially filled in sample chart encourages students to use their senses along with available texts, notes, other research, and peers to make *sensible deductions!* Remember to combine research with observation.

Figure 8.17

Materials	What happens when it's wet?	Describe its color.	What's heard if you shake it in a container?	Does it have an odor? Describe what you smell.	Use text, class notes, and/or online sites to tell why the material is important.
Sand	Sand forms clumps and crumbles when it is moistened	Color depends upon where the rocks and plants in sand come from—e.g., white or pink sand may come from rocks such as feldspars; black sand may come from rocks like obsidian or basalt			
Clay	Sticks together				
Soil					

TECHNOLOGY

Technology *is a tool for teaching, not the lesson itself.*

—Hiraoka, 2006

Baseline Knowledge Standards

Students will open a blank Word document and compose a three-paragraph report on a given topic, using a bulleted list of information gathered from their textbook or online sources. Students will select and insert appropriate clip art and charts.

Advancing Level

Other students will critique factual material read on assigned topics and compose a two- to three-page essay that evaluates the information from online sources and text.

Figure 8.18

Grades	Content Area/Skills and Standards: Technology
K–2	Learn about technology around us; e.g., computers, calculators, microwaves, cell phones. Identify types of technology in homes, schools, and communities. Able to explain how to access different computer and software programs. Knowledge of basic keyboarding skills.
3–5	Refine keyboarding skills. Produce computer charts and graphs. Create multimedia presentations. Edit documents using word processing tools. Apply graphic organizers. Insert images in Word documents. Locate information with search engines and Web browsers. Demonstrate ethical behavior when citing sources. Create a time line of technological products and services.
6–8	Actively use online library resources. Design spreadsheets and interpret data. Collaboratively complete Web searches. Investigate impact of technology in fields of medicine, agriculture, transportation, manufacturing, and more. Determine accuracy of electronic information. Create multipage reports/documents with references cited.
9–12	Create a research report with appropriate online citations. Prepare a resume using computer templates. Compare and contrast print and nonprint sources. Understand the costs, benefits, and risks of some technological developments.

More Challenging Assignments

Some students will write a research paper on a debatable teacher-assigned topic, detailing, supporting, and arguing contrary viewpoints, and using and citing all sources from online journals, Web sites, and texts.

Possible accommodations a child with *physical impairments* might need:

- Larger keyboard for typing
- Alternative trackball or control with on-screen keyboard
- Word prediction programs that ease additional fine motor strains
- Accessibility to all sites of information: classroom, library, computer labs
- Accommodations as needed; e.g., someone with cerebral palsy may have additional auditory needs and need a classroom amplification system or have speech/language communication requirements
- Coordination/collaboration with other health care providers, if there are medical concerns or specific physical demands to address
- Assistance from occupational and physical therapists
- More frequent breaks
- Additional time without penalties to complete assignments in class or at home
- Voice recognition software
- Arm support or footrest

Possible accommodations a child with *lower cognitive needs* might need:

- Alternative or parallel assignments related to daily living; e.g., functional topics such as importance of reporting to work on time, or appropriate dress in school, on a job, or during different seasons
- Oral reading of written directions or a scribe to write dictated responses
- Writing templates used to fill in words or pictures
- Peer coach or teacher assistant to monitor understanding of how to use technology
- Individual or repetitive lessons to reinforce computer knowledge and skills
- Guided list and direction on how to appropriately use online sites

Possible accommodations a child with *visual issues* might need:

- Larger font size
- Magnifier to enlarge printed directions; e.g., one mounted on a computer
- Sites and computers with speaking programs and tools
- Peer coaches
- Computer screen magnifier
- Alternative keyboard with larger, Braille, or tactile labels
- Screen color contrast
- Eyeglasses

Possible accommodations a child with *hearing issues* might need:

- Portable word processor or laptop computer
- Smart board in classrooms to aid with note taking
- Flashing signal on computer
- Teacher–student gestures or signals for transitions
- FM—a portable, wireless listening system that a teacher wears in the classroom to help students hear more clearly. The teacher wears a compact transmitter and microphone, while the students who need it are equipped with a portable receiver with earphones—or a Loop system
- Closed captioning for videos
- Avoidance of sensory distractions/interferences; e.g., carpeting on floor to aid with acoustics or cut-up tennis balls on the bottom of chairs to cushion extra noises
- TTY/TDD with or without relay for home communications with student and parents if they also have hearing issues
- Peer/staff education to face the student and speak in normal conversational tones if the student is lip reading
- Visual dictionary or concrete objects on hand to help explain abstract vocabulary
- Correcting but not penalizing student for grammar errors
- Written directions for oral assignments

Possible accommodations a child with *auditory processing issues* might need:

- Smart Board in classrooms to aid with note taking
- Accompanying written directions on chalkboard for verbal directions

- Frequent monitoring; e.g., ask student to paraphrase directions in own words to check understandings
- Additional visual cues or signals
- Preferential seating, closer to teacher
- Practice with conversational listening skills
- Handout of lesson's outline to follow along
- Terse but sequential directions
- Nonthreatening classroom environment that encourages students to ask questions

Lessons That P.A.Y.

Figure 8.19

Paraphrase	Agreement	Your Action
Steps: 1. Read the research and class notes. 2. Think about the information. 3. Write about what you read or heard, in your own words, summarizing the main points. You can use all computer tools—e.g., language, grammar, and spell checks—to correct written work.	1. Form your own opinion about what was heard in class, read in your textbooks, or researched online. 2. Tell whether you think this information is important or unimportant. 3. Do you agree with these facts?	1. Will this information affect you in any way? 2. What actions will you now take, based upon this information? 3. Have these facts in any way altered or changed your life and/or thinking?

9

Standards-Based Social Studies Objectives

What a shame that many students think social studies is boring! It's an incredible subject that, when excitedly taught, can engage learners to think about themselves as miniscule in relation to the long time line of written records and artifacts from prehistoric civilizations. Social studies is not a bunch of boring facts, but a way of looking at the past, present, and future. How can students be politically minded, culturally savvy, civic oriented, geographically aware, or economically conscious if they don't know what these terms mean? The following research, lessons, projects, and worksheets attempt to bring the excitement of learning social studies back to students and educators while honoring student strengths and academic standards.

RESEARCH IMPLICATIONS

Because geography is better described as the study of spatial aspects of human existence (Geography Education Standards Project, 1994, 18) rather than as the memorization of obscure information, children need to see how geography relates to their lives.

—Edgington & Hyman, 2005

Students have a preconceived idea that history is boring and insipid, because it deals only with events that have happened long ago and far away, making the history discipline irrelevant.

—D'Sa, 2005

Docudramas are appropriate and relevant tools for social studies instruction. . . . [They] focus the visual and auditory senses of the student . . . [and] engage the interest of the learner.

—D'Sa, 2005

Many at-risk students with learning problems struggle to understand social studies textbooks. . . . [A]uthors have relied on an expository, rather than narrative approach. . . . Narration can be used to instruct as well as engage children in learning social studies facts, concepts, and causation.

—Dull & Van Garderen, 2005

In order to help students become better equipped to conquer social studies textbooks and learn history . . . set a goal to find supplemental materials and engage students in interactive methods of building content and genre schemata for studying topics in history.

—Villano, 2005

If children are to become economically and financially literate adults, economics and personal finance need to become a stronger part of the school curriculum.

—Schug & Hagedorn, 2005

For most students, the functions of government and their historical roots are often little more than dry details with no real connection to their everyday lives.

—Manzo, 1998

Online Social Studies Sites for Further Insights:

National Council for the Social Studies: http://www.ncss.org

Information on how students can become involved democratic citizens: www.civiced.org, www.closeup.org

Social Studies Lessons: www.csun.edu/~hcedu013/plans.html

African-American History, Culture, and Black Studies Resources: www.blackquest.com/link.htm

American History: http://.school.discovery.com/schrockguide/history/hista.html

World History: www.socialstudiesforkids.com/subjects/worldhistorygeneral.htm

Museums and Exhibits: www.yahooligans.yahoo.com/School_Bell/Social_Studies/History/Museums_and_Exhibits/

Teaching Tolerance: www.teachingtolerance.org

SAMPLE LESSONS/CONNECTIONS FOR K–12

GOVERNMENT

Baseline Knowledge Standards

All students will understand that the U.S. government has written laws that guarantee rights to its citizens; e.g., the Bill of Rights (Amendments 1–10). Students will create a time line of amendment details by matching the dates and specifics through text or illustration.

Figure 9.1

Grades	Content Area/Skills and Standards: Social Studies: Government
K–2	Realize the reason for authority and basic rules and laws. Start by using the classroom, school, and home as examples.
3–5	Know that there are different levels and types of government.
	Distinguish differences between local, state, and national governments. Understand how laws protect citizens. Learn about the three branches of the U.S. government.
6–8	Identify how to contact government officials. Compare and contrast power vs. authority (e.g., democracy vs. autocracy). Understand necessary limits of the government. Define representative government. Outline major principles of the U.S. government. Know how citizens impact governments. Research documents; e.g., U.S. Constitution, Bill of Rights. Research famous law cases such as *Dred Scott, Plessy v. Ferguson*.
9–12	Compare and contrast governments around the world.
	Determine different philosophies within political parties.
	Debate contemporary issues the Supreme Court is facing.
	Know how citizens participate in the government. Understand global, political, and social conflicts.

Advancing Level

Students will learn about the amendments to the constitution beyond the Bill of Rights and how these amendments have been applied to people living in the United States, such as Native Americans (Indian Removal Act), black citizens such as Dred Scott or Rosa Parks, Chinese immigrants (Chinese Exclusion Act), and many other groups of people who faced or face discrimination in social and political arenas.

More Challenging Assignments

Discussion of civil liberties vs. situations such as concerns with national security and terrorism. Students will also research historical court cases and terms such as *Marbury v. Madison, Plessy v. Ferguson,* habeas corpus, secret ballots, and so on.

Possible accommodations a child with *learning/reading/auditory processing issues* might need:

- Other ways to demonstrate knowledge, aside from written assessments; e.g., illustrate a historical poem/text, critique a historical movie
- Instruction/guidance about the social studies textbook's format
- Rubric/model of appropriate written work and details needed for essays
- Practice with note-taking and outlining skills
- Help learning how to skim, highlight, and paraphrase important information
- Instruction on how to use a glossary or computer language tools to define and spell words
- Pre- or reteaching vocabulary to better understand unfamiliar words in context
- Rephrasing directions in textbooks during instruction or assessments
- Establishing of connections with relevance to students' own lives
- Preferential seating to better focus on or hear the teachers
- Closed captioning for videos shown
- Books on tape for easier reading, following, and processing of written words

Possible accommodations a child with *visual differences* might need:

- Kinesthetic opportunities to demonstrate knowledge; e.g., acting out roles of characters in a historical play about our government
- Braille texts and tapes or recordings of primary and secondary sources
- Enlarged computer screen or handheld magnifiers for research
- Graphic organizers that eliminate clutter
- Color code information
- Appeal to auditory strengths; e.g., create a song about the content or listen to historical fiction or nonfiction with books or voices recorded
- Books with the same content, but larger sized print

Possible accommodations a child with *developmental differences* might need:

- Parallel curriculum; e.g., *Bill of Functional Rights,* relating to personal daily freedoms that students may encounter in everyday situations
- Modification of assessments; e.g., changing multiple-choice or matching questions to true or false ones with only the most essential and basic ideas tested
- Rephrasing of directions using simpler vocabulary
- Determination of prior background knowledge
- Same exposure to the information, yet fewer demands in assignments given

Figure 9.2   Personal Freedoms

Amendments	Examples of Functional Bill of Rights
1. Freedom of speech, religion, press, assembly, and petition	1. You can tell others what you think and believe by speaking or writing down your words and getting together in a peaceful group with friends or to practice your religion.
2. Right to bear arms	2. You can protect yourself from people who would harm you.
3. No soldier quartered in any house without the consent of the owner	3. Nobody can force their way into your house without your okay.
4. No unreasonable searches or seizures	4. You have privacy rights.
5. Right to due process without bearing witness against oneself, not being held in jeopardy for the same offense twice, not taking private property for public use without compensation	5. You can never be forced to say bad things about yourself or if proven innocent be tried again in a court.
6. Right to a speedy and public trial by an impartial jury	6. If you do something legally wrong, you cannot be thrown into jail without a quick and fair trial by people like yourself.
7. Jury examines rules of common law	7. People that are similar to you form a jury that listens to the facts and decides the innocence or guilt if you are accused of wrongdoings, by following a code of written laws.
8. No excessive bail, fines, or cruel or unusual punishments inflicted	8. Nobody can do mean things to you or force you to pay large sums of money for your freedom after you are accused or convicted of a crime.
9. These rights shall not be construed to deny or disparage others retained by the people	9. These rights do not replace others.
10. Powers not delegated to the United States by the constitution, nor prohibited by it to the states, are reserved to the States respectively, or to the people	10. We live in a free country with national and state governments that protect people's rights and interests!

- Peer coach to assist with more difficult readings
- Communication with parents who can review, reinforce, or reteach learning at home
- Concrete examples of social studies content by watching more videos or hearing personal accounts from guest speakers
- Relating the learning to students' own lives

Learning About Countries: *A Broad* Appeal!

1. Choose a country in the _____ hemisphere.

2. Draw two proportional pictures of its flag, one smaller and larger.

3. Draw a map that includes the following:
   o Neighboring countries
   o Major cities
   o Bodies of water
   o Land forms
   o Scale of miles
   o Legend
   o Compass rose

4. Tell about the government of this country. Who are its leaders?

5. What languages do the people speak? What holidays do they celebrate? Make an illustrated glossary of five words, expressions, and/or customs from that country.

6. Find sheet music with lyrics from a song composed there.

7. Tell about the populations that live there:
   o Humans—Types of jobs, standard of living. Tell how the people have satisfied their basic needs. Did war, migration, or trade have an impact on the culture?
   o Animal—Habitats, interactions with humans. Choose one animal there and divide it into its Linnaean classification.
   o Plants—How does the climate affect the agriculture/crops?

8. Describe the impact of geography on historic events of this country.

9. Use a Venn diagram to compare and contrast your own culture or way of life to this country.

10. Choose another contemporary country and compare the economic systems to this one.

11. If you were a scientist living there, what invention would you create to better the population? Draw a diagram of the technological advance.

12. Create a poem, short story, or illustration with captions. Your product must include five facts about your country.

13. Would you want to live in this country? Explain why or why not.

14. Write the following two 5-paragraph letters:
   o Letter from a citizen of your country to the president of the United States
   o Presidential response to that citizen's letter

15. Write a pilot script for a television show that would be broadcast in that country.

Planning Form

Directions: Numbers 1–5 and bibliography are required. Choose five more from numbers 6–15.

Figure 9.3

1. Country approved	
2. Flag	
3. Map (a–g)	
4. Government	
5. Languages/Holidays/Customs/Glossary	
6. Sheet music	
7. Populations (a–c)	
8. Geographic impact on history	
9. Cultural Venn diagram	
10. Comparison of economic systems	
11. Technological invention	
12. Poem/short story/illustration with captions	
13. Desire to live there	
14. Two 5-paragraph letters	
15. TV script	

1. Include these terms when applicable in your completed works:

- political
- social
- economic
- cultural diffusion
- exchange of ideas
- historical conflicts
- production of goods
- subsistence agriculture
- market-oriented agriculture
- cottage industries
- commercial industries
- migration
- immigration
- demographic patterns
- population growth
- technological innovations
- physical landforms
- environmental conditions
- residential
- commercial
- industrial development
- free enterprise
- prosperity
- civil rights
- ethnicity
- cultural patterns
- standard of living
- individual rights
- primary source
- secondary sources

We the undersigned will cooperatively and proudly complete all requirements for this project. All sources used will be correctly cited in a bibliography and finished by the due date given below.

Signatures: _____

Due date: _____

WORLD HISTORY

Connective Academic Issues

Teacher request/question: How do archaeologists learn about the past?

Student response: "Archaeologists learn about the past by using weapons."

Just what was this sixth-grade student thinking? He was rather adamant about his response, and was puzzled that I didn't totally embrace his answer, but asked him to explain it instead. So much can be achieved by analyzing incorrect responses, rather than dismissing them and moving onward. It's the faulty reasoning that needs to be challenged and thwarted in its tracks before it snowballs into more incorrect concept formations, gathering momentum as the grades progress. Well, his explanation was based upon his textbook readings, but not upon the whole picture about archaeology. You see, this student read that archaeologists dig up weapons. He ignored the main idea, which was that one way they learn about the past is when they find artifacts. This student was a *mover and shaker,* who loved wrestling and action-packed sports, so the word *weapons* appealed to him, but the word *artifacts* had little connection to his life, since it was a novel vocabulary

Figure 9.4

Grades	Content Area/Skills and Standards: Social Studies: World History
K–2	Categorize past and present events with teacher guidance. Understand that the world has changed and not stayed the same through time; e.g., countries/areas have had different names. Know that the world was different in the past and will again change in the future.
3–5	Realize the connection between our contemporary world and prior generations. Identify characteristics of a civilization. Understand how the environment influences global communities. Begin to learn about agrarian societies.
6–8	Study the development of human civilization from prehistory to the Middle Ages. Learn about hunter-gatherer and agricultural communities. Understand why some civilizations have prospered, declined, or perished. Identify how and why societies changed. Know how Western civilization developed. Explore varying cultural and social factors of countries. Learn about economic, political, and environmental issues groups have faced. Explore different gender roles. Understand how technology shaped civilizations; e.g., stone vs. bronze weapons, chariot. Identify beliefs and accomplishments of different civilizations throughout time.
9–12	Identify the role religion has played in world events. Compare and contrast agricultural vs. urban societies. Understand how economic conditions influence world events. Realize how technological changes influenced world events. Analyze worldwide political, economic, and social changes. Compare and contrast sedentary agriculture and subsistence methods. Realize how the environment has positively and negatively shaped civilizations. Explore how cultural invention and diffusion has influenced regions and societies.

word. He needed to know that yes, archaeologists can learn about the past through the larger umbrella that is the artifacts, with weapons being only a sub-category or type of artifact, along with pottery, cooking utensils, jewelry, artwork, and more. This student was then given more practice with logical thinking, deductive and inductive reasoning, and outlining skills to prevent this type of faulty thought process from continuing in other content areas as well.

Baseline Knowledge Standard

Some students' reading comprehension levels interfere with their ability to extract important pieces of information from expository texts. This is especially true when they cannot draw connections among some events in world history that in their minds have no familiarities or importance to their lives. If the purpose of the lesson is to develop higher-order thinking skills and learn how to evaluate information, then students need to have a solid foundation of facts. A chart such as the following one with detailed facts allows them to take a broad jump into the given assignment. Students can then research and expand basic facts into sentences, paragraphs, and essays. At least a framework such as this one has some key world history facts outlined.

Figure 9.5

Cultures/ Religions/Societies/ Time Periods/Eras/ People/Ideas/ Developments	Who?	When?	Where?	What?
Judaism	Hebrews, Jews, Moses, Abraham, Solomon, David	More than 3,500 years ago	Ur, Babylon, Jerusalem, Israel, Judah	Ancient monotheistic religion, Torah, Talmud
Islam	Mohammed was a merchant in Mecca. Moslems	Founded in 7th century AD	Mecca, practiced in many regions	Ancient monotheistic faith, mosques, Koran
Christianity	Jesus Christ as savior and Messiah	BC (before Christ) AD (anno Domini: in the year of our Lord)	Spread throughout Roman Empire, then Europe, North and South America	Monotheistic religion based on the Old and New Testament of the Bible
Hinduism	Single deity with other gods and goddesses	Evolved since 1500 BCE	India, Nepal, and nearby countries	One of the major world's religions, Vedas, castes, reincarnation
Caste system in India	Brahman—priests Kshatriya—ruler, warrior, landowner Vaishya—merchants Shudra—artisans, farmers Harijan—once called *untouchables*	Evolved since 1500 BCE	India	Social system of hierarchical class orders

(Continued)

Figure 9.5 (Continued)

Cultures/ Religions/Societies/ Time Periods/Eras/ People/Ideas/ Developments	Who?	When?	Where?	What?
Buddhism	Siddhartha Gautama, known as Buddha	2,500 years ago	Spread from India to China	Four Noble Truths Eightfold Path
Athenian society	Aristocrats, citizens, metics, slaves	5th century BCE	Ancient Greece	Civic, economic and social tasks, democracy
Ancient Rome	Plebeians, patricians, slaves, emperor, Legend of Romulus, and Remus, Julius Caesar, Augustus, Constantine the Great	625 BC founding of Rome	Centered in what is now Italy	Ancient civilization, mythology, religion, slavery, aqueducts, Roman Empire, Pax Romana, Rise and Fall
Vikings	Warriors, explorers, Leif Ericson	8th–10th Century	From Scandinavia, but spread out and settled in other countries	Raided other countries, traveled and explored on the seas
Mayan society	Native American people	1st Century–1600s	Mexico and northern Central America	Ancient civilization, hieroglyphics, calendars, astronomy, pyramids
Incas	Native American people, conquered by Pizarro	15th–16th centuries	Western South America, what today is Peru	Ancient civilization, vast empire, nice to conquered people
Aztecs	Native American people, Cortes, Hernando, Montezuma	Started in 12th century	Mexico	Before the Spanish arrived—well-developed civilization, human sacrifice
Renaissance	People such as Galileo, Leonardo da Vinci, Michelangelo, Shakespeare	14th century–middle of 17th century	Europe	Rebirth of literature of ancient Greece and Rome, time of rediscovery of learning
Feudalism in Europe	Peasants, nobles, kings-aristocracy, vassals, serfs	Middle Ages	Europe	System in Europe where king owned all land and gave some to nobles for service who then let peasants and serfs farm the land
Ottoman Empire	Turks	14th century–1920	Present-day Turkey, parts of Middle East, southeastern Europe	Empire started by the Turks

Who Are These People?

Directions: In cooperative groups, divide the boxes to find out facts about people, exchange information, and then sequence all people on a time line.

Figure 9.6

Nelson Mandela	Benito Mussolini	Karl Marx	Frederick Douglass	John F. Kennedy
Abraham Lincoln	Franklin D. Roosevelt	Alexander the Great	Susan B. Anthony	Benjamin Franklin
George Washington	Martin Luther King Jr.	Julius Caesar	Ulysses S. Grant	Winston Churchill
Cleopatra	Gandhi	Charles de Gaulle	Henry VIII	Sitting Bull
Napoleon	Harriet Tubman	Socrates	Joan of Arc	Albert Schweitzer

Breaking Up the Learning: Ancient Israel

The following lesson demonstrates how generic learning principles can be applied to social studies, allowing students to take steps toward understanding required information for these standards. The topic here is ancient Israel, but these principles are expandable to help students master all sorts of social studies knowledge!

Topic: Events in Ancient Israel

Learning Objectives

- Increase reading skills; e.g., sequencing, cause–effect
- Develop social/interpersonal skills through teamwork and cooperative learning efforts
- Use research/study skill techniques
- Increase self-awareness of background knowledge
- Research skills

Figure 9.7

Social Studies Topic: Ancient Israel (scrambled facts)	After Solomon's death, Israeli tribes had rivalries or competitions that led to fights and the division into 2 kingdoms, Israel and Judah.	David, the man who slew Goliath, became the next king and united the Israelite tribes.
Abraham and descendants settled in Canaan.	King Saul was now the leader.	After the division, the kingdom of Israel was weaker.
Some of the Jewish people left their homeland, Canaan, because of a famine, lack of food, and went to Egypt.	The 2 kingdoms were invaded by the Chaldeans and the Assyrians.	Moses led Israelites in an exodus (out of) Egypt and back to Canaan.
The Assyrians scattered the people of Israel to different lands, while the Chaldeans took the people from the kingdom of Judah to Babylon, a period known as Babylonian captivity.	David's son, Solomon, became the next king and made Israel a wealthy nation; e.g., there was increasing building, trade, and manufacturing.	Jewish people were forced to be slaves by the Pharaoh in Egypt.

Anticipatory Set

Ask the students if they've ever eaten scrambled eggs. After students describe the characteristics of scrambled eggs, tell them that these facts are a bit like that, since they are not in any order, all jumbled together. Their job is to *unscramble* facts!

Procedure

These 11 scrambled facts are given to students in cooperative groups. Students divide the statements, and copy them on 11 different index cards, which they then together try to sequence, using class notes, text, and online research. When each group is finished, they are allowed to self-correct with the student answer key.

Evaluation

The best part of this lesson is that students are able to self-check answers as a cooperative group. Teacher observation can confirm this. A quiz the next day, or later that week, can ask students to complete the same task as individuals.

Why Do It This Way?

It beats reading from a textbook or strictly listening to class lectures. When students purposefully rewrite facts, they have better retention. In addition, peers are more attentive when actively learning with each other's support.

CULTURAL AWARENESS

Baseline Knowledge Standard

All students will share knowledge about themselves with their peers that includes information about family background. Students will be respectful of each other's differences, similarities, likes, and dislikes.

Advancing Level

Exploration of stereotypes through simulated activities.

More Challenging Assignments

Students will explore the results of inequities experienced by people at the hands of the government; e.g., land taken from Native Americans, tragedies under the influence of the Ku Klux Klan, injustices during the Holocaust, women fighting for equal rights, conditions before the civil rights movement gained recognition and fair laws were passed, Rwandan genocide, conditions in Darfur in the Sudan.

Possible accommodations a child with *learning differences* might need:

- Monitoring of prior knowledge and experiences so that misconceptions do not influence cultural learning
- Help with social interactions when sharing ideas with peers; e.g., appropriate listening skills, maturity when hearing unfamiliar ideas and experiences, and participation in simulations
- More self-awareness of own level of tolerance
- Reassurance that no one is judging the student's differing academic competencies
- Repetition of directions for activities
- Asking the student to paraphrase main idea of assignment
- Grading of written work based on content, not appearance or spelling errors
- Assistance with more difficult readings and vocabulary beyond the student's level

Possible accommodations a child with a *communication disorder* might need:

- Assistance from speech therapist to practice pronunciation and articulation of more difficult words or words outside the student's culture
- More visuals and realistic photos related to different cultures

- Use of total communication if needed; e.g., sign interpreter and finger spelling
- Teachers and peers should face the student if the student is lip reading
- Modeling of correct conversational tones and speech patterns by peers
- Digital tape recorder if student has poor receptive language or difficulties processing and remembering auditory information
- Same opportunities as others for peer social interactions
- Written outline of lesson to follow
- Repetition of directions with intermittent checking to ensure understandings
- Assistance with communicating thoughts in writing

Possible accommodations a child with a *conduct disorder* might need:

- Behavior modification program to reward positive behavior
- Consistent expectations
- Trusting adults and peers
- Nonthreatening and nonjudgmental environment
- Consistent limits and consequences preestablished
- Direct social-skills instruction, practice, and monitoring
- Opportunities for positive and meaningful interactions with peers
- Explanation of lesson before the rest of the class so possible impulsive or negative reactions can be dealt with, avoiding embarrassment in front of peers
- Contact and collaboration with therapists and parents
- Sensible discipline
- Guidance for self-monitoring to help student increase awareness of behavior
- Assistance to channel impulses and exhibit more self-control

Possible accommodations a child *from a different culture* might need:

- Validation about own culture
- Not to be made *an example of* _____, or a representation of an entire culture or race
- Chance to share knowledge and differences
- Explanation of more difficult vocabulary words
- More visuals; e.g., picture/visual dictionary or content-related clip art
- Communication with parents; e.g., letters sent home translated into native language, interpreters at conferences if necessary
- Understanding that the mainstream culture of the school, although in the majority, is not superior to the student's culture, nor can it replace the student's culture and beliefs
- Literature that includes writers and illustrators from diverse cultures

CURRENT EVENTS

Baseline Knowledge Standard

All students will read a grade-level news article and identify the following types of questions: *who, what, when, where, why,* and *how.*

Advancing Level

Some students will critique the reporter's objectivity to determine if the facts given support the article's tone or if there was an omission of any facts.

More Challenging Assignments

Other students will research the news topic and then rewrite the same article with additional facts or more background knowledge, as an editorial.

Figure 9.8

Social Studies Topic: Ancient Israel Student Self-Checking Correctly Ordered Answer Key	1. Abraham and descendants settled in Canaan.	2. Some of the Jewish people left their homeland, Canaan, because of a famine (lack of food) and went to Egypt.
3. Jewish people were forced to be slaves by the Pharaoh in Egypt.	4. Moses led Israelites in an exodus (out of) Egypt and back to Canaan.	5. King Saul was now the leader.
6. David, the man who slew Goliath became the next king and united the Israelite tribes.	7. David's son, Solomon, became the next king and made Israel a wealthy nation; e.g., there was increasing building, trade, and manufacturing.	8. After Solomon's death, Israeli tribes had rivalries or competitions that led to fights and the division into the 2 kingdoms, Israel and Judah.
9. After the division, the kingdom of Israel was weaker.	10. The 2 kingdoms were invaded by the Chaldeans and the Assyrians.	11. The Assyrians scattered the people of Israel to different lands, while the Chaldeans took the people from the kingdom of Judah to Babylon, a period now known as Babylonian captivity.

Figure 9.9

Content Area/Skills and Standards: Cultural Awareness	
"By welcoming a student's home language into the classroom, schools actively engage English language learners in literacy." (Cummins et al., 2005)	
K–2	Understand that different cultures exist in our school, community, country, and world. Learn about different ways people around the world celebrate life events. Develop positive self-image. Respect yourself and others.
3–5	Explore how ideas are exchanged within and outside countries. Define what prejudice is compared to discrimination. Report on contributions of different cultures throughout history. Explore family's own background through interviews.
6–8	Report on ways you could increase your own level of acceptance of yourself, peers, relatives, neighbors, and other citizens. Learn about how nations communicate and solve disagreements. Realize how stereotypes negatively impact people. Understand how world conflicts are based on different religions and cultures in the past and presently exist.
9–12	Research conflicts that surround diversity. Relate how technology has increased global communication. Identify purposes of international organizations. Compare and contrast immigrants, migrants, and refugees. Participate in activities designed to exchange and increase cultural knowledge. Identify national and global social inequalities.

Figure 9.10

Grades	Content Area/Skills and Standards: Social Studies: Current Events
K–2	Expand ideas beyond self. Discuss community news. Give everyday examples of neighborhood, country, and world happenings.
3–5	Read newspapers and locate articles about local, national, and world events. Identify all parts of a newspaper. Answer the *wh questions* about given articles: who, what, where, when, why.
6–8	Compare current and past local, national and global events. Investigate online news stories. Understand the meaning of plagiarism. Gather facts from a variety of sources to write own news article giving proper citations for sources.
9–12	Critically analyze the content and possible slant of news stories and editorials. Learn more about a journalist's responsibilities.

Possible accommodations a child with *dyslexia* might need:

- Easier version of the same news content on instructional reading level, not age/grade level; e.g., in a different format than a newspaper, such as *Scholastic News, Time for Kids,* or *Weekly Reader*
- Highlighting or preteaching more difficult vocabulary words
- Strategies to break up words in articles into syllables
- Access to an electronic speller
- Site online with current articles read to them
- Grading content, not spelling errors
- Writing templates for more organization

Possible accommodations a child with *emotional issues* might need:

- Closer screening of article choices or a given pile of teacher-preselected articles to choose from, if student might obsess or be depressed about certain violent news articles, or those dealing with personally volatile or depressing topics
- Additional monitoring of long-range assignments; e.g., help keeping a calendar for when articles are due, breaking up components of assignment
- Increased praise for time on task
- Structure and consistency in assignments
- Realistic praise for completion of work

Possible accommodations a child with *visual difficulties* might need:

- Newspaper articles with enlarged print
- Magnification page
- Articles in Braille
- Sheet to block out other articles to concentrate on selected visual text without other words or articles distracting student's focus
- Site online with current events articles read to them
- Peer reader or adult to help read articles
- Transcribing of articles on tapes for student to listen to, replacing requiring reading
- More frequent breaks if student has eyestrain

Examining News Articles

Read and write about different articles.

Title of the article: _____

Source (newspaper and reporter): _____

Answer who, what, when, where, and give your opinion.

Figure 9.11

Current Events (What's happening now–today)	Local (Your neighborhood)	National (Your country)	International (Other countries)	Sports	Entertainment (Movies, shows, Tv, etc.)
Who?					
What?					
When?					
Where?					
My opinion					

Possible accommodations a child with *Tourette's syndrome* might need:

- Assistance communicating and interpreting what was read
- Help with attention or focusing issues
- Fewer visual distractions
- More time to complete current events assignments
- Praise for efforts toward task completion
- Help organizing thoughts for written and oral report
- Graphic organizers to help with possible fine motor issues
- More frequent kinesthetic breaks

Possible accommodations a child with *traumatic brain injury* might need:

- Simpler articles with lower reading levels
- Teacher and peer modeling by extracting answers to questions from sample current events articles together
- Explanation of more difficult vocabulary words
- Giving student facts about prior knowledge related to chosen articles
- Narrowing down choices of articles to ones that suit instructional level of student
- Accompanying visuals that concretize articles
- Step-by-step directions for assignment
- Template to fill in facts for news summary

Possible accommodations a child with *Asperger's syndrome* might need:

- Clear-cut directions
- Rubric with expectations outlined
- Acknowledgement of individual interests by allowing student to have a free choice in selection of personalized current events articles related to his or her interests
- Peer coach to help student practice giving oral report to the class
- Established classroom routine
- Graphic organizer to sort responses to questions from the article
- Templates to sequence and structure writing
- Praise for task completion, increased social interactions, and communication

ECONOMICS

Baseline Knowledge Standard

All students will be able to identify types of goods and services. Students will know how the government pays for things like schools, parks, and police protection. Teacher can first define words together with the class, model a few sentences, and then ask students to apply the knowledge in constructive, yet *economical* paragraphs.

Figure 9.12

Grades	Content Area/Skills and Standards: Social Studies: Economics
K–2	Learn what money is, how we get it, and how we use it. Identify different types of ways to pay for items; e.g., coins, bills, credit cards, checks. Know that the same item can have differing prices Develop sense of monetary value of items; e.g., expensive, less expensive.
3–5	Define these vocabulary words: *goods* (objects), *services* (activities), *buyer, seller,* and *resources.* Explore the concept of trading or bartering goods and other forms of money; e.g., checks, credit cards. Identify qualities of an educated consumer. Understand types of resources: *human, natural,* and *capital.* Realize that resources can be scarce and affect societies. Define an *entrepreneur.* Learn about different types of economic systems. Know correlation of purchases made with rising or lowering of costs. Realize that the government pays for its goods and services through taxing and borrowing.
6–8	Understand the concepts of increasing and decreasing prices and the relationship between supply and demand. Explore the government's role in the economy of a country. Know that personal, societal, and political decisions affect economies. Identify how labor productivity/force is related to an improved standard of living. Understand correlation of wages, responsibilities, and salaries. Compare self-sufficiency with interdependence. Research the unemployment rate. Understand about personal finance and money management.
9–12	Learn how the gross domestic product relates to inflation and deflation. Identify *marginal benefits* and *costs,* along with *negative* and *positive incentives.* Learn about *corporations* and *labor unions.* Understand how *competition* is affected by *collusion* Critique *natural monopolies.* Explore situations that affect unemployment rate. Identify where most federal tax comes from along with other tax basics, knowing what taxes are used for. Continue learning about personal money choices; e.g., earning, spending, and saving money. Include facts about the stock market and how to read a stock table.

Advancing Level

Some students will understand the relationship between *scarcity, choice,* and *cost* and how families allocate their incomes. Exploration of relationship between *consumers, producers,* and *price elasticity.* Some more kinesthetic learners or concrete learners can even act out *store situations.*

More Challenging Assignments

Students will explore public goods concepts of shared *consumption, nonexclusion,* the idea of *marginalism,* and how the money supply from the Federal Reserve System relates to national spending.

Economical Words

Choose any 10 of these words, and write a thoughtful, yet *economical* paragraph that demonstrates your understandings of the vocabulary.

Figure 9.13

Economics Words	Definitions (Synonyms)	Sentence Examples
want	would like, desire	"I *want* that video game."
need	can't do without, required, essential	"I *need* food and water to live."
buyer		
seller		
barter		
money vs. credit		
supply		
demand		
goods		
services		
price		
consumer		
economy		
labor		
business		
entrepreneur		
incentive		
monopoly		
checks		
capital		
taxes		
stocks		
scarcity		

My Economical Paragraph:

GEOGRAPHY

Baseline Knowledge Standard

All students will know the physical and human characteristics of the region where they live. They will be able to compare and contrast their community to a different type of geographic region. Students will also be able to identify all continents and oceans and read a compass rose to locate places on a map.

Advancing Level

Students will be proficient in identifying the latitude and longitude of places around the world. Students will also be able to identify how societies are influenced by geographic features.

More Challenging Assignments

Students will investigate how environmental factors influenced past civilizations and continue to impact upon present societies.

Possible accommodations a child with *oppositional defiant disorder* might need:

- Empowerment and allowances to select an assignment from a teacher-given list; e.g., locate 7 out of the 12 places
- Chart to self-monitor accuracy
- Praise or tangible student centered rewards; e.g., computer time, homework pass for correctly completed work

Figure 9.14

Grades	Content Area/Skills and Standards: Social Studies Geography
K–2	Learn about representations of the Earth's surface; e.g., maps and globes. Know the difference between human and natural features and places; e.g., river vs. buildings. Identify characteristics of different areas and landforms in their community, state, country, and world. Learn how compass rose directions are associated with left, right, up, and down.
3–5	Explore physical and human characteristics of places. Learn how human actions can modify the environment. Identify different types of regions and their characteristics. Use map keys, scales, and legends. Create own maps of their classroom, school, neighborhood. Use an atlas and world maps to identify different hemispheres, continents, countries, and cities.
6–8	Learn about patterns of human settlement. Identify interdependence of regions. Explore impact of society on the environment and the impact of the environment on society. Continue development of map skills, locating places with latitude and longitude.
9–12	Know how geography is used to interpret the past. Explore global and environmental issues. Tell how the Earth's surface can be affected by cooperation or conflicts. Identify world cities, corresponding countries, and changing political boundaries.

- Rubric to gauge parameters required
- Structured environment with consistent rules

Possible accommodations a child with *AD/HD* might need:

- Help with compass rose, latitude and longitude, and other map-reading requirements if the student has visual perception issues; e.g., standing up and waving arms in correct directions (arms raised up for north, down for south, or physically modeling degrees of latitude and longitude with numbers and locations such as the equator placed on floor tape that is a midpoint of the classroom)

Figure 9.15

- Opportunity to constructively release excessive motoric energy through appropriate means; e.g., holding cards with continent names and bodies of water and placing students around the room to physically indicate proper location
- Unobtrusive teacher redirection to focus on classroom instruction; e.g., hand signal, increased eye contact
- Teaching self-monitoring strategies to maximize attention
- Help with organizational skills; e.g., accordion folder to keep papers in order
- Direct study-skill instruction

Possible accommodations a child with *Down syndrome* might need:

- Concrete presentation of learning; e.g., aerial photographs of the community available online or pictures of the student and other people he or she knows in different community locations
- Concrete objects to solidify abstract concepts; e.g., leaves in the fall, flowers in the spring, sand, snow, and more
- Explanation of how geography influences students' everyday lives; e.g., type of clothing they wear, food they eat, homes where people live
- Videos and movies of different geographic regions
- Explanation of more difficult vocabulary terms
- Exposure to the same curriculum on the student's independent or instructional level, to eliminate frustrations or shut-downs, yet keep high expectations
- Consistent praise for learning strides
- Direct social-skills instruction
- High-interest but lower reading-level texts

Where in the World Is . . . ?

Can you identify countries at these numbered locations?

Label oceans in proper locations.

Use an atlas if you need extra help.

Figure 9.16

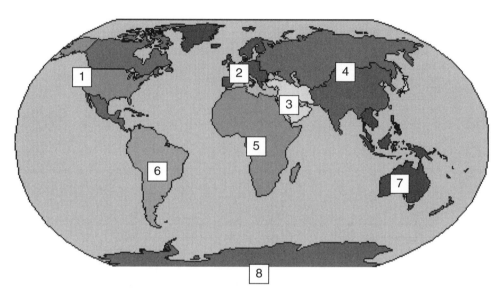

1. North America

2. Europe

3. Middle East

4. Asia

5. Africa

6. South America

7. Australia

8. Antarctica

Further Investigation

Compare and contrast the governments and cultures of two countries.

Fun Assignment

Different students personify the continents and oceans by placing numbered corresponding Post-its on themselves and then kinesthetically moving to correct locations in the room. Hint: First establish north, south, east, and west.

SOURCE: Karten, T. (2005). *Inclusion strategies that work!* Thousand Oaks, CA: Corwin Press.

Geography of Sports Stadiums

Stadium _____ Date built _____

Classroom team: _____

_____

Due date: _____

    Answer all of these questions in report form, with a separate paragraph for each column (Topics 1–4, Questions A–D). Check off the column space next to those questions you have completed. Use the *Stadium Notes* sheet as your paragraph planner.

Figure 9.17

1. Location/Region	√	2. Place	√	3. Human–Environmental Interaction	√	4. Movement	√
A. Where is this stadium? Name the state/country and in what part of the state/country the stadium is located. Name the region of the United States or location in the specific country.		A. Describe the land around the stadium.		A. How are the players and spectators influenced by the climate and location?		A. What are some ways that fans can travel to this stadium?	
B. What is the latitude and longitude of the stadium?		B. Why did people settle in the area near the stadium?		B. What kinds of businesses are close to this stadium?		B. Has the team that plays there now ever moved from another city?	
C. Name some nearby cities and/or countries.		C. Tell about the natural features, resources, and landforms nearby.		C. In what way does the stadium affect the economy of its city? Is there more than one sport that is played in the stadium? What other events take place there?		C. What is the shortest and longest distance this team travels to play *away* games?	
D. Was there anything else at this same location before this stadium was built?		D. Name the bodies of water close by.		D. Name some employment (jobs) available at this stadium.		D. Where do some players originally come from (other countries)?	

Stadium Research Documentation/Bibliography

Texts: _____

_____

_____

_____

Online articles/sites: _____

_____

_____

_____

_____

Other sources: _____

_____

_____

_____

_____

The stadium report is in our own words and we have cited all sources:

Signatures: _____

_____

_____

_____

Figure 9.18 Stadium Notes

1. Location/Region
A.
B.
C.
D.
2. Place
A.
B.
C.
D.
3. Human–Environmental Interaction
A.
B.
C.
D.
4. Movement
A.
B.
C.
D.

SOURCE: Adapted material from "Using Baseball in Social Studies Instruction: Addressing the Five Fundamental Themes of Geography," by Bill Hyman and Bill Edgington. Used with permission.

10

Standards-Based Art, Dance, Theater, and Music Objectives

Many students with cognitive, physical, communicative, and perceptual disabilities may exhibit difficulties with creative understandings or fine or gross motor coordination in art, music, and dance. Should these students then be exempt from improving their competencies in these areas? Of course not! That's even more of a reason to break up the learning here and use these subjects as a way to build students' self-esteem through creative and guided exercises that acknowledge the lower starting levels and build a foundation where further growth is pedagogically nourished! Other students who exhibit difficulties in subjects such as reading, social studies, or science may very well excel in drama, music, and art and need these types of creative outlets for expression. Art, music, and dance will aesthetically enhance their world, and schools are the places to nourish these skills.

RESEARCH IMPLICATIONS

The arts play related integral roles in the development and maintenance of many of our brain's processing systems . . . allowing us to explore topics in a nonthreatening playlike manner . . . [and] helping us to develop and maintain the emotion, attention, and problem-solving systems that normally challenge the problem.

—Sylwester, 2005

The National Association of State Boards of Education has a study group on the Lost Curriculum charged with designing recommendations that arts curricula not be lost in any reshuffling occasioned by the No Child Left Behind Act(NCLB:U.S. Congress 2001) or other educational reform efforts. . . . [D]ata show that students graduating from strong arts programs are more successful in navigating their way through other subjects in the curriculum . . . [are more] interested in school, more self-disciplined, know about practice and persistence, and self-responsibilities for learning.

—Colwell, 2005

Expected outcomes . . . using dance as a vehicle for building self-esteem and developing confidence and a sense of self-respect . . . round out the curriculum.

—Jones, 2005

It appears that private music lessons, community music experiences, museum programs, the school play, and participation in dance organizations contribute as much or more to arts outcomes than does formal schooling. . . . Public opinion polls provide overwhelming support that the arts should be available to all interested students.

—Colwell, 2005

The Music Educators National Conference (MENC) believes that every student, at every level, PreK–12, should have access to a balanced, comprehensive, and sequential program of instruction in music and the other arts, in school, taught by qualified teachers.

—Music Educators National Conference, n.d.

It's time to stop thinking about the arts as fluff. They make schools better places to learn and they raise student achievement.

—Rabkin & Redmond, 2006

SAMPLE LESSONS/CONNECTIONS FOR K–12

ART OBJECTIVES

Baseline Knowledge Standard

All students will view a famous picture and identify the major shapes, colors, and locations of images.

Figure 10.1

Grades	Content Area/Skills and Standards: Art
K–2	Observe surroundings. Identify shapes in everyday objects. Create a collage with given shapes. Identify patterns in art. Realize the shapes of objects. Experiment with different colors and textures. Use diversified materials; e.g., crayons, markers, paints, pens, pencils. Identify all primary and secondary colors. Realize that pictures tell stories and express ideas; e.g., illustrations in books, charts, advertisements.
3–5	Explore different media, textures, and tools through classroom-related assignments across the curriculum that value visual-spatial intelligences of students. Understand how art is a form of communication. Explore art from different cultures. Realize purpose of creating art. Critique own artwork. Begin to learn about famous past and present artists.
6–8	Relate art to world cultures, history, and society. Apply learned art techniques to an assortment of works. Learn about symbolism in art. Continue exploration of different forms and media. Investigate different art periods and styles of artists.
9–12	Critique art. Create art with increased confidence. Identify sophisticated subjects, symbols, and ideas in art forms throughout history. Differentiate between personal and commercial art forms. Identify artists with their works and time periods. Know that art can be evaluated and interpreted differently.

Advancing Level

Students replicate the main elements of a chosen famous picture. Students can be allowed to choose their own *master* picture to copy from art books, online museum sites, background knowledge, or other artistic encounters.

More Challenging Assignments

Students create their own picture, copying the same style and colors as a master artist, but using a different subject.

Possible accommodations a child with *physical difficulties* might need:

- Alternative writing supplies; e.g., pencil grips, thicker crayons, and wider handles on paintbrushes
- Templates; e.g., differently sized circles and other shapes to trace
- Slant board or paper taped to a desk if hand control is not steady
- Computer art tools to express thoughts; e.g., allowance to use word art and other drawing tools with a modified mouse, if fine motor control is weak
- Computer speech recognition program to accept commands
- Peer assistant to help with more difficult fine motor tasks; e.g., cutting with a scissor, holding a ruler steady
- Someone to follow student's verbal instructions for exact placement of picture's elements, if student cannot maneuver cutout shapes by him- or herself

- Environments that allow for optimum physical inclusion if student is in a wheelchair; e.g., correct height of desks, correct classroom/bathroom door widths, appropriate level of toilet tissue and mirrors in bathrooms, and more
- More frequent breaks if drawing task is too physically taxing

Possible accommodations a child with *visual impairments* might need:

- Braille or raised pictures to copy from tactile art books; e.g., Sanchez & McGinnis (2003), *Art and the Alphabet: A Tactile Experience* (Puerto Rico: Creative Creativo)
- More verbal directions or descriptions of pictures
- Help and more practice matching different shades of same colors
- Increased auditory clues about masters' works
- A *touch-me environment* that has a variety of art supplies and manipulatives accessible that student may be able to substitute for visual elements by adding varying tactile ones
- Parallel assignment if copying a master's work is too difficult; e.g., simple outline of a shape that is filled in with a design, pattern, or just elements to differentiate between foreground and background
- Access to voice programs on the computer that describe printed words and images

Possible accommodations a child with *lower cognitive levels* might need:

- Step-by-step modeling of how to copy a master's work that introduces art directions in smaller *artistic bites*
- Practice drawing straight lines and basic shapes
- Instruction on directionality; e.g., right, left, overlapping shapes
- Allowance to trace art, instead of drawing freehand, if task is too difficult
- More patience and time to complete tasks
- Copying a chosen picture from a photograph from student's own reference point; e.g., school, home, community environment instead of a picture that imitates a master's work
- More monitoring to ensure accuracy
- Frequent praise to reward *artistic* efforts instead of final product

Putting It All Into *Perspective!*

The place where both diagonal lines intersect is your vanishing point. In this case, *x marks the spot!* All lines would finish at that point if they were to continue onward. Try adding elements to this road scene to personalize it. For example, maybe you'd like to draw a movie theater or find a picture of the mall, a video store, or pet shop to add to the side of the road. Be certain to decrease their size as you head toward the x. Look around your community and pick a street to draw. Choose whatever scenes or pictures you'd like; remember, it's your perspective!

Figure 10.2

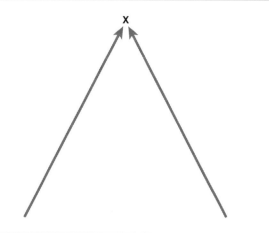

Creating and Understanding Tessellations

Tessellating Facts

- Can be designs, drawings, or patterns
- Made with overlapping shapes of polygons
- Date back to the Sumerian times in 4000 BC
- M.C. Escher, Bridget Riley, and Victor Vasarely are some famous artists whose works demonstrate tessellations
- Islamic art contains a lot of tessellations, since the Islamic religion does not allow the drawing of recognizable people, animals, or living forms.

View the video *Tessellations: How to Create Them* by Crystal Productions (www.crystalproductions.com). Also view this online, step-by-step tessellation site: http://www.jimmcneill.com/demo.html.

Students can create their own tessellations using these materials and directions:

- Oak tag or heavy construction paper marked into 3″ × 3″ gridded squares
- Scissors
- Glue/tape

Figure 10.3

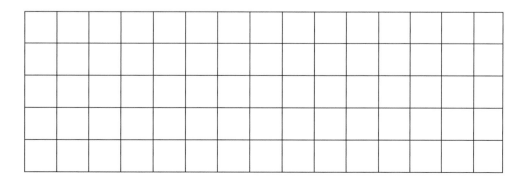

- Markers
- Index cards, cut into 3″ × 3″ squares
- Eraser
- Creative mind!

Figure 10.4

Translations	Rotations	Reflections
1. On an index card cut into a 3 × 3 size, draw a freeform line from the top left corner, to the top right corner.	1. Same as Step 1 in Translations	1. On a squared 3 × 3 index card, draw a freeform line from the bottom left corner to the top left corner.
2. Then draw another abstract freeform line from the top left, ending at the bottom left corner.	2. Same as Step 2 in Translations	2. Then draw another freeform line from the bottom right to the top right corner
3. Then cut out both of the shapes you drew on the index card and save for next step.	3. Same as Step 3 in Translations	3. Then cut out both of the spaces outside the lines you drew on your 3 × 3 square, and save for next step.
4. a. Slide cut top piece to bottom edge of the squared index card and tape it to the index card. b. Then slide cut left edge from left side to edge on right, and tape it to the index card.	4. a. Swing the top piece to the right, like a door on a hinge, and tape it to the straight edge of the index card. b. Then, take the left and swing it clockwise to the bottom and tape it to index card.	4. Flip both pieces in opposite directions and place them on opposite sides of the index card, bottom to bottom. Tape them in place on the index card.
5. Line up the corners of the index card that you have made into a translation by placing it on the oak tag, which is marked in 3 × 3 lightly penciled squares. Trace around the index card template on this large-grid paper and repeat.	5. Line up the corners and trace around the index card template on large-grid paper with 3 × 3 squares.	5. Line up corners and trace around the index card template on larger-grid paper on oak tag square.
6. Continue tracing and sliding shapes from the index card template, then erase grids and color.	6. Continue tracing and swinging shapes, then erase grids. Then color in the negative space.	6. Continue tracing and flipping shapes, then erase grids. Then color in the negative space or draw repeated designs.

DANCE OBJECTIVES

Baseline Knowledge Standard

Students will be able to master basic dance steps to given music pieces. Some students will also demonstrate response to different tempos and beats in their movements.

Figure 10.5

Grades	Content Area/Skills and Standards: Dance
K–2	Be able to move body to beat and rhythm. Explore personal space and movement skills such as bending, stretching, leaping, and sliding in various directions. Understand that dances can express a feeling or emotion.
3–5	Respond to different tempos. Understand how dance can be a form of communication. Continue movement exercises and increase kinesthetic awareness. Collaborate with others in dance; e.g., mirroring, leading, following. Perform for audiences. Understand the differences between types pf dance; e.g., folk dance vs. ballroom style.
6–8	Memorize and repeat more intricate dance steps and patterns from oral and visual directions. Learn associated vocabulary. Be able to reorder dance steps in different sequences and repetitions. Explore dances in various cultures. Understand the emotions dances can express for dancers and audiences.
9–12	Demonstrate more flexibility, agility and strength with locomotor movements. Choreograph own dance steps. Understand time elements. Continue exploration of various dance styles. Display emotion in dance movements. Critique professional dance in musicals and other performances.

Advancing Level

Some students will be able to choreograph and emotively express their own dance movements with partners.

More Challenging Assignments

Students will coordinate varying dance steps and styles with curriculum topics. They can cooperatively perform a *dance skit* that relates to the curriculum by expressing a mood or concept; e.g., solids, liquids, and gases moving closer or further apart, or the movement of Native Americans on the Trail of Tears.

Possible accommodations a child with a *hearing loss* might need:

- Available accommodations to hear the beat; e.g., placing hands near or on drums or speakers to *feel* vibrations
- Sensitivity from peers to include students in all conversations and decisions by practicing the best mode of communication; e.g., sign language, lip reading
- Accompanying verbal directions of dance steps with written ones
- More visuals that pictorially demonstrate dance step sequences or concepts they want to perform
- Explanation of the *hidden curriculum* of social/dance interactions, in case instructions or nuances are missed
- Asking students to act out situations with dance movements vs. speech

Possible accommodations a child with *more advanced skills* might need:

- Opportunities to work with *masters* or resident artists skilled in more sophisticated dance steps; e.g., local dance or theater troupes
- Social-skill instruction to work cooperatively with peers of differing abilities
- Awareness of ways to self-monitor progress
- Responsibility to choreograph own dances and movements
- Oversight to assure that emotions and cognitive levels match

Possible accommodations a child with a *physical impairment* might need:

- Parallel assignment that includes student in a productive way if unable to manage dance steps; e.g., student in a wheelchair could clap the beat or tempo, video classmates, or be the *dance director*
- Additional rest time or more breaks if the physical assignment is too taxing
- Modified environment if student has extra or uncontrolled movements; e.g., moving objects that could cause harm out of reach
- Increased coordination and collaboration with occupational therapist to maximize physical dance opportunities
- Realistic opportunities, objectives, and dance assignments that have high expectations, but do not physically frustrate, strain, or tire the student
- Proper usage of available technology that is appropriate for each situation; e.g., a standing-up wheelchair to be on eye-level with peers or interactive white board to help with note taking if fine motor issues interfere with scribing during dance step instruction
- Patience and support from adults and peers
- Increased, yet realistic praise for progress and efforts

THEATER OBJECTIVES

Baseline Knowledge

Students will identify basic plot elements of stories or plays viewed or read; e.g., television show, movie, Broadway play, *Scholastic News/Weekly Reader* article, historical fiction, and then reenact scenes with themselves as the main characters

Advancing Level

Students will create their own plays that dramatize concepts from social studies, science, or math lessons; e.g., *Mr. Rigid* (algebra), *Ms. Latitude* (walking across only, never up or down), *Mr. Benjamin Franklin* (coming up with inventions). Students will deliver these plays in short skits, narrations, or soliloquies.

More Challenging Assignments

Some students will copy styles of famous playwrights—e.g., Tennessee Williams, Wendy Wasserstein, Ibsen—to rewrite the plays or create and enhance existing or additional acts or scenes

Possible accommodations a child with *dyslexia* might need:

- Enlarged cue cards with words or lines phonetically (fo-net-ik-ly) spelled out
- Direct, intensive, structured, consistent, and multisensory phonics instruction

Figure 10.6

Grades	Content Area/Skills and Standards: Theater
K–2	Collectively think of simple dialogue for story characters with teacher guidance and scribing. Identify elements of a story; e.g., characters, plot, setting, ending. Simplify this to words such as *who, what, where, when, beginning, middle,* and *end.* Act out characters from stories read in teacher-guided dramatizations. Learn about props and visual items to enhance a play or story read to them. Know the difference between make-believe and real.
3–5	Act out plays with appropriate emotions that communicate a mood and relate to concepts learned; e.g., *Performance Station.* Write personal and expository scripts in cooperative groups. Use narration. Find materials for scenery and costumes. Develop imagination through improvisation.
6–8	Create emotive scripts that appeal to different audiences. Write dialogue for different characters. Incorporate all of the elements of a play. Establish a mood based on different settings, characters, and time periods. Cooperatively work on plays with peers. Include scenery, lighting, costumes, and makeup with musical and artistic elements in plays.
9–12	Refine all elements. Use literature, history, and research skills to create plays in a variety of genres set in different environments and time periods. Give characters credence with different voices and movements. Design scenery and costumes for plays. Investigate and imitate styles of selected playwrights from various cultures across history.

- If available, videos and DVDs of scripted plays for students to view
- Matching of recordings with CDs that have scores from original soundtracks
- Plays transcribed on tape (Recording for the Blind & Dyslexic, www .rfbd.org)
- Help and accommodations to spell more difficult words; e.g., able to use the language tools on the computer, pocket dictionary, handheld electronic speller, list of frequently spelled or curriculum-specific vocabulary words
- Patient peers and teachers who encourage, not discourage
- Grading on communication of concepts, not penalized for lower reading ability
- More time to rehearse lines
- Less reading and more accompanying visuals
- Direct teaching of instructional strategies on how to block out other words; e.g., with a paper or a ruler highlighting each line
- Lines in play enlarged, highlighted, or written on separate index cards for student to hold to memorize and practice
- Practice on how to locate plays, scripts, and other resources in a library or online

Possible accommodations a child with a *conduct disorder* might need:

- Specific guidelines on how to cooperatively work with peers during auditions, rehearsals, and performances; e.g., show up on time, share workload
- Monitoring of behavior during different times of the day to note any patterns or side effects of medications
- Structured environment with consistent rules and expectations

- Advanced preparation for scheduling or program changes
- Sensitive peers who are aware of student's behavioral needs
- Use of puppetry as a way to express a character's feelings
- Opportunities for maximum social interaction
- Preplanned ways to channel inappropriate impulses under teacher's and other trusting adults' auspices
- Parallel assignment if student's strength is not dialogue; e.g., working on the artwork, scenery, or directing
- Assignments or directions that allow for student choices, giving structured empowerment to the student
- Increased times for self-reflection and analysis of behavior
- Behavior modification programs
- Reminders of correct posture, body movements, and eye contact
- Frequent praise or individual contractual rewards decided ahead of time; e.g., more computer time or homework pass for positive behavioral strides
- Explanation of different characters' emotions
- Coordination with parents and permission slips to ensure that student is communicating ongoing school activities with those at home

Possible accommodations a child with *lower cognitive/developmental issues* might need:

- Parallel assignment; e.g., holding up cue cards for performers or non-speaking roles if student has communication issues, collecting tickets and greeting the audience during performances
- Translation of dialogue into simpler vocabulary and shorter sentences that transmit the same thoughts without the *flowery words*
- Extra time to prepare for final performance such as practicing or memorizing lines
- Peer theater coach or mentor
- Increased home contact and collaboration to continue and repeat learning of lines to avoid regression the next day
- More concrete and tangible objects that translate abstract words and concepts (e.g., puppets, finger plays, realistic props kept in a classroom *prop box*, scenery, and costumes instead of just using pantomime)
- Field trips to museums to actually see historical costumes, face decorations from different time periods; e.g., Egyptians, French, Renaissance
- Masks that help students portray and concretely assume a new identity

MUSIC OBJECTIVES

Baseline Knowledge Standard

Students will listen to and identify selected pieces by different composers from varied eras in music history: Middle Ages, Renaissance, Baroque, Classical, Romantic, Modern.

Figure 10.7

Grades	Content Area/Skills and Standards: Music
K–2	Repeat pattern, verses, and stanzas in songs. Listen to, describe, and reproduce different types of sounds in their environment. Learn about simple musical instruments, child-made and commercial.
3–5	Learn to play an instrument alone and with others. Read and notate music. Follow musical direction with voice and instruments. Begin performing for an audience.
6–8	Evaluate musical performances. Compose and arrange music. Understand how music relates to other arts and content areas. Perform musical pieces for audiences. Choose musical pieces and songs of interest.
9–12	Improvise melodies and accompaniments. Understand how music relates to other arts and disciplines. Sophisticate instrumental and voice performances by adding more elements and intricacies.

SOURCE: Adapted from National Standards for Arts Education, Copyright 1994 by Music Educators National Conference (MENC). The complete National Arts Standards and additional materials relating to the standards are available from MENC—The National Association for Music Education, 1806 Robert Fulton Drive, Reston, VA 20191.

Sources consulted: Baxter, H., & Baxter, B. (1993). *Learn to read music.* New York: MJF Books; www.emcnotes.com.

Advancing Level

Students will create a *curriculum jingle* that demonstrates the correct beat, rhythm, tone color, tempo, and pitch, using their voices and selected instruments.

More Challenging Assignments

Students will sing or play songs in different melodies, rhythms, harmonies, and styles to successfully demonstrate their musical knowledge, creativity, and critical-thinking skills.

Possible accommodations a child with a *communication impairment* might need:

- Concrete objects such as maracas, rhythm sticks, hand bells, or drum tambourines to feel the vibrations and to demonstrate understandings of musical elements
- More instruction and practice with control of breathing techniques
- Accommodations as warranted by individual educational speech goals

- Practice/coordination with speech therapist for enunciations
- Vocal warm-ups; e.g., opening mouth to form singing vowels *A, E, AH, O, OO*

Possible accommodations a child with *autism* might need:

- Direct and repetitive instruction to understand the difference between a beat (steady pulse heard) and instruments or melodies that surround the beat
- Instruction that includes familiar songs; e.g., younger students could practice with singing or animating nursery rhymes, while older students can change the lyrics of familiar tunes from television shows, movie scores, or commercial jingles
- Teaching of instruments of interest to students one by one
- Structured grouping units of study with categories; e.g., woodwinds stringed, brass, and percussion instruments
- Testing of cognitive skills by correctly selecting and matching pictures of people and instruments to lyrics or sounds
- Teaching practices that ensure complete participation in lessons, despite cognitive levels displayed; e.g., even if student might be participating in a parallel assignment. For example, if the child with autism has a lower cognitive level, he or she could be listening to a different, but perhaps more familiar or favorite song with simplified directions and varied but high expectations
- Modified grading that rewards progress, rather than mastery, after informal assessment of baseline musical knowledge and competencies
- Help with social interactions; e.g., practice and praise to increase eye contact and display appropriate social awareness and reciprocities
- Applied behavioral analysis to target certain social or musical skills

Possible accommodations a child with *AD/HD* might need:

- Assistance to understand musical notations; e.g., graphic organizers and more practice writing and identifying the values of notes
- Musical instruction on independent, not frustration level
- Writing the lyrics on an overhead projector or interactive board to increase attention and help student who may also have difficulties with fine motor issues such as taking notes or keeping pace during classroom lectures
- Playing of a song or instrument more than once
- Using multiple intelligence surveys and personal interest inventories to determine student's interests to tie song selections with individual choices and thereby increase focus during lessons
- Extra time to complete assignments or modification of requirements
- More opportunities for acceptable classroom motoric or kinesthetic releases if student has impulse or hyperactivity issues; e.g., finger plays, creating a dance to a choice of songs, guidance and instruction to play the role of the musical conductor while other students are seated

Musical Terms and Concepts

Create flash cards with illustrations to study these terms:

Figure 10.8

sound	caused by something vibrating
beat	steady pulse or sound heard, which is made up of notes of different lengths
rhythm	melody and instruments that surround the beat
tone	quality of a sound
pitch	highness or lowness (depth) of a sound
note	each written one has a sound
rest	written sign for silence, which is note's equivalent
sharp	half step higher in pitch
flat	half step lower in pitch
natural	sign used to cancel the sharp or flat
accidentals	sharps, flats, and naturals
scale	a ladder of notes, each with a different letter name; e.g., scale of C: C, D, E, F, G, A, B, C
harmony	combination of sounds heard; e.g., piano chords
stave or staff	set of five lines with four spaces between
whole note or whole rest	4 beats
half note or half rest	2 beats
quarter note or quarter rest	1 beat
eighth note or eighth rest	½ beat
sixteenth note or sixteenth rest	¼ beat
octaves	8 notes of the scale; e.g., C, D, E, F, G, A,B, C. The distance from C to C is an octave.
treble clef or G clef	used to write notes for high sounds
bass clef or F clef	used to write notes for low sounds
allegro	fast speed
largo	slow speed
moderato	moderate/medium speed
wheel of fifths	order of sharps
wheel of fourths	order of flats
theme	musical idea
variations	changes
rondo	simplest form of a song—A-B-A-B-A
unison parts or singing	two notes on the same line or in the same space that are sung or played at the same time. Unison singing means that one part is being sung at a time, except if performers are separated by octaves
verse	part of a song that can lead to the chorus and gives details about the subject of the song
chorus	important part of a song's lyrics that is repeated and may also contain the song's title

11

Standards-Based Health/Physical Education Objectives

T he connection between physical education and good health choices with academic classroom successes is enormous. Students, when asked to indicate their favorite subject, will most often claim it's PE. Including movement in classrooms certainly moves many students toward better achievement of the standards by honoring their bodily-kinesthetic strengths. Knowledge here is crucial for all!

RESEARCH IMPLICATIONS

A sample of physical educators noted that they require more staff development and resources to help students with disabilities successfully be included within physical education classes.

—Block & Zeman, 1996

Attitude is believed to play a significant role in explaining physical educators' actions toward teaching students with disabilities in regular classes.

—Folson-Meek, Rizzo, 2002

In an inclusive physical education class, individual differences are not hidden or ridiculed but rather shared among students who simultaneously learn to respect a wide variety of abilities and skills, value personal uniqueness, and recognize their own strengths.

—Obrusníková, Válková, & Block, 2003

Eighty-nine percent of 112 elementary physical educators who taught at least one inclusion class felt that they should be a part of the IEP planning process for students with disabilities.

—Hackney, French, & O'Conner, 2000

For students to reap the maximum benefits of exercise, it's important that physical activity be conducted in three stages: the warm-up, the main event, and the cool down.

—Crupi, 2006

When asked to rate the most important reasons why students choose to participate in physical education, most students agreed that they liked to get out and move, they liked competitive sports, it made them healthier, and they had fun.

—Couturier, Chepko, & Coughlin, 2005

Significant issues exist for students who do not like physical education. . . . [The] curriculum is boring, lacks personal meaning, the environment is too competitive, or they are likely to be ridiculed or embarrassed.

—Couturier, Chepko, & Coughlin, 2005

Young athletes need positive, appropriate and constructive role models to teach and reinforce sportsmanship and moral reasoning.

—Nucci & Young-Shim, 2005

You still have physical education teachers who are dinosaurs, who are unwilling to accommodate. We've been able to increase the knowledge of the regular physical education teachers. We get them to see the possibilities.

—Gehring, 2004

SAMPLE LESSONS/CONNECTIONS FOR K–12

HEALTH/PHYSICAL EDUCATION

Research shows that nutrition and physical activity affect student academic achievement.

—Satcher, 2005

Figure 11.1

Grades	Content Area/Skills and Standards: Health/Physical Education
K–2	Identify personal needs and *healthy behavior* appropriate for school and home; e.g., washing hands and face, brushing teeth, eating the right snacks. Develop motor skills through a variety of cooperative and team building activities. Understand basic emotional and physical needs. Identify *good, healthy choices.*
3–5	Identify strategies to prevent injuries and maintain health. Describe stressful situations and coping strategies. Identify functions of body systems. Set personal health goals. Expand view on physical fitness, learning about benefits of regular exercise for self and social interaction; e.g., teambuilding vs. competition. Continue nutrition training.
6–8	Understand how decisions about health, nutrition, and taking care of one's own body have positive and negative consequences. Express health decisions based upon information and current research. Know how the media influences health outlook. Decide how to manage conflict in *healthy ways*; e.g., communication and negotiation. Apply movement activities to everyday routines for self-improvement, physical expression, and personal well-being.
9–12	Analyze impact health decisions have on self and others; e.g., nutrition, diet choices. Compare and contrast physical vs. emotional health. Understand how government decisions influence populations (e.g., medical advances, financial support). Exhibit knowledge of school and community professional health services. Develop individual responsibility for own health. Demonstrate understanding of how communication influences positive interpersonal relationships. Achieve a physically healthy, active lifestyle.
	Healthy sources: www.actionforhealthykids.org, www.cdc.gov/healthyyouth

Some Adaptive Health/PE Suggestions

- Recognize that differences in physical, sensory, and cognitive abilities exist.
- Obtain financial support from administration for adaptations.
- Train personnel for inclusion at undergraduate and school building level.
- Break skills down into steps.
- Provide clear, concise directions.
- Model concepts.
- Use repetition and reinforcement.
- Reduce competition; focus more on team activities.
- Use different assessments, not only norm-rated ones, but also ones based on improvements and efforts.
- Evaluate frequently, not only with written assessments, but also by observing students and keeping accurate dated records
- Note changes in the quality of skill, rather than solely recording the outcome.
- Let student demonstrate knowledge in different ways; e.g., create a game that uses the skill, illustrate a storyboard, design a 5-minute.

videotape, interview other people and record their opinions about the learned activity or skill, keep a graph of improvements toward skill mastery.

- Individualize instruction; capitalizing on students' strengths to maximize participation and confidence levels.
- Even if a student cannot participate in an activity, he or she can keep a log of observations, coach others from the sidelines, or write a *sports article.*
- Make sure activity is age appropriate, regardless of motor or cognitive skills of students.
- Include these four components: Safety, success, satisfying, and skill appropriate

---

SOURCE: Adapted from Reeves & Stein, 1999.

Baseline Knowledge Standard

Students will understand basic rules of games; e.g., tennis, volleyball, basketball, capture the flag.

Advancing Level

Through play and observation, students will demonstrate 90% mastery.

More Challenging Assignments

Increase or vary directions or complexity of the games.
Possible accommodations a child with *physical differences* might need:

- Modeling and step-by-step demonstration and reinforcement; e.g., correct racquet grip or volleyball serve if student has fine motor issues
- Repositioning or lowering of the net for volleyball
- Differently sized or weighted volleyball or racquet
- Extra time allowance for practice of motor skills required before actual commencement of class game
- Enough room to maneuver in PE setting, if child is in a wheelchair
- Explanation to other students about specific needs and sensitivities; e.g., do not touch someone's wheelchair since it can be considered an extension of his or her body
- Peer or partner to help and coach with rules or motor movements
- Alternative or parallel assignment if physical demands exceed student's safety level; e.g., team captain, compare and contrast the actions of two friends for 15 minutes of observation and describe what they were doing during game play, or intermittently monitor and graph your team's pulse rate
- Assessment based upon improvements or efforts vs. winning the game

Possible accommodations a child with *auditory processing/learning/reading concerns* might need:

- Mnemonic devices to remember the rules, for capture the flag, volleyball rotations, how to keep track of who serves in tennis
- Visual aids when explaining a new game; e.g., videos of students engaged in the sport, storyboard with illustrative *sporting steps*, captions with pictures, using overheads or Smart Boards
- Privately ask student to paraphrase the game rules to proactively circumvent possible peer embarrassment when play begins
- Sensitivity when asking students to read in front of others in class with handouts or worksheets, if there are below grade-level decoding issues
- Sound out words in readings and divide them into syl-la-bles
- Offer step-by-step, terse directions
- Give praise for partial mastery to recognize efforts
- Offer a *game rubric* with expectations and criteria spelled out
- Demonstration/observation of game with experienced players from another class before actual competition
- Establish prior knowledge and current understandings before game play

Possible accommodations a child with *visual concerns* might need:

- Tennis ball, volleyball, or capture the flag item with a bell or squeaky noise placed inside or attached
- More auditory feedback; e.g., *listen to this*, instead of *watch . . .*
- Allow modifications in rules; e.g., positioning student in the first row in volleyball instead of rotating, if seeing from a distance is an issue, or change of boundaries for tennis, allowing player to stay closer than given boundaries
- Additional tactile, visual, and auditory stimulation; e.g., tape on floor indicating where to stand or how to rotate, whistle to signal movements

Three Stages of Exercise

For students to reap the maximum benefits of exercise, it's important that physical activity be conducted in three stages: the warm-up, the main event, and the cooldown.

Step 1: The warm-up

The purpose of the warm-up is to prepare your body for physical activity and to prevent injury. Warm-up activities should last a minimum of five minutes. There are various warm-ups that you can do with your students. Some possibilities include marching in place, backward and forward arm circles, jumping jacks, windmills, jogging in place, etc.

Step 2: The main event

The main event is the focal point of the day's physical education lesson. While your students are engaged in the main event, their heart rates should increase and major muscle groups should be utilized. Some examples of main event activities include the following:

- **Sharks and Minnows:** This is a fun one for younger students to play outside. Divide the class with half of your students playing sharks and the other half minnows. Next, divide the blacktop in half—sharks on one side and minnows on the other. Each side should have a five-foot area on their turf called a "safety net." When everyone is ready, call out "Sharks!" and all the sharks will then try to tag the minnows. If the minnows make it to the shark safety net, they are safe. If a minnow gets tagged, he or she becomes a shark.

- **Jump Rope Relay:** Divide your class into two teams. Each team is presented with a jump rope. All members of each team jump rope for one minute. While a person is jumping, the other teammates count how many times he or she jumps rope. Once a minute is up, the jump rope gets passed to the next teammate. The team with the most jumps wins.

Step 3: The cooldown

The main purpose of the cooldown is to gradually reduce one's heart rate. Students should perform five minutes of cooldown activities. Possible cooldown activities for both elementary and middle school students include static stretching exercises and walking. Have fun!

SOURCE: From the March 2006 issue of *Teaching K–8* magazine, Norwalk, CT. Reprinted with permission of the publisher, Early Years, Inc.

Empowering and Appetizingly Nutritional Choices

The Child Nutrition Reauthorization Act (2004) states that schools must stress student wellness with food guidelines for beverages and foods sold in schools, along with staff training on nutrition to create healthy environments.

—Satcher, 2005

Baseline Knowledge Standard

Students will understand that eating properly and maintaining a balanced diet is a way to stay healthy. Procedure asks class to sort a teacher/student list of a variety of foods into the following groups: grains, fruits, vegetables, protein, dairy, fats/sweets. The correct number of recommended servings of each group should be noted: grains (6–11), fruits (2–4), vegetables (3–5), protein (2–3), dairy (2–3), fats/sweets (not a lot).

Advancing Level

Cooperative groups will investigate how making poor food choices leads to negative physical effects. Student researchers will collate information about food neglect and its potential negative effects; e.g., anorexia, obesity, low energy level.

More Challenging Assignments

Some students survey both peers and adults about their eating patterns to see how their choices match recommended food guidelines. Students then cooperatively graph results after collectively sampling a minimum of 25 people.

Possible accommodations/modifications a child with *communication impairments* might need:

- Rehearsed speech with exact interview questions written on note or index cards
- Modeling proper tones by listening to peers in classroom conversations
- Easier classification assignment, with actual foods/packaging to sort
- Visuals that match the spoken or written word if student has language difficulties; e.g., vocabulary issues
- Tape of more difficult words articulated properly so that student can copy proper speech patterns and fluency
- Facing student when speaking, if person is lip reading
- Providing a copy of teacher's lesson plans or teacher's manual to follow along if hearing is not optimum
- Appropriate seating away from extraneous interfering noises

Possible accommodations a child with *visual differences* might need:

- Concrete foods to accompany abstract words
- Enlarged graphics and worksheets
- Raised food pictures and Braille books
- Computers with speech programs and accessible Web sites for research
- More auditory and kinesthetic/tactile cues and lessons

Possible accommodations a child with *emotional concerns* might need:

- Frequent monitoring to ensure task focus and completion
- Guidance on how to appropriately interact with peers
- Rehearsal on how to handle possibly stressful interviewing situations
- Praise or individual tangible and personalized rewards; e.g., more computer time, *healthy* lunch treat, recognition on behavior modification program; e.g., stars, happy faces, points for completion of assigned task: cooperating with peers and following teacher's classroom rules and lesson
- Relate nutrition lesson to own life and daily diet concerns
- Trusting and caring support system; e.g., peer chat group

Appetizing Nutritional Choices

Directions: Place the letter of food choice below in its correct food category. Then cooperatively think of some other favorite foods and draw pictures or write words in matching columns.

Figure 11.2

Grains Portions: (6–11)	Fruits (2–4)	Vegetables (3–5)	Protein (2–3)	Dairy (2–3)	Fats/Sweets (not a lot)

a. bagel
b. apple
c. yogurt
d. fish
e. eggs
f. pasta
g. cereal
h. cheese
i. broccoli
j. nuts
k. corn
l. apple
m. chocolate
n. grapes
o. beans

12

Standards-Based Career Education and Life Skills Objectives

I f the goal of special education, or all education, is in fact to prepare students to lead productive adult lives, then shouldn't schools be the place where students are taught marketable and employable skills? Why wait until career demands are thrust upon them? This training can begin at early ages and expose students to many learnings that reach out far beyond the classroom walls. The following lessons ask students to focus on their neighborhoods, increase awareness of career options, and set personal goals for future aspirations. Life skills and career skills must certainly parallel students' strengths, with high standards and expectations for all!

RESEARCH IMPLICATIONS

Vocational education—underfunded and underappreciated—has been overlooked in recent years. Tight budgets and increasing pressure on educators to improve standardized test scores have brought about a growing concentration on core subject classes. . . . We must focus on helping all students, not just those who are college bound, gain the marketable skills required for well-paying jobs that contribute to the economy and the well-being of the populace.

—"Preparing Students for Jobs," 2006

"The parents of today have their exposure to career tech as when they were in high school and the vo-tech kids were the dummies," said Jan Bray, executive director of the Association for Career and Technical Education. "No longer. Even the name for the programs has been revamped—it's now "career and technical education. . . . [T]he kids who come here are no less bright than the kids in regular high schools—as many go on to college as don't."

—*"Vo-Tech as a Door to College," 2006*

We need to stop addressing school improvement by focusing on academics in isolation from career and technical education, or career and technical education in isolation from academics. These two need to work together.

—Gary Hoachlander, president of ConnectEd, as cited in Olson, 2006

Teachers did not consider access to the general education curriculum important for students with severe disabilities, but instead ranked functional and social skills as most important.

—Agran, Alper, & Wehmeyer, 2002

SAMPLE LESSONS/CONNECTIONS FOR K–12

CAREER EDUCATION

K–2

Baseline Knowledge Standard

Students will identify different types of workers in their school and community.

Advancing Level

Students will associate different skills and abilities of workers with jobs, occupations, and careers.

More Challenging Assignments

Some students will be able to understand how a worker's efforts can result in better job performance.

Possible accommodations a child with *Down syndrome* might need:

- Real photographs of people he or she knows at work
- Field trips/outside visits or guest speakers to concretely identify types of community jobs and workers

Figure 12.1

Grades	Content Area/Skills and Standards: Career Education
K–2	Describe different careers. Identify different jobs in home, school, and neighborhood environments.
3–5	Know the reasons why people work. Realize that the work quality is related to knowledge, preparation, and efforts. Understand interpersonal skills and cooperative efforts.
6–8	Know the difference between the terms *job, occupation*, and *career.* Explore skills needed to obtain and retain employment. Research an array of employment possibilities in different fields, knowing how academics relate to the learning.
9–12	Self-assess personal interests, intelligences, and aptitudes. Set long-range goals. Outline a possible career plan. Work as teams to model appropriate work behavior. Analyze, model, and apply leadership skills.

- Chart to point to that matches jobs with skills, or *performance* verbs; e.g., mailperson—delivers mail, pilot—flies a plane, hairdresser—cuts hair
- More visuals with readings and texts
- Less written material
- Guided questioning with more discussion
- Modified or parallel academic assignments and assessments
- Relating learning to functional issues; e.g., *Who do you know that works?*

Possible accommodations a child with *cerebral palsy* might need:

- Instruction and discussion on how specific accommodations can erase job barriers
- Equal access for all community site visits by ensuring ahead of time that the enforcement of all Americans with Disabilities Act (ADA) codes are in effect
- Positive role models with physical disabilities who are gainfully employed
- Extra time for student to speak if there are communication issues
- Sensitivities based upon varying cognitive and physical levels of each student with cerebral palsy
- Disability awareness for peers and staff to circumvent mobility issues and ensure full social participation in the classroom and community
- Allowances for parallel assignments to gain same skills if activities are too physically taxing

Possible accommodations a child with *hearing issues* might need:

- Accommodations dependent upon severity of hearing loss
- Clearly spoken but not overemphasized speech

- Sign language interpreters
- More written directions and *tell-all* pictures that illustrate novel vocabulary words as related to community jobs
- Social encouragement for maximum peer interactions; e.g., increase knowledge about students' needs for peers
- Facing the student if he or she is lip reading
- Closed captioning for videos shown

3–5

Baseline Knowledge Standard

Students list the reasons why people work.

Advancing Level

Students match school subjects to careers that use those skills

More Challenging Assignments

Students interview family members and school personnel, listing skills that different jobs require.

Possible accommodations a child with *dyslexia* might need:

- Books on tape about different careers
- Break down of larger vocabulary words into syllables so students will not be intimidated by longer words; e.g., em-ploy-ment
- Talking handheld electronic speller
- Digital recorder to review, if student has spelling issues, transcribing employment/career interview answers from family members and school personnel

Possible accommodations a child with *lower cognitive abilities* might need:

- Pictures that match careers with names
- Explanation of *who, what, where, when, why,* and *how* questions through clear-cut graphic organizers
- Description of some community careers that are part of their lives; e.g., dentist, teacher, storekeeper, mailperson, doctor

Possible accommodations a child with *visual differences* might need:

- Worksheets with enlarged print
- Auditory and kinesthetic opportunities to compensate for visual weaknesses
- Talking computer programs about careers/employment
- Braille texts or worksheets
- Reduction of glare; e.g., not sitting by a window

6–8

Baseline Knowledge Standard

Students identify own interests through self-assessment.

Advancing Level

Knowing that there are differences between a job, career, and occupation

More Challenging Assignments

Cooperatively choose a career, and with your group, identify the challenges of that career or job.

Possible accommodations a child with *learning differences* might need:

- Better understandings about own personal likes and dislikes; e.g., interest inventory or checking off favorite activities from a teacher-given list
- Explanation of how multiple intelligences relate to employment choices
- Three-columned chart that gives examples of specific jobs, careers, and occupations
- High-interest but lower-level reading materials if decoding words is an issue
- Help paraphrasing information read and more frequent checks on understandings about different careers
- Guidance and reassurances that learning differences do not translate to career deficits
- Increased contact with adults who had learning differences in school and figured out how to compensate for weaknesses to become gainfully employed in chosen fields
- Study-skill instruction

Possible accommodations a child with *aggressive behavioral issues* might need:

- Frequent adult or self-monitoring of attitudes toward the future
- Structured environment that values student's issues
- Trusting adults that like the child, but dislike the behavior
- Access to medical knowledge; e.g., communication with the school nurse and family to find out if student is on medication to know possible side effects
- Explanation of rules for outside community visits
- Consistency of rewards along with frequent, yet realistic praise
- Avoidance of negative attention; e.g., yelling at the child or calling additional attention to inappropriate behavior
- Individual signals to interrupt poor behavioral choices and increase metacognition
- Education for peers about appropriate ways to interact with student, when to withdraw from unsafe situations, or when to ask for adult assistance and supervision

- Collaboration with home environment to ensure consistency in behavioral management programs
- Guidance to help with future job choices and direct instruction on how present behavior will affect future employment
- Daily or hourly behavioral logs stated in positive terms; e.g., appropriate and productive cooperation with peers

Possible accommodations a child with *autism* might need:

- Individualized PECS that lists realistic career choices
- Education on how to behave on a job; e.g., practice with phone skills, eye contact
- Behavioral analysis to increase appropriate *job behaviors*
- More practice with social skills to work in cooperative groups
- Peer coaches to monitor appropriate choices
- Acknowledgement and matching of student's individual interests with employment decisions; e.g., if the student loves horses, he or she could volunteer helping out in a riding stable, or if the student likes music, help out with the school band

9–12

Baseline Knowledge Standard

Identify own career goal or wishes and match personal character skills needed

Advancing Level

Think about the next steps involved in achieving goals. Write a personal essay about three ways that career can be achieved. Use technology to write a student resume.

More Challenging Assignments

Cooperatively choose a job or career, then invent, discuss, and formulate a plan to solve a workplace problem that might arise.

Possible accommodations a child with *depression* might need:

- More contact with guidance counselor or chat groups to explore future career, job, and occupation choices available
- Positive reinforcement for increased social interactions
- Graph to plot daily mood swings to increase self-reflections and identify possible antecedents for depression
- Identification of personal choices to channel and replace sadness; e.g., exercise, yoga, listening to music, sketching, chatting with friends online
- Increased contact with trusting adults and understanding peers
- More contact and ongoing communication with home environment

- Encouragement and job placement with volunteer organizations to experience satisfaction in helping others and to increase responsibility and feelings of self-worth
- Monitoring of student and communication with school nurse if the student is on certain medications
- Help to fill out college applications and assistance getting positive and cohesive thoughts together for personal essays

Possible accommodations a child with *attention issues* might need:

- Organizational skill instruction
- Help to understand how present needs and decisions affect future goals
- Assistance organizing and sequencing a job resume
- Nonverbal reminders to focus on lessons
- Increased self-monitoring of time on task
- Instruction on *self-talks* to raise confidence levels

Possible accommodations a child with *traumatic brain injury* might need:

- Repetition of oral and written directions
- More concrete exposure to career choices available
- Structure and consistency in school and work environments, with tasks clearly explained
- Step-by-step written or pictorial chart to ensure accurate completion of tasks
- Peer coach to help compose a resume
- Available guidance counselors, trusting adults, or peer coaches to talk to, ask questions, and help minimize frustrations
- Nonthreatening work and school environment
- Assistance with academic skills needed, such as reading or math requirements in school or on the job
- Help to match preferences with career choices
- Encouragement to continue and advance schooling in a supportive college environment or training program

LIFE/FUNCTIONAL SKILLS

Baseline Knowledge Standard

Students will develop an understanding of the cost of basic food items and the ability to estimate if they have enough money for purchases.

Advancing Level

Students will compare prices of items listed in different measurements and figure out the unit rates of different food brands to determine which is the *better buy.*

Figure 12.2

My Strengths (What I'm good at!)	Interests (What I like to do!)	Goals (What I hope I will do!)

Figure 12.3

Grades	Content Area/Skills and Standards: Life/Functional Skills Objectives
K–2	Increase awareness of others. Cooperatively help peers and family. Understand about respect and fairness. Learn about the value of money. Identify hygiene items. Demonstrate appropriate personal hygiene; e.g., combing hair, covering your mouth when you sneeze or cough. Learn vocabulary about their own body, clothes, grooming, and other health words. Use appropriate communication and behavior to make needs known. Identify community and school signs; e.g., keep out, don't walk, girls'/boys' room. Know that it costs money to buy things. Begin learning how to listen and talk to peers and adults.
3–5	Develop interpersonal skills to solve problems. Learn how to count coins and make change. Become aware of own body language. Practice conversational skills. Keep a personal calendar. Explore more outdoor community signs and symbols. Realize importance of honesty and showing kindness and respect for self and others. Develop listening skills. Follow school rules; e.g., waiting in line, talking in the hallway. Develop responsibility; e.g., doing school jobs, home chores.
6–8	Work cooperatively in teams. Continue development of character education; e.g., citizenship, responsibility. Solve everyday problems with feasible solutions. Develop shopping skills and etiquette. Have a spending plan and learn how to manage personal finances. Continue making good health and hygiene decisions. Learn about practical signs and labels; e.g., building signs, and labels on medicines. Understand about local public transportation. Learn ways to manage negative emotions. Demonstrate phone skills. Learn to think before you act; e.g., cope with failure, rejection, bullying. Develop cooking skills to prepare basic meals; e.g., use a microwave.
9–12	Demonstrate conflict resolution skills. Identify consequences when rules are not followed. Learn about motor vehicle safety. Establish a daily budget. Know how to obtain credit. Learn basic record keeping; e.g., how to balance a checkbook. Know how to act at an interview. Learn how to do laundry. Develop self-confidence. Learn to accept constructive criticism.

More Challenging Assignments

Students will investigate how and where goods are manufactured, knowing that variables such as the source of natural resources ingredients, packaging, and advertising factor into costs. Lessons on buying foods with better nutritional values, as opposed to buying the least expensive but lower-quality food item.

Possible accommodations a child with *lower cognitive/developmental differences* might need:

- Games to identify food types such as *Food, Money,* or *Career Bingo*
- Practice and drills with counting money or using food coupons
- Mock supermarket shopping in classroom setting
- Social-skills training in supermarket etiquette; e.g., checking out on certain lines such as 10 items or less, asking for help if you cannot find your item
- Use of a pocket calculator to help keep track of costs for selected foods
- Direct instruction on nutritional value of a balanced diet; e.g., limiting the junk food and impulse buying
- Peer/adult assistance to compose a shopping list
- Lessons on advertising and packaging, such as when it looks like there is more of an item, but the actual contents may be less than expected
- Help and practice reading labels
- Lessons on food categorization to know which foods are located in which aisles

Possible accommodations a child with *above average skills* might need:

- Opportunities to complete individual assignments that use higher-level thinking skills; e.g., comparing prices in different supermarkets or same items in different quantities or sizes
- Alternative assignments or centers to demonstrate same knowledge in creative ways; e.g., computer slide show, food art collage, personification of a food item
- Ability to cooperatively work with different types of student groupings that include both heterogeneous and homogeneous ones
- More self-awareness of levels through independent charting of progress
- Responsive teachers that value students' inquisitiveness and individual needs
- Structure and consistency
- Social-skills training if total focus is on academics
- Help to set up a team-building atmosphere vs. a competitive environment

Possible accommodations a child with *communication issues* might need:

- Paper to write down questions
- Practice with conversational skills
- Help listening to and interpreting advertisements
- *Shopping peer,* if appropriate, to help, not enable, the student

- Pre- or reteaching of food names or brands and appropriate consumer vocabulary
- Education of peers and others to speak in conversational tones, facing the student if he or she is lip reading
- PECS if student has lower cognitive level or cannot verbally communicate thoughts

Standards-Based Social/Behavioral/ Emotional Objectives

Even the best academically prepared lessons become futile ones to members of the classroom audience who are physically present, but emotionally disconnected from the academics. Teaching involves acknowledging the *huge* connection between emotions and how students will think, remember, and connect the learning to their lives. Even though emotions are more abstract than teaching a reading or math lesson, they can be taught with the same learning principles as other disciplines, in a step-by-step repetitive manner with much modeling. The following lessons and graphic organizers acknowledge the variability of students' emotions. Research supports the importance of teaching behavioral, emotional, and social skills.

RESEARCH IMPLICATIONS

Most researchers believe that as soon as we are born, the personal intelligences begin to develop from a combination of heredity, environment, and experience. . . . [I]ntrapersonal awareness is crucially important to developing learners who may grow increasingly ethical, productive, and creative, while simultaneously exhibiting positive independence and interdependence.

—Campbell, Campbell, & Dickinson, 2003

Students learn in different ways and that learning is influenced by social and emotional factors.

—Wang, Haertel, & Walberg, 1997

Social and emotional learning builds the foundation for accepting responsibility; managing emotions; appreciating diversity; preventing violence, substance abuse, and related problems; and succeeding academically.

—Zins, Weissberg, Wang, & Walberg, in press

In social and emotional learning programs, students develop skills to recognize and manage their emotions, develop caring and concern for others, make responsible decisions, establish positive relationships, and handle challenging situations effectively.

—Weissberg, Resnik, Payton, & O'Brien, 2003

Behavioral disorders may have a more adverse impact on academic achievement over time than do learning disabilities.

—Nelson, Stage, Epstein, & Pierce, 2005

Socialization can take place through participation in sports since sports provide learning environments where participants have the opportunity to learn competition, cooperation, role-playing and discipline regarding rules, regulations, and goals.

—Bloom & Smith, 1996

The ability to get along with people has more influence on career success than grade point average.

—Utay & Utay, 2005

When teachers stress social skills in the classroom and create a climate of cooperation and respect for each other there are fewer discipline problems and less negative behavior.

—McArthur, 2002

SAMPLE LESSONS/CONNECTIONS FOR K–12

SOCIAL/BEHAVIORAL/EMOTIONAL OBJECTIVES

Connective Academic/Social Issues

Teacher request/question: Use the word *does* in a sentence.

Student response: "There were *dose* amigos."

Figure 13.1

Grades	Content Area/Skills and Standards: Social/Behavioral/Emotional Objectives
K–2	Understand that people have different emotions. Learn ways to control impulsive behaviors. Know own likes and dislikes. Identify appropriate school/classroom behaviors. Realize the difference between speaking and listening; e.g., knowing that one person talks at a time, establishing eye contact. Understand that problems with peers can be resolved amicably, with compromises that minimize conflicts.
3–5	Profile own strengths and challenges. Increase knowledge about socially acceptable behavior. Learn how to chart progress toward achieving personal short-term goals; e.g., staying focused on task, improving a math grade, being a better friend. Learn about body language and moods of self and others. Develop more social reciprocity. Improve conversational skills. Know that conflicts with peers have varying causes and solutions.
6–8	Understand how school learning and motivation correlate to the achievement of future personal goals. Analyze and apply responsible behavior to everyday interactions. Evaluate ways to develop and express positive attitudes about themselves and others; e.g., peers, teachers, family. Understand how to set a plan into action to achieve short- and long-term goals. Learn to accept and respect differences and similarities between themselves and others' perspectives. Develop more empathy and respect for others. Take action to oppose bullying and the stereotyping of others. Continue development of effective interpersonal relationships.
9–12	Learn how emotions, attitudes, and thoughts affect and influence them and others in varying situations and environments. Evaluate obstacles presented in difficult social situations. Develop a plan to overcome or circumvent *difficult*, *unwanted*, and/or *unasked-for situations.* Understand and apply effective conflict-resolution skills. Compare own progress according to an acceptable *social rubric* or agreed-upon teacher and/or parent criteria. Know how to maximize available resources and services; e.g., guidance counselor, support groups, peers, daily planners. Identify and advocate for achievements of those from different cultural or social backgrounds. Oppose prejudicial actions of others.

SOURCE: Illinois Learning Standards: www.isbe.state.il.us/ils/social_emotional/standards.htm

Well, the Spanish teacher was totally delighted when I shared this sentence with her. This was from a student who has a low cognitive level and is a rote learner. What needs to be investigated here is this: does this student have perceptual difficulties, transposing letters within words? Also, the Spanish word for "two" was misspelled, yet the word "amigos" was spelled correctly. It might be coincidental, but this student is quite social and perhaps the word for "friends" in Spanish appealed to her and was something she wanted to remember. I had her highlight her mistake and self-correct, rather than marking her paper with the correct word. I did this so the student would increase her own level of self-awareness, and learn by doing! Experiential learning *does* work!

Baseline Knowledge Standards

Through sharing, modeled lessons, and class discussion, students will realize that their actions and behaviors influence others and themselves in both positive and negative ways. Students will also understand/discuss that the same situation or writing piece may evoke differing emotions in people, by examining fictional and historical characters in fairy tales, nursery rhymes, literature stories, newspaper articles, poems, and past and present world events.

Advancing Level

Students will interview adults and peers in their school, home, and community, and then record responses on a class graph that sorts and *analyzes* various possible emotional responses to the same hypothetical situations.

More Challenging Assignments

Students will write *emotive scripts* and role-play various hypothetical social situations, exhibiting appropriate but realistic emotions through fictional characters.

Possible accommodations a child with a *visual impairment* might need:

- Larger graph paper to record and tally interview results
- Peer or adult to read written directions and other printed requirements
- Technology to scan and then read aloud his or her own and others' written works/responses
- Magnification page to enlarge printed words in newspapers, poems, and stories
- Sensitivities regarding individual needs; e.g., more time and grading content, not appearance of written work
- Scripts, books, articles, or poems transcribed into Braille
- Listening to auditory tapes of writings
- Scribe or interviewee to record responses to interview questions
- Preferential seating; e.g., positioned away from glare from windows
- Mobility orientation training

Possible accommodations a child with a *hearing impairment* might need:

- More visuals; e.g., written directions, masking tape for cue on stage of where to stand during role-playing
- Signs/prompts that indicate the direction/source of sound or the student's turn to speak
- Having person face student during conversational interview or role-playing if student is lip reading
- Additional time or more practice rehearsals
- Environment that clears extra distractions or noises; e.g., carpeting, cut-up tennis balls on chair legs
- Sign interpreters as needed

Possible accommodations a child with *AD/HD* might need:

- Frequent breaks or intermittent kinesthetic activities during longer sitting sessions
- Peer, teacher, and/or parent to reinforce proper organizational skills
- Praise to reward partial mastery or efforts, if task is not completed at the same pace as peers; e.g., let student finish script at home or buddy up with a cooperative team

- Explanation of how body language is a form of communication
- Behavioral monitoring to graph positive periods of attention and focus

Possible accommodations a child with *oppositional defiant disorder (ODD)* might need:

- Teacher-directed allowances; e.g., "You can choose your own question to ask interviewees," or student chosen poem or story, rather than a teacher-selected one
- Closer monitoring during cooperative work with scripts; e.g., behavior modification program with self-selected reward, ranging from a lollipop to stickers, lunch with the teacher, homework pass, increased computer time; or helping the physical education teacher, art specialist, librarian, or music teacher with pre-, inter-, or follow-up class tasks
- Sensitivities when hypothetical situations or role-playing may mirror real-life situations
- Allowances to vary assignment without diluting requirements; e.g., journal writing of own emotional responses to daily situations for a week, rather than interviewing others or making up hypothetical ones
- Consultation/collaboration with parents, school nurse, school psychologist, or guidance counselor for their input regarding personal or home situations that they might be privy to that should be avoided in classroom discussion
- Tracking of student's emotions during different time periods
- Awareness of medications that must be taken, and their possible side effects

Possible accommodations a child with *lower self-esteem* might need:

- Praise for realistic social strides gained
- Journal writing to record daily moods and emotions
- Increased metacognition of own strengths
- Teacher guidance and monitoring to ease insecurities and raise confidence during both group and independent assignments
- Peer coach to support student's efforts
- School communication with family to reinforce and transition student's progress to home environment

Possible accommodations a child with *above average social skills* might need:

- More advanced or challenging assignments; e.g., publish his or her own poem, or current or historical news article, rather than reflecting on ones already written to express emotions
- Ways to increase, strengthen, and combine academic skills with social activities
- Realization that even though student might exhibit advanced skills in some social situations, this might not be evidenced *across the board*

Possible accommodations a child with a *cognitive/developmental issue* might need:

- Repetition, modeling, or explanation of *social rules*
- Sensitivity instruction for peers regarding level of cooperative work produced

- Step-by-step directions and breaking down of objectives; e.g., teaching about one emotion at a time
- Age-appropriate activities such as puppets for younger students and videos for more mature students
- Alternative or parallel assignments and assessments with daily living skills incorporated; e.g., asking students to identify specified emotions in realistic photographs of people's faces in daily encounters or settings

Possible accommodations a child with *autism* might need:

- Direct skill instruction to increase eye contact along with more inter- and intrapersonal gains
- Practice with peer coaches for improved conversational skills
- Listening exercises/training
- Collaboration with school speech therapists to improve vocabulary and language
- ABA (Applied Behavioral Analysis) to target specific skills; e.g., exhibiting appropriate body language
- Rewarding of strides
- Prompting and charting appropriate responses
- Increased praise for positive social reciprocity and more accurate behavioral awareness

T.O.T.A.L. MONITORING: TIME ON TASK ACCELERATES LEARNING

While academics are taught, where are the students? They may be physically present in classroom seats, but not on task! This chart allows for student monitoring and home–school communication. At first, the teacher rates the students' behaviors, monitoring their time on task. Older students can independently reflect upon their own concentration within given time frames, and chart themselves with coordinated adult supervision. Younger students can have a chart sent home for family members to review, since many families do not receive an accurate answer when they ask their child, "How was your day, honey?" The child's response might be a monosyllabic word such as "Fine." Not too revealing for a concerned parent who is eager to collaborate with the teacher.

In addition, children with AD/HD; learning, physical, or behavioral issues; and other disabilities may be taking different types of medication that could be interfering with their sleep patterns and attention. Parents and educators need to be doing systematic monitoring. Some students benefit from this type of behavioral scrutiny to determine if it's the cognitive level, pace of instruction, type of presentation, or in this case the inattention to the time on task that's the reason for learning discrepancies. Sometimes with maturation and hormonal changes, monitoring of this type could signal the need for changes in medication. Communication of behaviors now follows a structured routine, with a *total* approach, having *time on task accelerate the learning* of concepts.

Charting Behaviors

????? means that the behavior is questionable, and needs to be both improved and discussed. It allows the teacher to ask the student questions. For example, *Why did you _____?* or *When you _____, what were you thinking?* Students can also fill out a sheet titled *What's Going On?* if it's appropriate, allowing them to give free responses. Younger children may need shorter time increments tracked.

Figure 13.2

How I Was Today

TIME or DAY	WOW! ☺ 5 pts.	Good 4 pts.	Better 3 pts.	OK 2 pts.	????? 1 pt.

```
    ------        +-----        +-------       +------        +--------        = ____
Column totals:                                                                  Total
Name: _____
```

TIME or DAY	☆ ☺ ☆ ☆ ☆ WOW!	☆☺☆ ☆ GOOD CHOICE	Needs ? Reminders	Poor Choices ⬇

Figure 13.3 Behavioral Survey of Self and Others

How would you feel, and what would you do if . . . ↓	Your response	Teacher's response	Family member's response	Friend's response	Other person's response
someone was ignoring you while you were speaking to them?					
you didn't understand directions after they were repeated twice?					
you just won first prize in a writing contest?					
you and your best friend stopped talking to each other?					
your dog gave you a hug with his paws?					
you tried your best, but still failed a test?					
someone yelled at you and you didn't understand why?					
you found a $100 bill?					
you were granted 3 wishes?					

Emotions People Feel: Tally your emotions and the emotions of others on these charts.

Figure 13.4

(Continued)

Directions: Write the hour or day and keep track of different emotions by placing matching numbers in the boxes.

Figure 13.4 (Continued)

Hour/Date	Myself	Someone in my family	Teacher	Friend

1.
2.
3.
4.
5.
6.
7.
8.
9.
10.
11.
12.
13.
14.
15.

Resources to Consult to Develop, Foster, and Improve, Social and Independent Living Skills:

Council for Children with Behavioral Disorders (division of Council for Exceptional Children): www.ccbd.net. Promotes, advocates, and disseminates effective programs, resources, and more understanding for persons with emotional and behavioral disorders.

Illinois Learning Standards Social/Emotional Learning (SEL): www.isbe.state.il.us/ils/social_emotional/standards.htm

Dr. Mac's Amazing Behavior Management Site: www.behavioradvisor.com

Beane, A. (1999). *The bully free classroom: Over 100 tips and strategies for teachers K–8.* Minneapolis, MN: Free Spirit Publishing.

Johnson-Martin, N. M., Attermeier, S. M., & Hacker, B. J. (2004). *The Carolina Curriculum for infants and toddlers with special needs (CCITSN)* (3rd ed.). Baltimore: Brookes Publishing. Designed to assess, track, monitor, and implement social and academic interventions for young children with special needs from birth to age 5.

(Continued)

Creative Therapy Associates—Mood Dudes: www.ctherapy.com

School-Connect: Optimizing the High School Experience: www.school-connect.net

Program designed to improve social-emotional skills, raise academic achievement, and promote positive supportive relationships among students and teachers.

Hands on Tasks and Ideas: www.hot-ideas.org. Basic vocational skills activities and independent work habits.

Phillip Roy, Inc.: www.philliproy.com. Social behavior, transitional skills, character education, applied academics, independent living skills.

Charney, R. (2002). *Teaching children to care: Classroom management for ethical and academic growth, K–8*. Turners Falls, MA: Northeast Foundation for Children. www.responsiveclassroom.org

Karten, T. (2005). *Inclusion strategies that work! Research-based methods for the classroom.* Thousand Oaks, CA: Corwin Press.

Kriete, R., & Bechtel, L. (2002). *The morning meeting book.* Turners Falls, MA: Northeast Foundation for Children. www.responsiveclassroom.org

Tate, M. (2006). *Shouting won't grow dendrites: 20 techniques for managing a brain-compatible classroom.* Thousand Oaks, CA: Corwin Press.

TEACCH: Treatment and Education of Autistic and Related Communication Handicapped Children: http://www.teacch.com. Focuses on people with autism and has programs tailored to individual skills, interests, and needs.

PART III

Application of Strengths and Standards to Inclusive Environments

Standards-Based Interdisciplinary/ Cross-Curricular Lessons

Connections connect, while isolations isolate! Without seeing the big picture, many students are just regurgitating unrelated facts or tidbits of learning that are memorized for upcoming tests, and never stored in long-term learning. Interdisciplinary lessons accomplish just the opposite. They are

- Relevant to students' lives
- Useful
- Cross-curricular
- Motivating
- Challenging
- Stimulating
- Connective
- Retention oriented
- Fun to teach!
- Fun to learn!

The following lessons acknowledge and then apply the fact that subjects do not exist in isolation, but can very well be connected to other disciplines and students' lives. Academic and social skills are emphasized in these lessons. Not every subject is included, but all of these lessons acknowledge the value of linking ideas across and between the subjects through active learning and organized planning. There is a social component built into many of these lessons, with the encouragement of cooperative learning, team building, and home involvement. In addition, these lessons try to meaningfully engage the learners by tapping into their interests and allowing them learning choices, while at the same time addressing the standards. The goal is for students to achieve a sense of accomplishment upon the completion of these interdisciplinary lessons and projects.

Research as follows supports the interdisciplinary approach as a way to meaningfully boost students' skills.

> *Interdisciplinary units, which are project-based and team-based, motivate and challenge students while preparing them for the complexities that they will encounter in their education and in the real world of work.*
>
> —Jenkins, 2005

> *Transfer in learning from one cognitive domain to another isn't a one way process. . . . [R]ather [it's] a reciprocal one in which all curricular areas in a good school provide support for the mastery of other areas.*
>
> —Sylwester, 2005

> *Engineers tell us that in the schools algebra is taught in one watertight component, geometry in another, and physics in another, and that the student learns to appreciate (if ever) only very late the absolutely close connection between these different subjects, and then, if he credits the fraternity of teachers with knowing the closeness of this relation, he blames them most heartily for their unaccountably stupid way of teaching him. . . . [B]oth teachers and students not only see the important connections between the disciplines, but also understand how one discipline can support learning of the other.*
>
> —E.H. Moore's presidential speech in 1902
> to the American Mathematical Society,
> in Frykholm & Glasson, 2005.

The primary, intermediate, and secondary lessons that follow honor the standards as outlined by these national sources and many individual states across our nation:

Cross-Curricular Resources That Work:

Content Standards for Mathematics: www.standards.nctm.org

Developed by the National Council of Teachers of Mathematics (NCTM)

Science Content Standards: www.nsta.org/standards

Developed by the National Research Council

Content Standards for Social Studies: www.ncss.org

Developed by the National Council for the Social Studies (NCSS)

Content Standards for the English Language Arts: www.ncte.org

Developed by the National Council of Teachers of English (NCTE) and the International Reading Association (IRA)

Music Educators National Conference (MENC). The National Association for Music Education: www.menc.org

National Standards for Physical Education—American Alliance for Health, Physical Education, Recreation and Dance: www.aahperd.org/NASPE/publications-national standards.html

The Kennedy Center ArtsEdge: http://artsedge.kennedy-center.org/teach/standards .cfm

PRIMARY LESSONS TO SCALE UP OR DOWN

A Palette of Colors: Grades K–2 and 3–5

The objective of this interdisciplinary lesson is for students to learn about colors in the world to fill a palette of connective knowledge across subject areas.

Art

The obvious curriculum connection here is for students to begin with art. They start with the primary colors (red, yellow, and blue) and then mix paints to create secondary colors (orange, green, violet). Next, introduce the tertiary colors such as orange + red = orange-red, a primary color and the one next to it on the color wheel. As a culminating cooperative activity, in groups or individually, the class creates a collage of the colors. For example, they can imitate the styles of artists such as Jackson Pollack, Kandinsky, Jacob Lawrence, or Monet, changing the colors of a chosen picture from one of the masters, but keeping the other elements such as style and perspective identical. Later on, students can have a gallery walk and side-by-side comparison to see how selecting different colors creates different moods for paintings. Younger and more concrete learners can color in or paint over copies of digital grayscale photographs, templates of classroom scenes or masters' works, or, if more appropriate, simple outlines of familiar objects.

Math and Science

Students create their own color wheel by carefully measuring and dividing a large circle into equidistant spaces with radii or diameters. Other math connections ask the students to metrically discover how adding differing quantities of black and white paint pigment changes the tints and shades of hues. *Science: "Where do you see colors in nature?"* will be the leading question designed to increase students' observational skills to explore their environments. Students will record how daylight changes colors; e.g., late-morning light vs. the same scene after sunset. They will also note the position of the sun and how atmospheric conditions influence the amount of light that we see (e.g., clouds, moisture). Rainbows acting like prisms will also be studied. Students can also identify how animals use camouflage to blend in with the colors in their environments to avoid predators. Younger learners will identify and sort differently colored classroom objects according to similar traits and attributes such as size and shape.

Music and Reading

Class will listen to the song "Color My World", by the musical group, Chicago. Those who receive instrumental instruction will be asked to play along; e.g., a piano accompaniment. Then the class will be given the song's lyrics to read, and asked if they can interpret and relate them to the concept of *love*. In addition, some students will attempt to decipher the song's symbolism. Other students will explore expressions, such as, *He was as red as a beet*, or *She was talking until she was blue in the face!* As a primary activity, students can write or trace block letters of the alphabet with one color and then cut out letters and place them on differently colored backgrounds to notice which one is seen better (visibility); e.g., a black letter *A* on a yellow piece of paper or a black letter *A* on a blue piece of paper. Read *The Color Tree*, by Denise Bennett Minnerly, about a young boy changing a colorless landscape.

Social Studies

The baseline knowledge is that, regardless of what color skin people have on the outside, we all have the same inner biological makeup, and that no one country or race has a monopoly on culture. Older students will identify different reasons for structural differences. For example, many people in Africa have darker pigmentation because they are closer to the equator. In addition, older students will learn about racism based on skin colors. For example, in the former class systems in Mexico and the United States, and mulattoes, or lighter-colored slaves, were allowed to work inside homes on southern plantations before the Civil War, while darker-colored slaves were forced to work in the fields. Younger students will explore peoples' colors with multicultural crayons.

Model an example on the next chart before students complete it on their own. The purpose here is to neatly organize the information, but allow for individual creativity with illustrative responses.

Directions: Describe these colorful words!

Figure 14.1

Vocabulary Word	Sentence with this color	Illustration of the word/ Where it's seen
red		
yellow		
blue		
orange		
violet		
green		
hue		
tint		
shade		
complementary colors		
value		
intensity		

Inviting Lessons: Invitations to Famous People

Objective

Cooperatively create party invitations for a famous person. Then design the party. A sample listing of people to invite is included. You can use computer graphics or your own art work for the final product. If you want your invitation to be from someone else famous who is not on the list, you will need your teacher's approval. Younger students and more concrete learners can scribe (tell) ideas to an adult.

Invitation/Party From . . .

Primary (2–5): Little Red Riding Hood, Dr. Seuss, Curious George, Family member, president of the United States, Sir Isaac Newton, Christopher Columbus, Pocahontas, George Washington Carver, Derek Jeter, Judy Blume, Shel Silverstein, Martin Luther King, Jr., Ben Franklin, Sponge Bob

Middle School (6–8): Albert Einstein, Linnaeus, Julius Caesar, Rosa Parks, Pythagoras, Beethoven, Eminem, Leonardo da Vinci, Mark Twain, Eleanor Roosevelt

Secondary (9–12): Maya Angelou, Shakespeare, Aristotle, Thomas Jefferson, Jackie Robinson, John Lennon, Edgar Alan Poe, Woodrow Wilson, Sigmund Freud, Maya Lin, Helen Keller, Pablo Picasso

Figure 14.2

Answer these questions about your party:
Party given for _____ by _____   (your name)
What's the reason for the party?
Where is the party taking place?
When is the event?
Who will be attending? What's the floor plan and seating arrangement?
What will be served? Create a menu, listing ingredients and cooking directions.
Describe the entertainment (songs, music, dances, games).
Will dress be casual or formal? What are you wearing? Where did you purchase your clothing? What was the cost?
Design decorations for the party.
Describe the gifts the guests brought.
Was fun had by all?

Figure 14.3

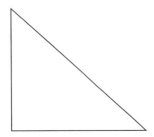

Invitations need to include facts that relate to the people. For example, maybe the shape of Pythagoras's invitation could be a right triangle, or Rosa Park's invitation could be a bus! Be creative!

ABCs of Sounds Around: Grades K–4

1. To make sounds, something must
   a. vibrate   b. talk to you   c. have lips

2. If something vibrates slowly, it makes a(an) _____ sound or pitch.
   a. boring   b. low   c. invisible

3. If something vibrates quickly, it makes a _____ sound or pitch.
   a. speedy   b. rushed   c. high

Obvious *resounding* answers:

1. a. vibrate
2. b. low
3. c. high

Try this following experiment to create a musical scale:

Materials:

- 6 glass jars of equal size
- metal spoon
- water

Procedure:

1. Fill each bottle with escalating (increasing) amounts of water.

2. Tap each bottle with a metal spoon

3. Listen to the sounds:
   a. What happens to the notes when you add more water to a bottle and there is less air?
   b. What happens when you take out water and there is more air?
   c. What is your *scientific musical* conclusion?

More Resounding Questions and Activities

- Make a two-columned list of opposite sounds; e.g., high and low.
- Take a walk around the school with a peer and record the sounds heard.
- Imagine a world without sound. What do you think it would be like? Give examples of how your life would be affected
- Research the following people, telling how they were affected by the sounds that they themselves or family members did not hear: Beethoven, Helen Keller, Alexander Graham Bell, Deanne Bray, Lou Ferrigno

Investigate how hearing works: Use this site for some answers: http://library.thinkquest.org/6419/hearing.htm.

Metamorphosis: Animate and Inanimate Changes: Grades 3–6

Directions: Review these life cycles of insects, frogs, and plants. Now choose an inanimate object (one that is not alive but man-made); e.g., a pencil, crayon, math book, lightbulb, trumpet, cell phone, video game, and more. Compare that item to one of the three life cycles below, to get ideas. Use some of the terms in these boxes to creatively describe the life cycle of your nonliving object. What metamorphosis or changes did it go through? Then compare the two items, animate (living) and inanimate (nonliving), to yourself. Tell what changes or metamorphosis you have gone through in your lifetime. Connect the inanimate to the animate, either an insect, frog, or plant, and of course *you*, too! Draw pictures; use clip art; write a play, commercial, poem, or news article; sing a song, play an instrument, and more!

Figure 14.4   Insect Life Cycles

Complete met-a-mor-pho-sis	Incomplete met-a-mor-pho-sis	Am-e-tab-o-lous stages
Egg	Egg	Egg
Larva	Immature	Larva
Pupa (cocoon)	Immature	Larva
Adult	Immature	Adult
Immature insect is different from the adult	Immature stage (nymph) looks like adult	Immature stage looks like adult, and may have no sex organs
Larva sheds its exoskeleton	Insect molts its exoskeleton in immature stages	No metamorphosis

SOURCE: www.ent.iastate.edu/zoo/lessonplans/lifecycles.html Iowa State University Entomology Department.

Figure 14.5

Life Cycle of a Frog
1. Egg—Female frog lays masses of eggs, which hatch into tadpoles.
2. Tadpole with gills (also called the polliwog)—Tadpoles hatch from eggs while they swim and grow in the water. Tadpole has a tail and breathes through gills.
3. Tadpole—The tadpole still has a tail, but now has legs, arms, and develops its head and body more, still breathing through gills at first, but then lungs start to develop. After it gets hind legs, it gets front legs, then becomes a young frog
4. Young Frog—The frog is becoming mature, loses its tail as it is absorbed by its body, has four legs and now uses lungs to breathe
5. Adult Frog—Frog continues to breathe with lungs, has no tail, and grows larger

SOURCES: www.enchantedlearning.com/subjects/amphibians/label/froglifecycle/label.shtml (Check out frog diagram and other animals on which you can label parts and cycles.); Great Source. (2005). *Sciencesaurus: A student handbook.* Wilmington, MA: Author.

Figure 14.6

Plant That Reproduces With Seeds
1. Seed has a root that grows in the soil to take in water
2. Root grows longer and stem develops from top of the seed, which will be used to carry water from the roots to leaves that come later
3. Leaves develop so plant can make its own food

SOURCE: www.fi.edu/tfi/units/life/

Moving Lessons: Grades K–4

Directions: Fill in the missing blanks under the correct columns. Follow the *nose!*

Language Arts

After students fill out this chart as their writing planner, they create a play with a cast of body parts personified as the main characters in whatever settings they choose, interacting with *everybody!*

Reading/Decoding

Students associate body parts with initial or final consonant sounds of words. For example, every time you say words such as, *house, hat, hello,* the students point to their *head* if they were learning the initial sound of *h.* If instruction was final sounds, students would point to their *noses* after hearing the words ca*n* and betwee*n.*

Science/Technology

Students learn about anatomy, human strength (e.g. muscles, exercise, stamina), medical advances, and proper care of body parts by cooperatively conducting online research to create a bodily Web search. Students will also compare the human body to different machines.

Math

Students measure hand spans, distances from knees to toes, circumference of head. Measure their height in quarters, nickels, and dimes. Compare body ratios to increase knowledge of number sense, fractions, proportions, scales, and measurements; e.g., use a string to measure their height, then wrap that string around the circumference of their head; the ratio should be 3:1.

Figure 14.7

Body Parts	Action— What it does	Quality/Degree— How it does it	Sentence Relationship— Combine it all!
Nose	sneeze, breathe	loudly inhale, exhale, lungs	I sneeze loudly when I have a cold. My lungs expand when my nose breathes in air.
Head			
Fingers			
Toes			
Ankle			
Shoulders			
Wrist			
Thigh			
Chin			
Knees			
Teeth			
Mouth			
Elbow			
Belly			
	twist		
	pull		
	stretch		
	catch		
	kick		
		always	
		happily	
		tired	
		whenever	
		quickly	
		slowly	

Art/Music/Dance

Trace hands and create abstract pictures. Sing *body songs*, do the *hokey-pokey* or *Simon Says* while playing different background music and beats.

Lessons for Every Body: Grades 4–6

Look at the answers to these questions, and then choose two of these questions you'd like to expand with details. Use your textbook or other additional sources in other books, or online sites. Gather more facts and present answers to the class in short essays, plays, poems, newspaper articles, dances, songs, pantomimes, sculptures, computer slide presentations, videos, or collages.

Figure 14.8

1. Why do we sweat?	It's a way to control our body temperature.
2. What are possible body reactions when a person is angry?	Pupils dilate, salivation stops, heartbeat increases
3. What are some of the effects of alcohol?	It's a drug that can negatively affect some organs, such as your liver. It blocks your true sensations and can make you tired and dependent upon it. With overuse, alcohol can destroy your neurons (brain cells) and be lethal (deadly).
4. Where does the human body get energy?	Your body gets energy from the foods it eats in a varied diet (different kinds of foods) with ones containing protein, carbohydrates, vitamins, fats, and fibers.
5. Can you sneeze with your eyes open?	No, it's impossible!
6. What happens when you exercise or experience stress?	Your nervous system stimulates your heart to beat faster.
7. What does our brain look like on the inside?	It's made up of 2 hemispheres, the right and left, each helping us in different ways.
8. What is a cough?	A cough helps clear dust and other irritants out of your windpipe and lungs.
9. What organ has no known function in your body?	The appendix appears to be useless. Some scientists think that one day it will disappear from the human race!
10. Why do you have a certain eye color?	Eye color is passed down through heredity, your parents' genes.
Interactive online source: www.bbc.co.uk/science/humanbody/body/interactives/3djigsaw_02/index.shtml?organs	

Nature Walk—Tree Unit: Grades K–4

Rationale

Students with learning disabilities may exhibit difficulties with reading comprehension, word decoding, mathematical reasoning, and computation. Many function best when learning is presented on a concrete level, with much practice and application.

Objective

Using their senses of hearing, seeing, smelling, and touching, students will take an outside nature walk to formulate questions about their environment. If students have visual or auditory deficits, then add more kinesthetic elements or ask a peer coach to describe the environment or help with communications.

Procedure:

1. With teacher supervision, students walk around the outside perimeter of the school:
   a. They smell, listen to, observe, and touch *appropriate* items (incorporation of sensory elements, bodily-kinesthetic/tactile, concrete presentation).
   b. Give each student an *official* clipboard to record their findings (to increase self-esteem and make it a valuing task).
   c. Ask each student to formulate one question about what he or she saw. For example, "Where do trees come from?"; "Why do leaves fall in the spring?" (establishing level and accuracy of prior knowledge, tapping individual interests). Later on in the lesson, you can clarify that leaves *fall in the fall,* not the spring!
   d. Since both questions were about trees, this can lead to *student-generated decisions* to begin a unit on trees (student empowerment and increased motivation).

2. Next, students conduct research by gathering information from computer Web sites (e.g., http://www.arborday.org) and library reference tools, properly citing sources consulted (reinforcing value of research, study skills, and technology).

3. After information is collected, students each make a tree folder. One folder is green, while the other is red. These complementary colors can lead to a discussion of the colors of leaves. The red folder represents autumn colors, while the green represents the color of leaves in the springtime (development of abstract thought, organizational skills).

4. Cooperatively peruse the information gathered, telling about parts of trees, how leaves change colors in the fall, why they fall off trees, how a tree develops from a seed to become lumber, photosynthesis, food chain, carbon-dioxide-oxygen cycle, and how leaves return to the soil, highlighting important vocabulary words, taking notes and paraphrasing key concepts (visual elements, research skills, reading comprehension, note taking).

5. Conduct a guided and supervised science experiment by gathering leaves, shredding them, covering them with alcohol in hot water, and inserting a coffee filter to separate the colors (concrete learning of chromatography, sequencing skills).

6. As a homework assignment, ask students to compile a list of 20 items in or around their homes that are made from wood, asking someone at home for help (parent involvement, observation skills). Hands-on learning further reinforces the fact that the trees have an age.

7. Students can touch a slice of a tree's bark, and count the rings to determine the tree's age. They can also count backwards from the year the ring was cut to its birth from a seed (kinesthetic/tactile, math integration, cause/effect).

8. Students learn more about different tree types by taking another nature walk to match given pictures of trees with ones outside the school or in their neighborhood (observational skills, kinesthetic activity).

9. Manipulate letters of tree words to discover a message and find hidden items in a nature picture (figure-ground, visual discrimination). Create a computer word search or crossword puzzle using graph paper or the site www.puzzlemaker.com (technology, vocabulary development).

10. As an evaluation, students answer questions, look at tree pictures, and list five things they've learned. In addition, they answer original investigative questions. For example, trees originate from seeds and fall in the fall because they do not have the same amount of chlorophyll for photosynthesis. The breezy winds help them drop their leaves (repetition and reinforcement of concepts).

Follow-Ups

- Teacher reads *The Fall of Freddie the Leaf,* by Leo Buscaglia, which is an allegory telling about a leaf's life as compared to a human life and death. Students then construct science poems based upon their reactions to the book and newly gained tree knowledge.
- Ask students to predict what would happen to the environment if all of the trees in their neighborhood were cut down to build more houses.
- After assessments, students will be asked to write down questions about their environment that they still wonder about.

More About Trees

Figure 14.9

> **Directions:**
> Label tree parts.
> Color in the leaves for each season.
> Draw some different types of trees.
> Identify where photosynthesis takes place.

SPRING   FALL

Draw pictures of trees you saw.

A Biomotic Challenge: Grades 5–8

Create and name your own biome, inventing plants, animals, seasons, songs, dances, a math system, alphabet, political system, and more!

Figure 14.10 Biomes

Step 1: Cooperatively choose one of these 5 biomes that you and your group will investigate.	Aquatic	Deserts	Grasslands	Forests	Tundras
Step 2: Expand the baseline facts under your biome's column by answering categories a–h in this column below:	Two aquatic types:	Four major desert types:	Two major grassland types:	Three major forest types (latitude):	Two tundra types:
a. Type of animals found in your biome	1. Freshwater regions— low salt concentration; e.g., ponds, lakes, streams, rivers, wetlands	1. Hot and dry; e.g., Sonoran, Mojave, Great Basin, Chihuahuan, Southern Asian realm, Ethiopian (Africa), Australian	1. Tropical grasslands— Savanna, central Africa, Australia, South America, India	1. Tropical; e.g., near the equator	1. Arctic tundra, northern Hemisphere, by north pole to coniferous forests of the taiga
b. average temperature range **c. seasons**	2. Marine regions; e.g., estuaries, oceans, coral reefs	2. Semiarid, sagebrush in Utah, Montana, Great Basin, Nearctic realm	2. Temperate grasslands; e.g., South Africa, Hungary,	2. Temperate; e.g., eastern North America, northeastern Asia, western	2. Alpine tundra— high altitudes, where trees cannot grow
d. rainfall/snow		(North America, Russia, Newfoundland, Greenland, Europe, northern Asia)	Argentina, Uruguay	and central Europe	
e. plants found there **f. canopy present**		3. Coastal; e.g., Nearctic and Neotropical realm, Antacama of Chile		3. Boreal forests (taiga), between 50 and 60 degrees north latitudes, Siberia, Scandinavia, Alaska, Canada	
g. Create a *biomotic* mural **h. Does your biome have any problems or concerns?**		4. Cold; e.g., Antarctic, Greenland, Nearctic realm			

SOURCE: www.ucmp.berkeley.edu/glossary/gloss5/biome/

Create-a-State: Grades 3–6

Primary Interdisciplinary and *Stately* Lesson

The below activities are first completed and modeled by the teacher and class working together, using a real state. For example, using the state of Texas, Massachusetts, Illinois, California, New Jersey, or Vermont, and so forth, students will learn about the physical features, climate, population, government, symbols, customs, and more. Then divide students into cooperative groups of 4 or 5 and tell them that they are explorers who have now discovered a new state, which they will name. The name of their state must include syllable parts of all of their own names. For example, Mary, John, Sue, and Tom might call their land Tojosuma or Majosuto. The reason for this? They've now taken ownership of their own state, buying into the lesson, and they learn about phonemes as well! Assign specific jobs such as researcher, recorder, artist, mapman, geogirl, state singer, focuser, planner, sports reporter, food critic, and more! All students must be active participants. As a challenge, more advanced students or groups can compare and contrast their created state with another real one.

Stately Objectives

Social studies: Understand the need for rules, laws, and government. Develop map skills. Understand about basic economic systems. Draw a connection between state and federal government. Realize that places had a history before other explorers entered the scene. Develop cultural awareness.

Math: Use a ruler. Draw a scale of miles. Understand charts, graphs, measurements, and ratios.

Reading: Explore syllables and sounds. Research skills developed and reinforced.

Science: Understand weather patterns and effects of climate. Study of animals and foods.

Writing: Plan and organize thoughts into cohesive sentences, paragraphs, and reports.

Art: Draw symbols, maps; understand perspective, negative space, and more.

Music: Awareness of different sounds, songs, instruments, rhythm, and dance.

Consumer awareness: Dynamics of buying and selling goods. Explore relationship between supply and demand. Learn about currency.

Technology: Use word processing skills, with tables and graphs, and computer graphics.

Physical education: Movement in groups, choreographing dances, sports awareness.

Stated Student Instructions:

1. Describe the geography. Include information about the average *cli-mate* in different parts of your state, seasonal weather, and *phys-i-cal fea-tures.* Name the cities, rivers, lakes, oceans, and mountains nearby. Draw a map of your state, with the capital. Include a scale of miles and compass rose. Name states that are near you. What is the range of your state's latitude and longitude. Create a *legend* that describes the physical features.

2. Give information about the *pop-u-la-tion* (people who live there). Who are the citizens and the leaders? What are the rules? Were there people living here when you entered? If so, do you get along? How do you treat each other? What kinds of jobs do the people in your state have? Tell more about the *gov-ern-ment* (people in charge) and what they do if someone does not follow the rules. What animals inhabit your state?

3. What do you eat? Draw pictures of the foods. Name the stores. Design some clothing for people in your state to wear. Do you buy or trade goods with other states or countries? Tell about your state's *e-con-o-my* and *cur-ren-cy.* Draw a diagram of the state capitol building, sports arenas, theaters, and shopping malls.

4. Name the holidays the people celebrate. What are your *cus-toms* during the year? Some *sym-bols* for the United States are the bald eagle and the American flag. Draw or create a symbol for your state.

5. What are your state's leisure or *rec-re-a-tion-al ac-tiv-i-ties* (interests, pastimes)? Tell what the people in your state do for fun and enjoyment. What kinds of musical instruments, dances, bands, and songs are popular in your state? Create a dance, song, cheer, or rap. Does your state have television or radio stations? What are some of the programs you watch or listen to? What are your state's favorite sports? Name the sports teams that play for your state. Write a state song.

Report Planner

Complete 1–15 below, and any other 5 topics, checking off each. *Co-op-er-a-tive-ly* (working together) and *si-mul-ta-ne-ous-ly* (everyone working at the same time—one person doesn't do it all!) divide work. As a challenge to earn more points, compare and contrast your state to one of the already existing 50.

Figure 14.11

Create-a-State Requirements (1–15) and any 5 more below that	*Check off when completed*
1. Name of state	
2. Capital of the state	
3. Cities in your state	
4. Map outline	
5. Scale of miles	
6. Compass rose	
7. Latitude/longitude	
8. Legend	
9. Bodies of water	
10. Mountains	
11. Climate/weather	
12. Neighboring states	
13. People living there	
14. Leaders	
15. Rules	
16. State capitol building	
17. Animals	
18. Food	
19. Clothing	
20. Stores	
21. Economy/currency	
22. Holidays	
23. Customs	
24. Symbols	
25. Recreational/fun activities	
26. State song	

Oh, the Places to Know! Monumental Momentum—Famous Architecture: Grades 4–6

With your peers, cooperatively list facts about these buildings. The one on the White House is shown as an example. The last step is to be architects and recreate your group's favorite building, using a variety of building materials. You can also creatively combine elements from different ones listed below. Then write *or build* 3 descriptive paragraphs, an epic poem, myth, legend, song, dance, or short skit!

Figure 14.12

Buildings	Year built	Culture/ Country	Reason built*/Uses	Materials used	Nearest city	Interesting facts/features
White House	Started work in 1792	United States	Political: president's home	Wood, steel, and more	Washington, DC	Architects copied Greek-European buildings
Sydney Opera House						
The Eiffel Tower						
St. Paul's Cathedral						
The Empire State Building						
Himeji						
Castle						
Tenochtitlan						
The Coliseum						
Stonehenge						
The Parthenon						

NOTE: *Reasons can include political, social, environmental, protection from weather or enemies, living accommodations, shelter, religious worship, relaxation, or business.

Challenge: Research these sites: Great Wall of China, Luxor Temple in Egypt, Coral Triangle in Indonesia, and Maldives, and tell how nature and/or man have influenced them in a negative way.

Writing From Picture Prompts: Grades 3–5

Okay, here's the assignment: Choose one picture and create a story that has details about the characters, setting, plot, and ending. Include at least 10 mathematical, scientific, historical, artistic, or musical words in your story, using your textbooks or other references for appropriate vocabulary! Remember that even though you are only choosing 10 words, they say that pictures are *worth a thousand words*!

Figure 14.13

Fables, Myths, and Legends Go to School: Grades 4–6

Directions: Read a version of one of these fables, myths, or legends with a small group of classmates. Then together, retell the story to the class, making believe that your characters have left the story and are now students in your class. Remember, the past is meeting the present and you are writing the script! Final project will be graded on the following:

1. Visuals such as illustrations, posters, drawings, clip art, props, and scenery

2. Computer-written, double-spaced text with a 3–5 page script handed in to teacher

3. How you tie together details from the fable and the school setting. Include a specific lesson with a story plot, setting, other characters, climax, moral, and ending. Choose what subject the characters are now learning about, or it could be a few scenarios during the course of the day; e.g., how would they act during lunch, on the bus, in an assembly, or during a geometry lesson? Be certain that the moral/theme of the *school fable* matches the original legend, story, or fable. It's like your characters have entered a time tunnel!

4. Dressing in costumes that characters from that time period would have worn

Some sample fables, myths, or legends to choose from:

The Maiden of the Northland

The Princess Libushe

The Story of MacDatho's Pig

Cuchulain's Fight Against the Sea

The Knight With the Lion

The Tale of Robin Hood

Mahabharata

Twin Rivers Rising

Fox and Grapes

Anansi Tries to Steal All the Wisdom in the World

Seven Old Samurai

The Legend of Osiris and Isis

The Ugly Duckling

The Children and the Hummingbird

Flying Rats

The Slave and the Lion

Aladdin and the Wonderful Lamp

The Tortoise and the Hare

Legend of the Phoenix

Prometheus

The Golden Fleece

Nolboo and Hungboo

The Blind Man's Daughter

Pig and Dog

The Golden Snail

The Odyssey

When the Animals and Birds Were Created

A Circle of GGS—Genre Games and Subjects: Grades 4–8

Choose one of these games, a genre, and a subject to design your own board game. You'll need the following:

- Rules for play with step-by-step directions
- Playing pieces or characters
- Board layout
- Box for your game

- Setting with drawings or clip art
- Information (facts and notes) about your subject
- Other materials; e.g., money, sound effects

Figure 14.14

Subjects	Games to Imitate	Genres
Math	Candyland	Fairytale
Science	Scrabble	Science Fiction
Social Studies	Monopoly	Biography
Reading	Trouble	Autobiography
World Language; e.g., Spanish, French, Italian	Life	Historical Fiction
Art	Checkers	Mystery
Physical Education/Gym	Chess	Nonfiction
Music	Chutes and Ladders	Fiction
Computers	Wheel of Fortune	Poem
Health	Jeopardy	Newspaper
Other	Other	Other

Figure 14.15

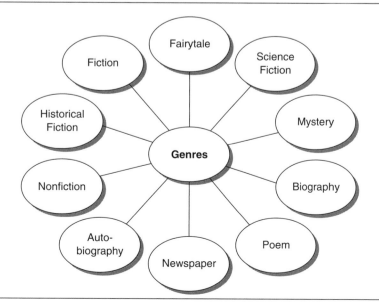

What If . . . ? Grades 6–8

Tuck Everlasting, by Natalie Babbitt, is an incredible story that asks us to think about the impossible: *What if people were immortal?* It's a story about a family that stops the cycle of life. The Tucks do not grow old or change. Symbolism in the story, such as the mention of the highest seat on a Ferris wheel that has stopped turning, repeats this theme. It's a fantasy that challenges us to rethink reality.

Directions: Now, here are some thought-provoking, *hy-po-thet-i-cal* (not true, but *what-if* situations) that ask you to think about possibilities beyond reality. Fill in the spaces for at least 5 of the ones given below.

Figure 14.16

What If . . .	My response:
1. There were other life forms like us in the universe?	
2. The world spoke the same language?	
3. Diamonds grew on trees, like leaves?	
4. Dogs could speak?	
5. There were no numbers?	
6. Mirrors reflected other people's images?	
7. Our bodies regenerated more than hair and nails?	
8. Time was measured in songs, instead of minutes?	
9. We had the cure for cancer?	
10. Babies were born knowing how to read?	
11. Cows could fly?	
12. There were no seasons?	

Training for Life Across the Curriculum: Grades 3–Beyond

Review the following list of occupations, jobs, and careers, and check off which subjects would be helpful for a person in that career. Then choose one job, career, or occupation that interests you the most, and on a separate piece of paper give specific examples of how each of your checked-off subjects would help you succeed in that job. You may also choose a career, job, or occupation that's not listed, but one that you might like more than the ones given here. Include graphics, clip art, or drawings to further illustrate your written points. You can use computer Web sites, interview someone in that job, or find out more information in books and magazines.

Nutritionally Sound Diets: Grades 2–5

Directions: With your group, cooperatively choose 5 of the foods to research. Each student in the group needs to hand in his or her own written report on the foods. Check off the boxes in your food's row, after you have completed each column. When you share your report with the class, you can also share samples (tastings) of the food, but check food allergies first!

Recipes for learning: Together, teachers and students cook up scrumptious lessons!

Math

Students bring in their favorite family or holiday recipe and then double or triple the recipe, learning about whole numbers, fractions, measuring, and cost analysis. Students can also figure out their body mass index with a calculator, using their own height and weight at http://www.cdc.gov/nccdphp/dnpa/bmi/index.htm.

Science/Health

Analyze food ingredients, fat or fiber content, amount of sugar, along with nutritional and vitamin content of recipes and food labels. Discussion about not only what you eat, but how much, learning about portion control, and maintaining a balanced diet.

Career Connections

Explore food-related jobs such as chefs, food servers, hosts, restaurant owners, food suppliers, farmers, cookbook writers, television personalities/cooks, food critics, butchers, bakers, supermarket cashiers, and more.

Art

Create a classroom food collage or mural with pictures of ingredients, which students then look at to guess what recipe is represented by each collection of ingredients.

Figure 14.17

Occupations, Jobs, and Careers ⇩	Reading	Science	Math	World Language	Writing	Social Studies	Music and Art
Accountant							
Architect							
Artist							
Baker							
Basketball Player							
Bus Driver							
Butcher							
Carpenter							
Coach							
Computer Specialist							
Dentist/Doctor							
Electrician							
Engineer							
Firefighter							
Hairdresser							
Hospital Worker							
Journalist							
Lawyer							
Mail Carrier							
Plumber							
Police Officer							
Salesperson							
Singer							
Soldier							
Teacher							
Veterinarian							
Another job, career, occupation: _____							

Figure 14.18

Food Choices ⬇	Places in world food is grown/ produced	If it could talk, what the food would say	Write a math problem using this food as the subject	Foods that share its plate	Cartoon/ Food picture	Living things that eat this food	Recipe with this food
Bagel							
Corn							
Milk							
Beans							
Orange							
Tomato							
Pizza							
Eggs							
Applesauce							
Milkshake							
Steak							
Lettuce							
Chocolate							
Potato							
Chips							
Butter							

Reading/Sequencing Skills/Cause/Effect

Students choose a recipe, copy each step on individual index cards, then scramble cards, and exchange an out-of-order sequence with a peer who tries to correctly unscramble the steps. Then *partnered peers* look at their ingredients and think about the effect deleting different ingredients would have on the taste of each other's recipe.

Social Studies/Cultures

Figure out where in the world ingredients are found. Which ingredients are imported from another country? Which ingredients are exported? Do certain cultures use some ingredients more than others? What similarities of ingredients are seen in different cultures? Investigate the origin of breads and grains such as pitas, matzoh, quesadillas, bagels, wheat, rye, and spelt.

Sporting Lessons and Reviews: Grades K–6

Teachers can review or introduce subjects as students score *points* (a.k.a., knowledge) for answers. In each of these games, the class is divided into two teams. Players from the same team consult with each other (*passing the ball, puck, and ideas*) before the designated player gives the answer to questions across the curriculum in science, social studies, music, art, math, reading, and more. Teachers can display a template of the rink, court, or field on an overhead, using differently colored transparent chips to designate whether players have scored points, goals, or runs. Drawing a rectangle or diamond shape on a chalkboard, with *Xs* and *Os* representing different teams and their positions, is also an option. Teachers can allow students to use notes and texts to find answers, making it an *open-ended sports event!* The *sporting rules* can vary as collectively agreed upon by the class. Major *points* here consist of the following:

- Students who love sports, but dislike the subject, are now listening to the content; e.g., they can even name and root for their teams!
- Attention issues decrease as students are focusing on the game *and* knowledge.
- Collaboration/teamwork is encouraged.
- Format varies from pencil-and-paper drill
- Research skills are encouraged.

Shooting Answers: Hockey Rules

1. Both students start at the center ice (circle in the middle) and receive the first question.

2. The player who answers the first question correctly, advances to the opponent's blue line.

3. That player then gets a bonus question, which if answered correctly, allows that team to score a goal.

4. If the answer is incorrect, then the other team gets to steal the puck and answer the question. If the question is answered correctly by the opposing team, they move to the other team's blue line and answer another question for a goal, their point. If they do not answer it correctly, then both players start over and face off at the center ice with a new question.

Bouncing Ideas: **Basketball Rules**

1. Both students start at the mid-court line and are asked the same first question.

2. The player who answers it correctly advances to the opponent's free-throw line.

3. Then that player gets a bonus question, which if answered correctly, allows his or her team to shoot a basket and score a point. If the answer is incorrect, then the other team gets to steal the ball, answer the question, and score a point for their team. If they do not answer the question correctly, then both players start over and begin with a new question.

4. Players can be assigned additional roles such as coaches, referees, and fans!

Figure 14.19

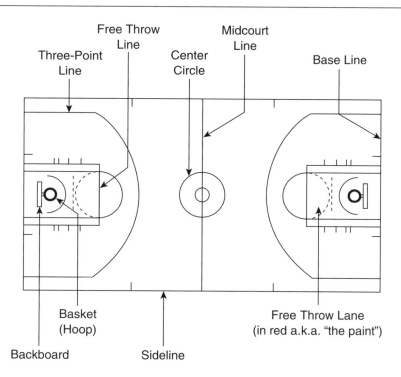

SOURCE: © Joanne B Mikola, http://www.lessontutor.com. Used with Permission.

Scoring Runs: Baseball Rules

1. Game begins with the first pitch—in this case, question! If the player on the starting team answers it correctly, then he or she advances to first base. If not, then the team gets an out.

2. The pitcher then gives more questions to the team, until there are 3 outs. The same rules apply as in baseball; e.g., if the team answers 4 questions in a row correctly, then they would have one run and the bases loaded, with nobody out.

3. Rules can be varied here, such as more difficult questions could be a double and then as complexities increase, they count as triples, and home runs.

4. After the team has 3 outs, the opposing team (other half of the class) is up at bat, with each player (student) on the team taking turns being *at bat.*

5. There are no strikes or fouls, unless of course teachers use these as part of a behavior management plan to maintain attention while other players are pitching or up at bat. Other rules include appointing players as coaches, cleanup crew, scorekeepers, vendors selling food and drinks, and even someone singing the national anthem!

Figure 14.20

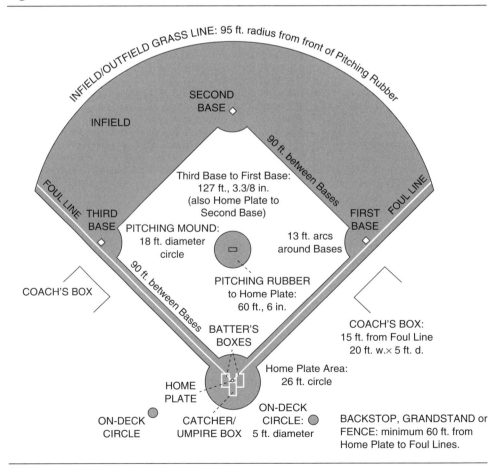

SOURCE: Image Courtesy of Baseball Almanac, www.baseball-almanac.com.

Tackling Review: Football Rules

1. Game begins with a *kick-off question.* The first player to answer the question correctly gets to carry the ball and then advances 10 yards.

2. For each question answered correctly, the team advances an additional 10 yards toward opponent's goal line.

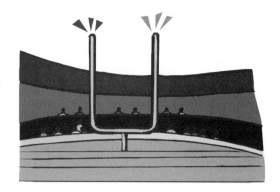

3. If a team gives an incorrect response, then they are tackled, and the other team answers the question.

As a variation, more difficult or multistep questions can be worth increasing numbers of yards.

Poetry Unit—"Albert on the Tee": Grades 3–6

Motivation/Anticipatory Set

Read your favorite poem to your students. If the vocabulary is too hard for them, paraphrase the thoughts the poet is conveying on a level that the students can understand. Then read a poem that you have written that mirrors this poet's style. As an example, a student wrote a poem titled "Albert on the Tee," which mirrored the style of "Casey at the Bat" by Ernest Thayer. Since Albert loves to golf, his choice was a perfect one for him! The best parts are when students share the poems with each other. They present or act out their poems and then share a collection/anthology of the entire class's *published* poems.

Procedure:

1. Obtain a collection of poetry books from the school library. Students in the class then each select one poem that they like and try to imitate the poet's style in their version. Students can add their own interests here, personalizing their poems.

2. Afterward, students type the poem they chose alongside their own version. Collectively, the class *publishes* their poems in a bound book, which can also be donated to the school library. These were some poems selected by a fifth-grade class.

3. Selection of poets/poems to imitate (students are encouraged to find other poems too!):

Figure 14.21

Poems	Poets
Casey at the Bat	Ernest Thayer
Whoops, Learning	Judith Viorst
Flat, Creep and Slither	J. Patrick Lewis
Smart What a Day! Invention My Hobby Moon Catching Net	Shel Silverstein
Daydream	Joyce Armor
The Hawk	Douglas Florian
On Our Way	Eve Merrian
Eyeballs for Sale! Suzanna Socked Me Sunday Monday's Troll I'm as Happy as Anyone Could Ever Be I Was Walking in a Circle A Nasty Little Dragon Song News Brief	Jack Prelutsky
Daisies	Frank Dempster Sherman

MIDDLE AND HIGH SCHOOL LESSONS

Like adults, high school students don't expect their workday to include only experiences they enjoy . . . but they need a sense of purpose . . . . And when we link a school's goals with that need for meaning, a stronger school culture will result.

—Cushman, 2006

The following lessons incorporate students' interests while stressing academic and social skills. The interdisciplinary lessons value research skills, cooperative learning, technology, and self-direction. The students become teachers, talk show hosts, video game creators, and film directors while learning about math, science, social studies, music, and art, as well as learning reading and writing skills. The *shapely lesson* topics range from lighthouses to becoming more culturally savvy students! The formats vary from more traditional lessons, but will hopefully transfer to valuable student lessons!

Media Genius

1. Choose 5 of these movies by Steven Spielberg and fill in the table below:

War of the Worlds

Raiders of the Lost Ark

Schindler's List

Close Encounters of the Third Kind

E.T. the Extra-Terrestrial

Saving Private Ryan

Indiana Jones and the Last Crusade

Indiana Jones and the Temple
of Doom

Jaws

Minority Report

Catch Me If You Can

Empire of the Sun

The Color Purple

A.I. Artificial Intelligence

Hook

Jurassic Park

Munich

Figure 14.22

Name of the movie	Year released	Theme	Description of characters	Setting	My critique or movie review

2. Pretend that Steven Spielberg has just hired you as his assistant director. He has allowed you to choose any time period from history to create a script. You can also cast whatever actresses or actors you'd like to portray your characters. Fill in the next table (Figure 14.23) that tells about your upcoming movie.

Title of Movie: _____

Figure 14.23

Setting (where and when)	Description of the characters	Theme	Plot/Climax/ Resolution	Actors/Actresses that will star in my movie

3. Mr. Spielberg would like you to select a score for the movie. You can choose 5 songs or musical pieces.

4. Design an advertising strategy for the movie. What will upcoming television or radio commercials tell about the movie? Create a prototype for a full-sized billboard or an advertisement for the entertainment sections of local newspapers.

5. Investigate the costs of production for your upcoming film, based upon other Spielberg movies. Which Spielberg movie will you have to surpass if your movie is to be the most profitable?

Video Game Learning

You have just been hired to design a video game. Decide the following:

1. Is your video game a fantasy one or reality-based?
2. How will violence be avoided in your game?
3. Is the game sports-oriented?
4. Who are the main characters?
5. How many people can play at one time?
6. Are there points scored? If so, describe the point system.
7. What is the theme/setting of your video game?
8. Describe the sound effects.
9. What audience are you targeting?
10. What will be the cost of production for your video game?
11. What will the public pay for the video game?
12. Where will your game be sold or played?

Now that you have planned your video game, go for it!

Figure 14.24

My video game will look like this:

Talk Show Formats

Congratulations! Television executives have decided that you have what it takes to host your own talk show. You select who to interview under the following categories. The best part is that your guests have the ability to travel through a time tunnel, so they can be living today or from the past. Then decide 2 questions you'd like each guest to answer.

Figure 14.25

Category	Person's Name	Question 1	Question 2
Actress/Actor			
Musician/Singer			
Author			
Scientist			
Politician			
Explorer			
Inventor			
Dancer			
Nobel Prize Winner			
Athlete			

Invisible Learning: Filling in the Missing Elements

Learning about words or concepts that you cannot see is a tough task. Because the facts are not visible to the eye or have no definite shape, you as a learner need to discover what's missing from the picture. Choose a topic from the ones listed below and tell about the *invisible*.

1. What proof is there that this concept exists?

2. Include a demonstration, model, poster, cartoon, drawing, graph, or any picture that shows the invisible concept.

3. Write a narrative that personifies the concept, from its point of view; e.g., "As the Black Hole, I . . ."

4. Who was the first to learn about this concept and/or when did you first learn about this concept?

5. Why did you select this concept?

6. Even though it cannot be seen, identify and explain how other senses may be able to detect this concept; e.g., hearing, smelling, touching, tasting. Or, what's another way you can understand or gather more insights and information about this concept? For example, could you see a movie, research online, or even interview an expert to learn more?

7. Is there more knowledge that needs to be discovered about this concept? Is this concept meaningful to you now or will it be in the future?

Figure 14.26

Math	Science	Social Studies	Reading/Writing	Art/Music
Rational Root Theorem	Black Hole	Latitude and Longitude	Figurative Language	Tempo
Probability	Food Chain	Imperialism	Literature Themes	Pitch
Negative Numbers	Radiation	Discrimination	Moods	Light Source
Matrices	Your Skeleton	Equator	Point of View	Perspective
Time	Gravity	Equality	Main Idea	Vibrations

Computer Web Searches

Web searches can involve all subject areas. Students are required to look up information, using given computer Web sites as their tool. Here is an effective way for educators to approach this:

Step-By-Step Webbing Procedure

- First off, find Web sites dealing with the topic you'd like to instruct.
- Next, construct questions from the information given on the *student friendly* Web sites chosen. That way you know that the answers are there. Again, first start with the site information, then construct the questions.

Figure 14.27 *Shapely* Lessons

Connect Subjects, Facts, and Issues to Shapes. Remember, a prism has rectangular faces, while a pyramid has triangular ones.	Rectangular Pyramid	Triangular Pyramid	Rectangular Prism	Triangular Prism
Number of Faces	5	4	6	5
Number of Vertices	5	4	8	6
Number of Edges	8	6	12	9
Identify an equal number of details or viewpoints about a historical issue or current event as the number of faces, vertices, or edges of one of these shapes.				
Select one of these shapes and draw it in the left-hand corner of a piece of graph paper. Then, with a ruler, grid your picture. The next step is to decide upon a scale and proportionally enlarge the shape onto the larger grid.				
Write a paragraph about this shape and translate it into the language you are studying; e.g., Spanish, Russian, Arabic, Hebrew, Italian, French, and more.				
Use yarn, pipe cleaners, or toothpicks to recreate these shapes.				
Identify where you see these shapes in our environment, naming similarly shaped objects in nature, your classroom, or home.				
Tessellate one of these shapes on a grid, showing your knowledge of rotation, reflection, and translation.				

SOURCE: www.mathworld.wolfram.com/TriangularPyramid.html

- Then, insert a two-columned table with the questions on the left side, and place the Web site locations where the students can find the answers on the right side.
- Later on, some students can design their own Web searches from teacher-given Web sites, using this identical procedure.
  - The Web search about disabilities appeared in *Inclusion Strategies That Work!* (Karten, 2005).

Figure 14.28

1. What's the difference between the diagnosis of autism and that of Asperger's disorder? 2. What are the best strategies parents and teachers can use to help students with a. Autism b. Asperger's disorder	www.autism-society.org www.asperger.org
3. What types of modifications can be made in a classroom for children with hearing loss? 4. How do cochlear implants work?	www.agbell.org http://www.bionicear.org/mhg/cichowcochlearimplants work.htm
5. Name some areas that can be affected by a learning disability. 6. Tell some strategies that help children with auditory processing difficulties.	www.ldinfo.com www.ncld.org
7. What are the most common types of anxiety disorders in children?	http://www.nmha.org/
8. Name some multimodal treatments for AD/HD.	www.chadd.org/ http://nichcy.org/
9. What are the educational/employment implications for a child with Down syndrome?	http://nichcy.org/ www.ndss.org www.ndsccenter.org/
10. Name some sensitivities that need to be exhibited toward children with Tourette's syndrome.	www.tsa-usa.org/ www.tourettesyndrome.net/
11. Why is self-determination an important outcome for people with mental retardation?	http://www.thearc.org
12. What are some sports programs available to people with cerebral palsy?	http://www.ucpa.org

HS Media Technology Project

Bonus:

a. Write a song, poem, or brief skit about one of your inventions.

b. Make a pictorial time line of your 10 chosen inventions.

Figure 14.29

Choose 10 inventions from the list below and answer these questions about each. →	1. a. When was this discovery? b. In what century did this happen? c. Estimate how many years have lapsed since this invention.	2. a. Who was or were the initial person/people most important in making this discovery? b. Were there other people who were later involved?	3. a. Name the continent, country, or city/state where the invention was first developed. b. Was this idea then diffused to other countries?	4. a. Why was this invention important? b. What other inventions similar to this one followed? c. Any other interesting facts to include?
Example: Typewriter	a. 1867 b. 19th century c. About 150 years lapsed	a. Christopher Latham Sholes, Carlos Glidden, and Samual W. Soule b. Sholes and Glidden sold the rights to James Densmore who had a gun and sewing machine company (Remington & Sons), and who then produced the typewriter with the help of an artist-mechanic named William Jenne	a. Continent: North America Country: United States State: New York b. The Underwood No. 1 of 1895, by German inventor Franz Wagner, considered to be the first modern typewriter	a. increased legible business and personal communications b. computers, fax machines c. The first commercial typewriter had a foot pedal to move the paper and decorative flowers on the side!
lightbulb				
printing press				
automobile				
bicycle				
traffic lights				
washing machine				
bubble gum				
Velcro				
digital cellular phones				
CD-ROM				
hybrid car				
ATM machine				
Post-it note				
artificial heart				
credit card				

Lighthouses

Directions: Cooperatively explore the locations, history, and physics of lighthouses. Take the *enlightening* facts and vocabulary here and expand them into a written report about lighthouses. Then, choose *one* of the following formats in which to present the facts in your written report to the class:

1. Quiz game format; e.g., *Wheel of Fortune, Jeopardy, Who Wants to Be a Millionaire?*

2. Poster board with realistic pictures, hand-drawn illustrations, diagrams, and/or clip art

3. Song with lyrics and stanzas that include these facts and more about lighthouses; e.g., "You Light up My World!"

4. A dated time line of 5 lighthouses and a world map that shows their locations

5. A replica of one of the lighthouses built using a variety of building materials

6. A play or a skit. Pretend that you are the lighthouse keeper of one of the lighthouses and write a skit about what happened one day.

Figure 14.30

Expand upon at least 5 of these facts below in your group's written report. Afterward, pick one project (chosen from a–f above) on which to present your facts:
1. bonfires on hillsides, which were the earliest lighthouses
2. location of first lighthouse in Alexandria, Egypt, 285 BC
3. first American lighthouse in Boston Harbor, 1716
4. special powerful (Fresnel) lens to focus light that replaced candles. Talk about Fresnel lens uses today; e.g., solar energy
5. Other lighthouses in the United States; e.g., Havre de Grace
6. Other lighthouses around the world; e.g., Roben Island Lighthouse, Hesaki Lighthouse, Warden Head Lighthouse, Nash Point Lighthouse
7. Explanation of terms: fixed beam, flashing light, occulting lights
8. Descriptions of how they work/ed: lighthouse keepers vs. electricity
9. Compare the design and construction of early to later lighthouses
10. Identify the lighthouse contributions of these people and civilizations: Egyptians, Phoenicians, Greeks, Romans, British, George G. Meade, John O'Neill, Professor Alexander D. Bache, Augustin Fresnel
11. Explore conditions of lighthouses today. Are they operational? Should they be preserved?
12. Include at least 2 examples of figurative/descriptive language about lighthouses in your final written report; e.g., similes, metaphors, personification, alliteration
Resources: http://www.buddyproject.org/thematic/lighthouse.asp http://www.worldlights.com/world, http://library.thinkquest.org/5286/lighthouses_of_the_world.htm Books/Poems: *Historic Lighthouse Preservation Handbook* by National Park Service, *Beacons of Light* by Gail Gibbons, *The Little Red Lighthouse and the Great Grey Bridge* by H. H. Swift and Lynd Ward, *The Lighthouse* by Henry Wadsworth Longfellow, *A Light in the Storm* by Karen Hesse

Curriculum Timelines: "If I was the Teacher . . ."

Directions: With a partner, choose *one* topic under each heading and discuss the following:

1. How will you teach each topic to the rest of the class?
2. Will you lecture or have students complete work together or independently?
3. Will you have visuals such as a PowerPoint presentation, digital story-telling, worksheets, Smart Board, or overheads with clip art?
4. What important facts/details do you want students to learn?
5. Can you create a game for the other students to play that will help them to learn more about the topic?
6. How will you and your partner coteach the lesson?
7. What quiz or test will you give to the students to find out if the lesson was successful?
8. What homework will you assign?

Be prepared to teach your lesson!

Figure 14.31

Social Studies	Math	Science	Art/Music	Writing	Reading
World Geography	Division	Recycling	Abstract Painting	Figurative Language	Context Clues
World War II	Probability	Human Life	Watercolor	Capitalization	Literary Elements
Civil Rights	Algebraic Equations	Astronomy	Rhythm	Verb Tenses	Syllables
American Revolution	Graphs	Chemistry	Classical Music	Business Letter	Poetic Terms
Economics	Solving Word Problems	Plants	Reading Music	How to Prepare for a Debate	Sequencing Events
Political Systems	Tessellations	Physics	Famous Composers	Transitions	Genre Types
Ethnicity	Geometry	Animal Types	Perspective	Writing an Essay	Using a Dictionary
Imperialism	Patterns	Oceans	Sketching Still Life	Outlining/Note Taking	Identifyingthe Main Idea
Cultural Diffusion	Estimation	Food Chain	Impressionism	Proofreading Skills	Vowel Sounds

The Culture of . . .

Culture can be defined as a way of life of a given people. Groups of people who have similar beliefs, religions, or ideas are said to *share a culture* with each other. Sometimes, when someone who is *different* enters another culture, the person might be surprised at the way things are done because the rules, language, places, and people are so different from what he or she is accustomed to seeing or doing in the person's own culture or country. A perfect example of this can be seen in the book, *In the Year of the Boar and Jackie Robinson*, by Bette Bao Lord. When the main character, Shirley, a recent immigrant from China who came to live in Brooklyn, is playing a game of baseball and is told to go home, instead of running to home plate, she leaves the game and heads for her house! Sometimes in the real game of *life*, complications and global misunderstandings escalate beyond the complexities of ball games. The following activity brings this to mind for middle and high school learners.

Figure 14.32

Culturally Discomforting Situations Directions: Research a cultural group or race from the list on the right and explore how some of these culturally discomforting situations would be handled:	Cultural Groups/Races Chinese Mexican
What if your clothing was *not in style?*	Vietnamese Native Americans
What if you were taught not to question authority?	African American
What if your parents only wanted you to be friends with or date your own cultural group or race?	Jewish Japanese
What if you are a recent immigrant?	Russian
What if others made fun of the way you looked?	Puerto Rican
What if you had no friends?	Cuban Americans
What if you did not understand what the teacher was saying and found that the English language was very difficult to speak, write, or read, making most subjects tough to learn?	Dominican Arabic Korean
What if no one in school understood your religious practices?	Asian Indian
What if other kids would not sit next to you?	Hispanic
What if the food you ate was different from that of other kids?	Filipino
What if your family could not afford to see a doctor or dentist?	Irish
What if your parents wanted you to follow their rules despite school demands?	Italian Islamic
What if political situations were so bad in your former country that you could never return?	Czech Swedish
What if you want to assimilate, but are continually faced with prejudicial remarks and discrimination from peers?	German Other culture

Student Directions:

1. Choose the perspectives of a student from a culture or race different from your own. This student may have recently immigrated to the United States or may have lived here for his or her whole life, but is practicing a culture at home that is quite different from the *school culture.*

2. Research the background of *one* of these different cultures or groups. Remember that even if you know one person from that culture, he or she does not represent the entire culture. There are differences within groups too!

3. How might the person react to the following school or social issues?

4. How could you assist this person's transition or help them learn how to handle these different and sometimes difficult situations, if he or she does not know about, share, or agree with the thinking of the *majority culture?*

5. Identify how stereotypes, prejudicial remarks, and discrimination experienced by these different cultural groups in the past and present have impacted their lives.

Analyze the Quotes

Directions: First off, rephrase all of the quotes in your own words. Then pick *one* quote and answer the following:

1. Who was this person? Tell when and where this person lives or lived.

2. Then choose a quote to illustrate, giving the words a picture with drawings, cutout pictures, or clip art

3. Pantomime the quote (just use actions and gestures, no words!)

Figure 14.33

Quote: What someone else said.	Rephrase: What I think the quote means to me.
1. "I've failed over and over again in my life, and that is why I succeed." Michael Jordan	
2. "We make a living by what we get; we make a life by what we give." Winston Churchill	
3. If you judge people, you have no time to love them." Mother Teresa	
4. "Only the educated are free." Epictetus	
5. "When one door of happiness closes, another opens; but often we look so long at the closed door that we do not see the one that has opened for us." Helen Keller	
6. "Judge a man by his questions rather than his answers." Voltaire	
7. "Common sense is seeing things as they are, and doing things as they ought to be done." Harriet Beecher Stowe	
8. "The great mistake is to imagine that we never err." Thomas Carlyle	
9. "If we all did things we were capable of, we would astound ourselves." Thomas Edison	
10. "Nobody gets to live life backward. Look ahead; that is where your future lies." Ann Landers	
11. "Life is like riding a bicycle. You don't fall off unless you plan to stop peddling." Claude Pepper	

SOURCE: Inspirational Quotes on Life: www.indianchild.com/quotations on_life.htm 1/11/06

Attaining Inclusion

CPR FOR INCLUSION

Figure 15.1

C	P	R
CONTENT	PROCESS	RESULTS
CHALLENGE	PREPARE	RESEARCH
COLLABORATE	PERSONALIZE	RECOGNIZE
CONSISTENCY	PARENTS	REEVALUATION
CONNECTIONS	PARTNERS	RESPONSIBILITY
COMPASSION	PATIENCE	REPETITION
COMPREHEND	PARAPHRASE	REPHRASE
COGNITION	PRODUCTS	REVISITATION
COOPERATIVE	POSITIVE	RESPONSIVE

Use some of these words to fill in the sentences below.

Inclusion can be successful when _____

_____

_____.

I still wonder if _____

_____.

One day _____

_____.

TEACHER PLANNING

Think of your own curriculum and write an objective you would like your students to achieve.

Figure 15.2

Grades/Students	Skills/Content Areas
K–2	
3	
4	
5	
6	
7	
8	
9–12	

Baseline Knowledge Standard:

Advancing Level:

More Challenging Assignments:

Possible accommodations a child with _____ might need:

Possible accommodations a child with _____ might need:

Possible accommodations a child with _____ might need:

HOW BECOMES WHO

What you teach is based upon the standards, but how you teach those standards depends upon who is in your class. Educators, administrators, curriculum supervisors, staff developers, and families can help children understand a given topic when they address who the learners are as individuals. Each learner deserves optimum attention, whether the learner is in a school classroom, or asking a family member for help with homework at the kitchen table. Maximizing each child's potential is the ultimate goal. Accomplishments for all are attainable with the right attitude, strategies, and support, and most important, by not viewing differences as obstacles, but as challenges to be properly addressed!

It's quite true that educators are faced with complex classrooms. Are there students with above average skills mixed in with students with lower cognitive levels? Are there students in your class who have difficulties sitting still for extended periods of time? Are there students with communication needs mixed in with students with visual needs? Do some students have emotional issues that interfere with their understanding of new learning materials? Do some students need frequent repetition since they have memory issues or trouble understanding abstract concepts, or are some missing prior background knowledge? Do some students have great comprehension, but poor decoding skills? Do other students read printed words well, but do not understand what the words mean? How many of your students have difficulties with basic computations or cannot solve word problems? And, which students have a strong motivation to succeed? As a consequence of this diversity in your classroom, *how* you teach becomes influenced by *whom* you are teaching.

Educators work with other educators, yet the combinations can be compared to the elements in the periodic table, with some mixing better together than others. Teachers need to be on the same learning page when students who are classified with specific learning, emotional, physical, and developmental needs are placed in the same classroom as students who don't need more, but sometimes need less academic help or social guidance. Who is the *real teacher?* Erasing that *yours or mine* mentality and replacing it with shared responsibility for all of the students quickly dissolves any combative relationships that are counterproductive to students' achievements. Although a teacher of students with special needs wants to accommodate and at times modify the curriculum to best meet the needs of *special learners,* aren't all students within the classroom *special* as well? The group that sometimes misses out on the most learning and may become bored or distracted is composed of the students with above average, rather than below average skills. The curriculum and assignments need to challenge all students, yet not frustrate others. That's where careful planning regarding who is in the classroom supersedes how you teach. When teachers have ample activities prepared for such occasions, students are then in *automatic pilot,* able to adjust their own pace of learning under the teacher's auspices if more advanced standards can be matched to their advanced needs.

Families must also understand that young person, not just as a relative, but as a learner. Here the task is even more difficult, since objectivity is often replaced by *subjective, blood-related interfering thoughts.* Do families have the skills in the content areas or know the right strategies to implement? Do some family members have the required time or patience to devote to the child's education, after a long hard day at work? A student with special learning, emotional, behavioral, physical, visual, or auditory needs may require more attention. Do some families support the school's program when all is working well, or do some blame the educational system for their child's lack of progress?

When bridges of communication between the school and home environments are in place, possible negative and counterproductive relationships can be circumvented and replaced with *collegial–parental collaboration.*

And this starts from the top! Administrators and staff developers need to slot ample time into teachers' schedules to collaborate and plan for individual students' successes. Staff trainings, although mandatory, should at the same time be relevant ones that parallel the constantly changing roles, needs, and feedback from educators. Overcoming barriers is best addressed if the administration proactively removes those very administrative barriers before they have a negative impact on staff morale. If this negativity is not properly corked, then there's a trickling down of this negativity to the students, which then becomes translated to frustrating experiences for all. Reversing this to a *positive domino game* would be most beneficial to all! Perhaps it's a matter of having more supportive services such as OT, PT, or speech in the general classroom setting for more frequent teacher and student consultations along with increased nonjudgmental observations with recommendations. When administrators are more visible in school buildings, then their understandings of the *classroom culture* take on a more realistic view. Administrative decisions that ignore, undervalue, and underscore the daily stress and demands teachers face hinder mutual respect. The obverse is this: communication, collaboration, and high esteem belong on a *two-way street,* with students of all abilities reaping the benefits.

So *how* becomes *who.* Just rearrange this three-letter word and realize the impact it has on not just everything to be instructed, but everyone involved! Education does not exist in a vacuum or on a page of classroom strategies, but in a narrative script with a huge cast of characters delivering the best educationally award-winning roles imaginable, with the students screaming for encores! Yes, *how* means *who!*

FAMILY AND HOME SUPPORT

Integrating what is done at school and at home helps children move up the developmental ladder.

—Greenspan, 2005

Families' roles are enormous. When families are involved in their children's lives from an early onset, this vital line of communication continues to grow with their children throughout the years. Here are some questions for educators to ask, to begin thinking about home dynamics, perspectives, and extent of family involvement:

- What values are instilled in the home?
- How is education viewed?
- Are social skills more important than academics?
- Do children receive adequate medical care?
- Are they raised in a nurturing environment?
- Is creativity emphasized?
- Are school assignments valued?
- Are the children praised for their achievements?

- Are they mocked or ridiculed for their failures?
- Do the children participate in outside activities that emphasize community involvement such as sports or religious groups or volunteer work?
- What amount of time do children spend with their families?
- Do they eat dinner together?
- Is anyone home when the child returns from school?
- Does anyone check the children's homework, or ask if they need help with reports? Do some families actually do the reports *for* their children?
- Are some families so burdened with financial or medical concerns that they just can't physically or emotionally devote as much time as they would like to be part of their child's daily activities?
- Are some families guilt ridden if their child has a disability and do they blame themselves?
- Do some families deny that their child has difficulties in school?
- Do some families accept their child's individual needs and work as partners with the school to help their child develop compensatory strategies to implement in all environments?
- Are some families not intact?
- Does every child have a parent?
- Do all children have equal beginnings?

Educators have little control over what happens when students physically leave the school building. If possible, establish an ongoing communication system with families or caregivers that values consistent home support. Yes, difficulties arise in all environments, but children are only children for a short amount of time. We don't get that time back with them to have *do-overs!* Together, the schools and families must be cognizant of how this crucial collaborative role will impact future generations, personally and collectively. Schools can support families, families can support each other, families can support schools, administrators can listen to both groups, and we can ultimately all learn from each other.

To close this section on family advice, I'd like to recommend the following book to those who want further insights into the complex parent-child relationship. It's a fiction book that a student recently shared with me, titled *101 Ways to Bug Your Parents*, by Lee Wardlaw. My point here is that a little levity carries a huge impact! Other resources that are nonfiction follow:

Resources That Work!

- *Yardsticks: Children in the Classroom Ages 4–14: A Resource for Parents and Teachers* by Chip Wood
- *The Child With Special Needs: Encouraging Intellectual and Emotional Growth* by Stanley I. Greenspan, Serena Wieder, & Robin Simons
- *The Big Book of Special Education Resources* by George Giuliani & Roger Pierangelo

PRINCIPALS' AND ADMINISTRATORS' SCRIPTS: PROACTIVELY ADDRESSING, SOLVING, AND PREVENTING DILEMMAS

The principal may be the building leader, but at the same time, he or she must respect the staff as being adult learners with unique personalities. A principal who does this will in turn gain *reciprocal respect* from the staff. In addition, the building principal sets a *teaching tone* that permeates both faculty meetings and classroom instruction. Administrators must be at the helm, offering direction, but at the same time value teacher input in a nonthreatening professional environment. Communication and cooperation go hand in hand in an educational school climate that both guides and applauds its staff.

Even though teachers, just like students, have unique personalities, all teachers need to be on the same school team. Valuing teachers as contributors honors their adult life experiences and knowledge. A principal who not only talks to the staff, but also listens to their needs, is encouraging their input and fostering a collaborative spirit for the school. This comfortable atmosphere yields escalating positive results. Happy educators trickle down to happier students, which makes for a productive social and academic environment for learners to thrive.

Administration is also ageless. What this means is that the principal may be older or younger than his or her staff. Inversely true is that the staff may be older or younger than the principal. Age here is irrelevant. What matters most are the mind-sets. An administrator who is not intimidated by the older staff members or does not feel the need to dictate to the younger staff members, is valuing the contributions of his or her entire staff. Everyone has ideas to share. Some may be veteran ideas, tried and tested, while others may be a novel approach with a fresh idea or twist to a concept. The administration should encourage staff collaboration and acknowledge the contributions of all.

Yes, administrative support and training are needed, as well as outlining roles and responsibilities. However, administrators who listen to educators' feedback expand their knowledge of just how their *inherited scripts* from the central office often play out in their school building. Shared discussion time may not change existing policies, yet it might just be a time for teachers to vent frustrations over the application of a new reading series, an objectionable instructional directive, or the child or parent who refuses to follow school procedures.

This is the conundrum: how do you develop and foster this type of atmosphere? One way to accomplish this is through efficient and productive faculty meetings. Compare and contrast the following administrative faculty meeting scripts. Then fill out the checklist that compares the scenarios. Which script does your school follow? Could you write a different and even more productive script? (These sources were consulted for some of the information above Leib [n.d.] and Gerlach [2004].)

Script 1

Narrator: Faculty Meeting Script Number 1

Principal: Okay, staff, everyone should have a copy of today's agenda that was distributed two days ago. Those of you who have not brought your agenda, please look on with someone who was more prepared. The first item that concerns me is the time you are arriving at school. The contract states that you are expected to arrive at 8:15. That does not mean 8:16, 8:20, or 8:29. Is that understood by all? (Blank stares from teachers) Good, let's move on to the next item. This next item on the agenda is of huge concern. Every student in this district is expected to achieve adequate yearly progress on the upcoming standardized tests. Some of you have class records that do not reflect this. Yes, Ms. Objection.

Ms. Objection (fifth-grade teacher): How can we be held accountable for all students' progress, if they do not enter our classrooms with the same academic levels? My class last year had eight classified students who were reading more than two grade levels below. How can these students be given this same test and be expected to achieve the identical results as students who are more advanced?

Principal: You are missing the point here, Ms. Objection. Yes, Common, what is your comment here.

Mr. C. Sense (eighth-grade teacher): I agree with my colleague, Ms. Objection. Common sense tells us that she's right!

Principal: Common sense has nothing to do with this, and you are taking us away from the bottom line of improving test grades. Yes, there are difficulties, but if you are unable to properly do your job, then please let me know and I will find the necessary replacements who are willing to follow the program. Don't forget, you will not be entitled to the merit pay offered to those teachers whose students are showing significant improvements. Now, let's move on to the next item, before more time is wasted.

Item 3 concerns the boy's bathroom in the seventh-grade corridor. The custodian has discovered that the students are wetting the toilet tissue and throwing it on the ceilings. As of tomorrow, there will be no more toilet tissue in this bathroom. Please inform your students that this is a lesson about consequences for their inappropriate actions.

The next item concerns the new literature series. As directed by the language arts supervisor, there will be no more reading of novels. You are to use the short stories in your anthologies along with the accompanying reading and language worksheets. Yes, Whatta.

Ms. Whatta Future (fourth-grade teacher): I totally disagree with this method, since students are not taught the joy of reading, but only get small clips of stories. It's like a snapshot, without knowing what happened at the beginning or end of the story. Many of my students want to know how the story ends, but these passages lack closure.

Principal: Well, the only thing I have to say here is, how do you expect standardized scores to improve if we have no consistent structured language arts program?

Mr. Sense:	This is senseless.
Ms. Objection:	I object!
Ms. Future:	Just wait!
Principal:	Again, those of you who disagree with this policy will not be entitled to the merit pay we are now offering. Are there any other questions or comments? Good. That's it for the faculty meeting today. We would have ended sooner, if the comments were curtailed. See you at 8:15 sharp tomorrow morning. You are dismissed!
Narrator:	Teachers then race out of the school.

Script 2

Narrator:	Faculty Meeting Script number 2
Principal:	Welcome, everyone. I know it's been a long day, but I do hope to cover our agenda within the next 30 minutes. If you did not bring it with you, I have a few extra copies on the *Oops, I forgot* table. First off, thank you to those staff members who are reporting to school on time. Our sign-in time is 8:15. Just like trains and planes have schedules, we need to adhere to them as well. My main concern here is safety. Teachers arriving later are conflicting with the buses as they are pulling into the school. Your absence at 8:15 also worries me since I am uncertain about substitute coverage. Yes, there is something called *life* that happens; please see me privately if on a given day there are extenuating circumstances. Again, thank you to the majority of the staff who are reporting to school on time. Okay, let's move on to the next item. This next item on the agenda is of huge concern. I just returned from a meeting at *Progress Street.* According to our superintendent, every student in this district is expected to achieve adequate yearly progress on the upcoming standardized tests. Some of you have class records that do not reflect this. I think at this point I would like to open up the floor for discussion. Yes, Ms. Objection.
Ms. Objection (fifth-grade teacher):	How can we be held accountable for all students' progress, if they do not enter our classrooms with the same academic levels? My class last year had eight classified students who were reading more than 2 grade levels below. How can these students be given this same test and expected to achieve the identical results as students who are more advanced?
Principal:	I hear your concerns, Ms. Objection. Yes, Common, what is your comment here?
Mr. C. Sense (eighth-grade teacher):	I agree with my colleague, Ms. Objection. Common sense tells us that she's right!

Principal: Yes, some valid points are noted here. Common sense has everything to do with the bottom line of improving test grades. However, our ultimate goal is to improve students' levels. The way to do this is by monitoring these standardized tests, which are snapshots of students' academic levels on any given day. Then we can see if yearly progress was achieved. I think that perhaps we need to revisit this item in a separate meeting where I invite people from the central office to listen to your concerns. Together we can chart out a course to figure out the best route to follow to improve students' levels. I know some of you have been very successful and innovative in this area. Perhaps we can also allot some time on one of the professional days to have a strategy-sharing session, where we collectively communicate some positive strides and at the same time iron out some of our concerns. Yes, there are difficulties, but I think we need to stand together and help each other out in any way possible. If any of you have further thoughts or comments to share, please see me at your convenience. Thanks to Ms. Objection and Mr. Sense for their candid remarks. Remember, we are all in this together.

Now, let's move on to the next item. Item 3 concerns a lighter, but shall I say *uplifting concern,* regarding the boy's bathroom in the seventh-grade corridor. The custodian has discovered that the students are wetting the toilet tissue and throwing it on the ceilings. Rather than placing surveillance cameras in the bathroom, which would be most inappropriate, we need to monitor the students' behavior more. I am requesting that the seventh-grade teachers be more vigilant on the times students sign out for the bathroom and their return time.

The next item concerns the new literature series. Our language arts supervisor wants to suspend the reading of novels. He would like you to use the short stories in your anthologies along with the accompanying reading and language worksheets. Yes, Whatta.

Ms. Whatta Future (fourth-grade teacher): I totally disagree with this method, since students are not taught the joy of reading, but only get small clips of stories. It's like a tease, without knowing what happened at the beginning or end of the story. Many of my students want to know how the story ends, but these passages lack beginnings and closure.

Principal: Well, I understand his reasoning to have a consistent structured language arts program, but I also sympathize with your students' plight. Perhaps we can reach a compromise here.

Mr. Sense: That would make sense.

Ms. Objection: No objections from me!

Ms. Future: I can't wait!

Principal: Those of you who teach reading and are affected by this decision, please form a committee that would offer a pliable solution that

I can present to the Language Arts Supervisor, Mr. Novelless. Are there any other questions or comments? Okay, I get it, your silence tells me you're tired and just want to chill. I was walking around the building today and heard many of your well-planned lessons. I understand your exhaustion. Well, the meeting was within the 30-minute time frame I hoped for. That's it for today. Have a wonderful afternoon everyone, and I'll see you in the morning.

Narrator: Teachers smile and collegially walk out of the faculty room together. Some have brief conversations with the principal, thanking her for her ongoing support.

Principal Evaluation

Directions: Check off which faculty meeting describes the given statements.

Moral: Respect is mutual!

Figure 15.3

Statement	Faculty Meeting #1	Faculty Meeting #2
1. Principal showed respect and appreciation to her staff.		
2. Staff showed respect and appreciation to the principal.		
3. Teamwork is valued.		
4. Principal listens to the staff.		
5. Teachers' concerns are validated.		
6. Principal uses humor with the staff.		
7. Principal shares power with the staff.		
8. Principal treats the staff as individuals.		
9. All staff is concerned with students' needs and levels.		

CLASSROOM DOCUMENTATIONS AND COMMUNICATIONS

Teachers can communicate with families without using an inordinate amount of forms and time. Academic or behavioral logs are brief and structured ways to link homes and schools, so that everyone including the student is on the right page, literally and figuratively!

Figure 15.4

> BEHAVIORAL
>
> JOURNAL
>
> HOME–SCHOOL
> COMMUNICATION

> **Sample entry:**
>
> Date:____/_____/____
>
> Today was a great day for Stella Student.
>
> She cooperatively worked with peers and was attentive during classroom lessons. She did not have enough time to finish her math assignment (Worksheet #55), but promised to complete it at home and return it to school tomorrow.
>
> Parent/Guardian Signature: _____
>
> Comments/Concerns: _____

> **Sample entry:**
>
> Date:____/_____/____
>
> Harry Help had a difficult time in school today during the Chemistry lesson.
>
> His inattention to classroom rules was a safety issue for himself and his group. He did not have enough time to finish the assignment. At this point, I am concerned about his disregard for procedural safeguards in the laboratory setting. Rules are listed in the handbook, which can be found on our district's Web site at www.followrules.com. Please encourage Harry to review these rules with you. He needs to paraphrase these rules in a brief 50-word paragraph to be returned to school tomorrow. Please write any comments or concerns below or contact me at ms.let'smakethisbetter@teachthem.net. With our coordinated efforts, hopefully Harry's behavior in Chemistry class will improve. He shows excellent potential for good progress once these safety issues are addressed.
>
> Teacher Signature: _____
>
> Parent/Guardian Signature: _____
>
> Comments/Concerns: _____
>
> _____
>
> _____

IMPLEMENTING MODIFICATIONS BY CHARTING LESSONS

Teachers observe and review children's progress during class lessons and chart individual modifications, as they are needed. For effective class management, the table below can be used as documentation for 10 students, or to record the progress of one child over a period of time.

Content Area: _____

Objectives: _____

Figure 15.5

Student (name or initial) and/or Dates	Able to participate in the same lesson as peers	Needs modified expectations and/or materials within the lesson	Can independently participate in a different but related activity in the room	Requires supervision/ assistance to complete assignments	Needs to complete assignment in different setting	Other Comments Observations Areas of Need Modifications V/A/K/T Concerns Future Plans

SOURCE: Karten, T. (2005). *Inclusion strategies that work!* Thousand Oaks, CA: Corwin Press.

Teachers can keep notes from IEPs read, and monitor how lessons align with modifications and goals listed in the IEP.

Figure 15.6

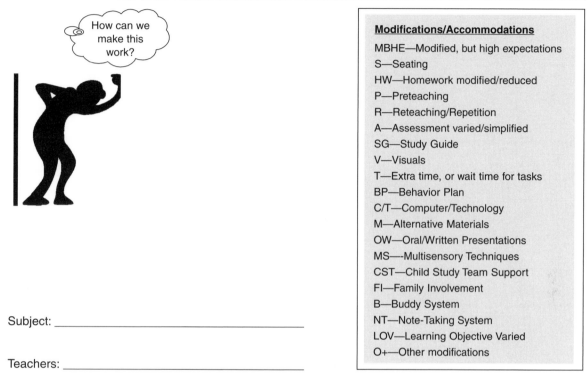

Subject: _____

Teachers: _____

Modifications/Accommodations

MBHE—Modified, but high expectations
S—Seating
HW—Homework modified/reduced
P—Preteaching
R—Reteaching/Repetition
A—Assessment varied/simplified
SG—Study Guide
V—Visuals
T—Extra time, or wait time for tasks
BP—Behavior Plan
C/T—Computer/Technology
M—Alternative Materials
OW—Oral/Written Presentations
MS—-Multisensory Techniques
CST—Child Study Team Support
FI—Family Involvement
B—Buddy System
NT—Note-Taking System
LOV—Learning Objective Varied
O+—Other modifications

Students	Modifications/ Accommodations	Assessments/Dates Mastery Level	Comments

SOURCE: Karten, T. (2005). *Inclusion strategies that work.* Thousand Oaks, CA: Corwin Press.

16

Rewards for All!

There are various inclusion models that can be implemented in classrooms, ranging from instructing small groups to partners team teaching, independent classroom study, and peer tutoring. No matter what model is chosen, teachers must be cognizant if the chosen approach is right for the students and the class as a whole. Structure must go hand in hand with variety to address both the standards and individual student strengths. As shown with the standards-based, inclusive principles listed in this book, students must reflect on their learning achievements and be instructed in a way that honors their multiple intelligences. Academic and emotional growths go hand in hand, with each fueling the other.

The positive effects of inclusion cannot always be measured on a daily basis, but the seeds of inclusion sprout throughout the years as students with and without special needs grow into adults in an inclusive world. Acceptance at early ages ensures acceptance later on in life. To include is to really model what will follow as students mature. Attitudes are developed by educational staff who have the significant responsibility to lead and guide students into those positive mind-sets, having high expectations for all students. Inclusive education relates to both general and special education students. Hopefully, one day the lines will blur and all students will be recognized for their strengths. Education will never become a standardized rubber stamp, since the population varies so greatly. However, exposing all students to curriculum standards is surely the way to include vital academic nourishment and assure that life will offer the same opportunities via inclusive and accepting educational environments.

The benefits of inclusion *include* the following:

- Higher motivation for students to succeed, wanting to fit in with their peers
- Access to the general education curriculum
- Improvement in academics due to higher expectations from teachers

- More organizational skills within the classroom and at home
- Better study skills under teacher's guidance and instruction
- Increased conceptual understandings as a result of specialized instruction received by pedagogical experts in content areas

In addition, inclusion maximizes communication skills:

- Conversational speaking
- Participating in diverse classroom discussions
- Listening skills for students with both verbal and nonverbal needs
- Potential social benefits with peers as role models
- Development of friendships
- Higher self-confidence levels
- Overall osmosis, learning about the *hidden curriculum*; e.g., following directions or *intelligent disobedience* too!
- Opportunities to cooperatively complete assignments with peers
- Greater tolerance and acceptance for people with and without differences
- Growth for peers, which later translates to coworkers' acceptance
- Transference of academic and social learning to other venues outside the classroom
- Easier transitions to the community and workforce
- Societal gains, when people with disabilities are given opportunities to learn necessary academic and social skills to join the workforce, thereby becoming active and productive members of the community

And last, but not least, there are these points from the inclusion puzzle:

Embracing the fact that we all coexist on this planet and perform on different levels, with varying strengths, needs, and abilities, is not meant to be a puzzling concept. Some horizontal or vertical clues are challenging or even missing. Some students and classroom situations are more puzzling than others. However, solving puzzles requires researching, understanding, and self-discovery of the clues to fill in the answers.

Realize that there is no hierarchy in life for people with differing abilities or an *educational monopoly philosophy* telling us which students are allowed access to success—or the right to be included in the learning experiences and then community integrations.

The reason for this? Everyone's life is meritorious!

This book offers many clues, which you now possess to solve classroom puzzles. And besides, inclusion . . .! (You can fill in the blanks now!)

Figure 16.1

| |
| |
| |
| |
| |
| |
| |
| |
| |
| |
| |
| |
| |
| |
| |
| |
| |
| |

References

Agran, M., Alper, S., & Wehmeyer, M. (2002). Access to the general curriculum for students with significant disabilities: What it means for teachers. *Education and Training in Mental Retardation and Developmental Disabilities, 37,* 123–133.

ASCD Education Update. (2002, January). Vol. 44(1) [entire issue]. Alexandria, VA: Association of Supervision and Curriculum Development.

Asha, J., DiPipi, C., & Perron-Jones, N. (2002). An exploratory study of schema-based word-problem-solving instruction for middle school students with learning disabilities: An emphasis on conceptual and procedural understanding. *Journal of Special Education, 36*(1), 23.

Ayvazoglu, N., Ratliffe, T., & Kozub, F. (2004). Encouraging lifetime physical fitness. *Teaching Exceptional Children, 37,* 16–20.

Barlow, D. (2005). The teachers' lounge. *Education Digest, 70*(8), 63.

Bauminger, N., Shulman, C., & Agam, G. (2003). Peer interaction and loneliness in high-functioning children with Autism. *Journal of Autism & Developmental Disorders, 33*(5), 489–508.

Baxter, H., & Baxter, B. (1993). *Learn to read music.* New York: MJF Books.

Beale, A. (2005). Preparing students with learning disabilities for postsecondary education. *Techniques: Connecting Education & Careers, 80,* 24.

Bellis, T. (2002). *When the brain can't hear.* New York: Atria Books.

Biancarosa, G. (2005). After third grade. *Educational Leadership, 63*(2), 9–14.

Bina, M. (1999, March). Schools for the visually disabled: Dinosaurs or mainstays. *Educational Leadership,* 78–81.

Black, S. (2003). New remedies for high-school violence. *Education Digest, 3,* 43–48.

Block, M., & Zeman, R. (1996). Including students with disabilities in regular physical education: Effects on nondisabled children. *Adapted Physical Education Quarterly, 13,* 38–49.

Bloom, G. A., & Smith, M. D. (1996). Hockey violence: A test of cultural spill-over theory. *Sociology of Sport Journal, 13,* 65–77.

Bowen, C. (1998). *Children's speech sound disorders.* Retrieved October 2005 from http://www.members.tripod.com/Caroline_bowen/phonol-and-artic.htm

Bower, B. (2004, November 6). Brain-based help for adults with dyslexia. *Science News, 166,* 19.

Broomfield, H., & Combley, M. (2003). *Overcoming dyslexia.* London: Whurr.

Brown, K. (2003, July 11). New Attention to ADHD genes. *Science, 301,* 5630.

Burstein, N., Sears, S., Wilcoxen, A., Cabello, B., & Spagna, M. (2004). Moving toward inclusive practices. *Remedial and Special Education, 25,* 104–117.

Bustamante, E. (2003, Fall). Treating the disruptive adolescent: Finding the real self behind oppositional defiant disorders [Book Review]. *Bulletin of the Menninger Clinic, 67,* 4.

Callard-Szulgit, R. (2005). Teaching the gifted in an inclusion classroom. Lanham, MD: Scarecrow Education.

Campbell, L., Campbell, B., & Dickinson, D. (2003). *Teaching and learning through multiple intelligences.* Boston: Pearson Education.

Cascella, P., & McNamara, K. (2005). Empowering students with severe disabilities to actualize communication skills. *Teaching Exceptional Children, 37*(3), 38–43.

Child and adolescent conduct disorder. (2005, April). *Harvard Mental Health Letter, 21*(10), 4–8. Available online at www.health.harvard.edu

Chisolm, J., & Johnson, M. (1993). *An Usborne introduction: Chemistry.* Tulsa, OK: EDC Publishing.

Cline, S., & Hegeman, K. (2001, Summer). Gifted children with disabilities. *Gifted Child Today, 24*(3), 16–25.

Colwell, R. (2005). Wither programs and arts policy? *Arts Education Policy Review, 106*(6), 19–29.

Content Standards for the English Language Arts. (n.d.). Developed by the National Council of Teachers of English (NCTE) and the International Reading Association (IRA). Available online at http://www.ncte.org

Content Standards for Mathematics. (n.d.). Developed by the National Council of Teachers of Mathematics (NCTM). Available online at http://standards.nctm.org

Content Standards for Social Studies. (n.d.). Developed by the National Council for the Social Studies (NCSS). Available online at http://www.ncss.org

Coster, W., & Haltiwanger, J. (2004). Social-behavioral skills of elementary students with physical disabilities included in general education classrooms. *Remedial & Special Education, 25*(2), 95–104.

Couturier, L., Chepko, S., & Coughlin, M. (2005). Student voices—What middle and high school students have to say about physical education. *Physical Education, 62*(4), 170.

Craig, A., & Rosney, C. (1993). *The Usborne science encyclopedia.* London: Usborne Publishing/Tulsa, OK: EDC Publishing.

Crupi, J. (2006). In just three steps. *Teaching PreK–8, 36*(6), 18.

Cummins, J., et al. (2005). Affirming identity in multilingual classrooms. *Educational Leadership, 63*, 38–43.

Cushman, K. (2006). Help us care enough to learn. *Educational Leadership, 63*, 34–37.

Denworth, L. (2006, April 10). The sun has finally come out for Alex. *Newsweek, 147*(15), 26.

Dillon, S. (2006, March 26). Schools cut back subjects to push reading and math. *New York Times*, p. A1.

Downing, J. (2005). *Teaching literacy to students with significant disabilities.* Thousand Oaks, CA: Corwin Press.

D'Sa, B. (2005, January/February). Social studies in the dark: Using docudrama to teach history. *The Social Studies, 96*(1), 9.

Dull, L., & Van Garderen, D. (2005). Bringing the story back into history: Teaching social studies to children with learning disabilities. *Preventing School Failure, 49*(3), 27–31

Dunn, A. (2005, September). Get happy. *Real Simple*, 248. Available online at http://www.realsimple.com/realsimple/

Dunn, W. (n.d.). *The sensory profile.* The Psychological Corporation. Available online at http://harcourtassessment.com/hai/Images/resource/techrpts/senspr01.html

Dycke, J., Martin, J., & Lovett, D. (2006). Why is this cake on fire? Inviting students into the IEP process. *Teaching Exceptional Children, 38*(3), 42–47.

Dyslexia theory. (2005, May 30). *The Times* (United Kingdom), p. 17.

Dzaldov, B., & Peterson, S. (2005). Book leveling and readers. *The Reading Teacher, 59*(3), 222–229.

Edgington, W., & Hyman, W. (2005, May/June). Using baseball in social studies instruction: Addressing the five fundamental themes of geography. *The Social Studies,* 113–117.

Faherty, J. (2006, June 1). Can't read this? *The Arizona Republic.* Retrieved June 2, 2006, from http://www.azcentral.com

Farrell, L., & Barrett, P. (2006). Obsessive-compulsive disorder across developmental trajectory: Cognitive processing of threat in children, adolescents and adults. *British Journal of Psychology, 97,* 95–114.

Folson-Meek, S., & Rizzo, T. (2002, April). Validating the physical educators' attitude toward teaching individuals with disabilities. *Adapted Physical Activity Quarterly, 19,* 2.

Foster, H. (2003). The crazy curriculum: Teaching that matters. *Educational Horizons, 81*(4), 174–177.

Franklin, J. (2005, June). Mental mileage: How teachers are putting brain research to use. *ASCD Education Update, 47,* 6.

Freiberg, K. (2002). *Annual editions: Educating exceptional children* (14th ed.). Guilford, CT: McGraw-Hill/Dushkin.

Frykholm, J., & Glasson, G. (2005). Connecting science and mathematics instruction: Pedagogical context knowledge for teachers. *School Science and Mathematics, 105*(3), 127–141.

Furner, J., Yahya, N., & Duffy, M. (2005). Teach mathematics: Strategies to reach all students. *Intervention in School and Clinic, 41*(1), 16–23.

Gardner, H. (2006). Orchestrating multiple intelligences. *Educational Leadership, 64*(1), 22–27.

Gehring, J. (2004, October 27). Moving in a special direction. *Education Week, 24,* pp. 9, 36.

Gerlach, K. (2004). *Let's team up! A checklist for paraeducators, teachers and principals* (3rd ed.). Washington, DC: NEA Professional Library.

Glasson, G. (2005). Connecting science and mathematics instruction: Pedagogical context knowledge for teachers. *School Science and Mathematics, 105,* 3.

Grados, M., Labuda, M., Riddle, M., & Walkup, J. (1997, March). Obsessive-compulsive disorder in children and adolescents. *International Review of Psychiatry, 9,* 1.

Grandin, T. (1995). *Thinking in pictures and other reports from my life with autism.* New York: Vintage Books.

Greenland, R., & Polloway, A. (1994). Handwriting and students with disabilities: Overcoming first impressions. Position paper. (ERIC Document Reproduction Service No. ED 378 757)

Greenspan, S. (2005, September). Inside the inclusive classroom. *Scholastic Parent and Child, 13,* 1.

Gregory, G., & Chapman, C. (2007). *Differentiated instructional strategies* (2nd ed.). Thousand Oaks, CA: Corwin Press.

Guastello, E., & Lenz, C. (2005). Student accountability: Guided reading kidstations. *The Reading Teacher, 59*(2), 144–156.

Hackney, K., French, R., & O'Connor, J. (2000). Perception and knowledge of inclusion of students with disabilities by elementary physical educators. *Research Quarterly for Exercise and Sport, 71,* A-106.

Hallowell, E., & Ratey, J. (1995). *Driven to distraction: Recognizing and coping with Attention Deficit Disorder from childhood through adulthood.* New York: Touchstone Books.

Harriott, W. (2004). Inclusion inservice: Content and training procedures across the United States. *Journal of Special Education Leadership, 17,* 91–102.

Harvey, R. (2006, March 13). "Broken person" defies the odds. *Toronto Star Canada,* p. E1.

Hiraoka, L. (2006, March). All this talk about tech. *NEA Today, 24,* 6.

Hodapp, R. M. (2004, February). Studying interactions, reactions, and perceptions: Can genetic disorders serve as behavioral proxies? *Journal of Autism and Developmental Disorders, 34*(1), 29–35.

Idol, L. (2006, March/April). Toward inclusion of Special Education students in general education. *Remedial and Special Education, 27*(2), 77–94.

Illinois Learning Standards. (n.d.). Available online at http://www.isbe.state.il.us/ils/ social_emotional/standards.htm

An "invisible" disability. (2005, May/June). *FDA Consumer, 39*(3), 40.

Ivey, G., & Broaddus, K. (2001). Just plain reading: A survey of what makes students want to read in middle school classrooms. *Reading Research Quarterly, 36,* 350–377.

Ivey, G., & Fisher, D. (2005). Learning from what doesn't work. *Educational Leadership, 63*(2), 9–14.

Jenkins, R. (2005, May/June). Interdisciplinary instruction in the inclusion classroom. *Teaching Exceptional Children, 27,* 5.

Jensen. E. (1998). *Teaching with the brain in mind.* Alexandria, VA: Association for Supervision and Curriculum Development.

Jones, M. (2005). *Letter of Feb. 7.* Boston: Bank of American Celebrity Series.

Karten, T. (2005). *Inclusion strategies that work!* Thousand Oaks, CA: Corwin Press.

Kelly, G. J., & Ying-Tien W. (2005). Development of elementary school students' cognitive structures and information processing strategies under long-term constructivist-oriented science instruction. *Science Education, 89*(5), 822–846.

Kendall, J. S., & Marzano, R. J. (2004). *Content knowledge: A compendium of standards and benchmarks for K–12 education.* Aurora, CO: Mid-continent Research for Education and Learning. Available online at http://www.mcrel.org/standards-benchmarks

Kent, A., & Ward, A. (1984). *An Usborne introduction: Physics.* Tulsa, OK: EDC Publishing.

Kettler, T., & Curliss, M. (2003, January 1). *Gifted Child Today, 26*(1), 52.

Kight, K. (n.d.). *Executive dysfunction.* Retrieved February 8, 2006, from http://www .mywebpages.comcast.net/kskight/EFD.htm

Klass, P., & Costello, E. (2003). *Quirky kids.* New York: Ballantine Books.

Kozleski, E., Mainzer, R., & Deshler, D. (2000). Bright futures for exceptional learners: An agenda to achieve. Reston, VA: Council for Exceptional Children. (ERIC Document Reproduction Service No. ED451668)

Kramer, J. (2004, February 9). Tourette's syndrome deserves TV respect. *Television Week, 23*(6), 9.

Landsman, J. (2006). Bearers of hope. *Educational Leadership, 63,* 26–32.

Lantz, J., Nelson, J., & Loftin, R. (2005). Guiding children with autism in play: Applying the integrated play group model in school setting. *Teaching Exceptional Children, 37,* 8–14.

LeDoux, J. (1997). Emotion, memory, and the brain. *Scientific American 7*(1), 68–76.

Leib, S. (n.d.). *Principles of adult learning, adults as learners.* Retrieved October 11, 2005 from http://honolulu.hawaii.edu/intranet/committees/FacDevCom/guidebk/ teachtip/

Little, C. (2001, Summer). A closer look at gifted children with disabilities. *Gifted Child Today, 24*(3), 46–55.

Manzo, K. (1998, September 23). A lesson in civics. *Education Week, 18*(3), 1–4.

McArthur, J. R. (2002, July/August). The why, what, and how of teaching social skills. *The Social Studies,* 183–185.

McParland, M. Q. (2003, Fall). Treating the disruptive adolescent: Finding the real self behind oppositional defiant disorders. *Bulletin of the Menninger Clinic, 67*(4), 373–374.

McTighe, H., Seif, E., & Wiggins, G. (2004). You can teach for meaning. *Educational Leadership, 62,* 26–30.

Meador, K. (2003). Thinking creatively about science. *Gifted Child Today, 26*(1), 25.

Meagher, S. (2005). Reading about writing. *Teaching PreK–8, 35*(8), 76–78.

Mooney, J., & Cole, D. (2000). *Learning outside the lines.* New York: Fireside.

Moore, J. (2003). The act of sorting. *Science Activities, 39*(4), 17.

Most teens oblivious to the threat of loud music to hearing. (2005, May 12). *New York Amsterdam News, 96*(20), 33.

Munk, D., & Bursuck, W. (2003). Grading students with disabilities. *Educational Leadership, 61*(2), 38–43.

Music Educators National Conference (MENC). (n.d.). Reston, VA: The National Association for Music Education. Accessed online at http://www.menc.org

Myles, B. (2005). *Children and youth with Asperger syndrome.* Thousand Oaks, CA: Corwin Press.

National Center on Educational Outcomes. (1997). *High stakes testing for students: Unanswered questions and implications for students with disabilities* (Synthesis Report 26). Available online at http://education.unm.edu/nceo/OnlinePubs/Synthesis26.htm

National Council of Teachers of Mathematics. (2000). *Principles and standards for school mathematics.* Reston, VA: Author.

National Reading Panel. (2000). *Report of the National Reading Panel: Teaching children to read.* Bethesda, MD: National Institute of Child Health and Human Development. Available online at www.nichd.nih.gov/publications/nrp/smallbook.htm

National Standards. (n.d.). Education World, U.S. Education Standards. Retrieved December 21, 2005, from www.education-world.com/standards/national

National Standards for Physical Education (n.d.). American Alliance for Health, Physical Education, Recreation and Dance. Available online at http://www.aahperd.org/NASPE/publications-nationalstandards.html

Neff, R. (2006). Teaching phonological awareness with deaf and hard-of-hearing students. *Teaching Exceptional Children, 38*(4), 53–58.

Nelson, J., Stage, S., Epstein, M., & Pierce, C. (2005). Effects of a prereading intervention on the literacy and social skills of children. *Exceptional Children, 72*(1), 29–45

News. (2005, July). *Journal of Visual Impairment and Blindness, 99*(7), 441-442.

Nolet, V., & McLaughlin, M. (2005). *Accessing the general curriculum: Including students with disabilities in standards-based reform.* Thousand Oaks, CA: Corwin Press.

Nucci, C., & Young-Shim, K. (2005, Fall). Improving socialization through sport: An analytic review of literature on aggression and sportsmanship. *Physical Educator, 62*, 3.

Nunley, K. (2003). Layered curriculum brings teachers to tiers. *Education Digest, 69*, 1.

Obrusníková, I., Válková, H., & Block, M. (2003). Impact of inclusion in general physical education on students without disabilities. *Adapted Physical Activity Quarterly, 20*(3), 230.

Odom, S., Brantlinger, E., Gersten, R., Horner, R., Thompson, B., & Harris, K. (2005). Research in special education: Scientific methods and evidence-based practices. *Exceptional Children, 71*(2), 137–148.

Olson, L. (2006, May 24). Vocational programs earn mixed reviews, face academic push. *Education Week, 25*(38), 21.

Olstead, J. (2005). *Itinerant teaching: Tricks of the trade for teachers of students with visual impairment* (2nd ed.). New York: AFB Press.

Orton Gillingham (n.d.). *Homepage.* Available online at www.orton-gillingham.com

O'Shea, M. (2005). *From standards to success.* Alexandria, VA: Association for Supervision and Curriculum Development.

Prause, J. (2005, August). Itinerant teaching: Tricks of the trade for teachers of students with visual impairment [Book review]. *Journal of Visual Impairment and Blindness, 99*(8), 504–506.

Preparing students for jobs: Governor's visit focuses attention on vocational education. (2006, March 25). Editorial. *The Fresno Bee.*

Prestia, K. (2003). Tourette's syndrome: Characteristics and interventions. *Intervention in School and Clinic, 39*(2), 67–72.

Quinn, P., & Stern, J. (2001). *Putting on the brakes: Young people's guide to understanding attention deficit hyperactivity disorder.* Washington, DC: Magination Press.

Rabkin, N., & Redmond, R. (2006). The arts make a difference. *Educational Leadership, 63,* 60–64.

Ravitch, D. (2006, January 5). National standards for "50 States" is a formula for incoherence and obfuscation. *Quality Counts at 10: A Decade of Standards-Based Education* [special issue]. Retrieved January 16, 2006, from http://www.edweek.org/ew/articles/2006/01/05/17ravitch.h25.html

Reed, E. (2005, December 9). OCD guidelines aim to raise awareness. *Practice Nurse, 30,* 10, Section: News.

Reeves, L., & Stein, J. (1999). Developmentally appropriate pedagogy and inclusion: Don't put the cart before the horse. *Physical Educator, 56,* 2–7.

Runyan, D., Marshall, S., Nocera, M., & Merten, D. (2004). A population-based comparison of clinical and outcome characteristics of young children with serious inflicted and noninflicted brain injury. *Pediatrics, 114*(3), 633–639.

Salend, S., & Sylvestre, S. (2005). Understanding and addressing oppositional and defiant classroom behaviors. *Teaching Exceptional Children, 37*(6), 32–39.

Samuels, C. (2005, August 10). Disability less likely to hold back youths following high school. *Education Week, 24*(44), 1–19.

Satcher, D. (2005). Healthy and ready to learn. *Educational Leadership, 63,* 26–30.

Scarpati, S. (2000). Assessment accountability and students with disabilities. *In Case, 41*(5), 1–3.

Scherer, M. (2006). Celebrate strengths, nurture affinities: A conversation with Mel Levine. *Educational Leadership, 64*(1), 8–15.

Schlozman, S., & Schlozman, V. (2002, November). Chaos in the classroom: Looking at AD/HD (Article 10). *Educational Leadership,* 28–33.

Schnorr, R., & Davern, L. (2005). Creating exemplary literacy classrooms through the power of teaming. *The Reading Teacher, 58*(6), 494–506.

Schug, M., & Hagedorn, E. (2005, March/April). The money savvy pig goes to the big city: Testing the effectiveness of an economics curriculum for young children. *Social Studies, 96*(2), 68–71.

Science Content Standards. (n.d.). Developed by the National Research Council (NRC). Available online at http://www.nsta.org/standards

Sharma, M. (2003, July). *Guiding principles and structure for a mathematics lesson.* Framingham, MA: Center for Teaching/Learning of Mathematics.

Shaywitz, S. (2005, February/March). Overcoming reading problems [interview]. *Scholastic Parent and Child, 12,* 4.

Shea, T. (2005, July). Uncommon skills. *HR Magazine, 50,* 7.

Sherlock, L. (2005, May/June). The last word: An "invisible" disability. *FDA Consumer Magazine.* Available online at www.fda.gov/fdac/departs/2005/305_word.html

Shprintzen, R. (2000). *Syndrome identification for speech-language pathologists.* Scarborough, Ontario, Canada: Delmar Singular.

Siegle, D., & McCoach, D. (2005). Making a difference: Motivating gifted students who are not achieving. *Teaching Exceptional Children, 38*(1), 22–27.

Silva, J. (2004). *Teaching inclusive mathematics for special learners, K–6.* Thousand Oaks, CA: Corwin Press.

Silver-Pacuilla, H., & Fleischman, S. (2006, February). Technology to help struggling students. *Educational Leadership, 63*(5), 84–86.

Simpson, R. L., de Boer-Ott, S. R., Griswold, D. E., Myles, B. S., Byrd. S. E., Ganz, J. B., et al. (2005). Autism spectrum disorders. Thousand Oaks: CA: Corwin Press.

Smith, S. (2005). On the move. *Scholastic News, 73,* 15.

Stough, L., & Baker, L. (1999, March/April). Identifying depression in students with mental retardation. *Teaching Exceptional Children,* 62–66.

Strassman, B., & D'Amore, M. (2002, July/August). The write technology. *Teaching Exceptional Children, 34*(6), 28–31.

Sullivan, A., & Perigoe, C. (2004, Winter). The association method for children with hearing loss and special needs. *The Volta Review,104*(4), 339–348.

Sylwester, R. (2005). *How to explain a brain.* Thousand Oaks, CA: Corwin Press.

Talking book machines. (2005). News section, www.humanware.com

Tang, G. (2003). *Math appeal.* New York: Scholastic.

Teicher, S. (1999). Virtually accessible. *Christian Science Monitor, 92,* 11.

University of Washington. (2001). *Working together: Computers and people with sensory impairments* (ED481297). Seattle: Author. Available online at http://www .washington.edu/doit/Brochures/Technology/wtsense.html

U.S. Census Bureau. (2000). Accessed online at www.factfinder.census.gov

U.S. Department of Education. (2005a, August). *No Child Left Behind: Alternate achievement standards for students with the most significant cognitive disabilities.* Washington, DC: Author.

U.S. Department of Education. (2005b). *Spellings announces new special education guidelines, details, workable, "common sense" policy to help states implement No Child Left Behind.* Available online at www.ed.gov/news/pressreleases/2005/05/ 05102005.html

Utay, J., & Utay, C. (2005). Improving social skills: A training presentation to parents. *Education, 126,* 2.

Vaidya, S. (2004, Summer). Understanding dyscalculia for teaching. *Education, 124*(4), 717–721.

Vail, K. (2005). Helping students through depression. *Education Digest, 70*(8), 36–43.

Villano, T. (2005). Should social studies textbooks become history? A look at alternative methods to activate schema in the intermediate classroom. *The Reading Teacher, 59*(2), 122–130.

Vo-Tech as a door to college, evolving programs draw on strong backs, strong minds. (2006, March 12). *The Washington Post,* p. C11.

Vurnakes, C. (1998). Words on a vine: 36 vocabulary units on root words. Grand Rapids: MI: Instructional Fair.

Walsh, J., & Conner, T. (2004). Increasing participation by students with disabilities in standards-based reform through teacher observations. *Journal of Special Education Leadership, 17,* 103–110.

Wang, M. C., Haertel, G. D., & Walberg, H. J. (1997). Learning influences. In H. J. Walberg & G. D. Haertel (Eds.), *Psychology and educational practice* (pp. 199–211). Berkeley, CA: McCutchan.

Ward, R. (2005). Using children's literature to inspire K–8 preservice teachers' future mathematics pedagogy. *The Reading Teacher, 59*(2), 132–143.

Warshaw, M. G. (2004). Motivation problem or hidden disability? *Pediatrics for Parents, 21*(1), 10.

Weissberg, R., Resnik, H., Payton, J., & O'Brien, M. (2003). Evaluating social and emotional programs. *Educational Leadership, 60*(6), 46–50.

Wiggins, G. (2006, April). Healthier testing made easier. *Edutopia*. Retrieved April 21, 2006, from http://www.edutopia.org/magazine/ed1article.php?id=Art_1498& issue=apr_06

Winebrenner, S. (2000, September). Gifted students need an education, too (Article 31). *Educational Leadership, 52*–56.

Winkler, H. (2005). The world's greatest underachiever. *Highlights for Children, 60*(3), 26.

Wolfe, P. (2001). *Brain matters: Translating research into classroom practice.* Alexandria, VA: Association for Supervision and Curriculum Development.

Wolk, R. (2006). It doesn't add up: Forcing kids to take higher math doesn't always compute. *Teacher Magazine, 17*(5), 4.

Yell, M., Katsiyanna, A., & Shiner, J. (2006). Improving student services: The No Child Left Behind Act, and adequate yearly progress, and students with disabilities. *Teaching Exceptional Children, 38,* 32–39.

Young, C. (1989). *Castles, pyramids and palaces.* London: Usborne.

Zametkin, A. J., & Monique, E. (1999). Current concepts: Problems in the management of attention deficit hyperactivity disorder. *New England Journal of Medicine, 340,* 40–46.

Zins, J. E., Weissberg, R. P., Wang, M. C., & Walberg, H. J. (Eds.). (in press). *Building school success on social and emotional learning.* New York: Teachers College Press.

Zull, J. (2004). The art of changing the brain. *Educational Leadership, 62,* 68–72.

Additional Web Sites

U.S. Census, Index of Population: www.census.gov/population
Project Criss: www.projectcriss.com
The Kennedy Center ArtsEdge: ArtsEdge.kennedy-center.org/teach/standards.cfm
Recording for the Blind & Dyslexic: www.rfbdinfo.org

Index

CORWIN PRESS

The Corwin Press logo—a raven striding across an open book—represents the union of courage and learning. Corwin Press is committed to improving education for all learners by publishing books and other professional development resources for those serving the field of PreK–12 education. By providing practical, hands-on materials, Corwin Press continues to carry out the promise of its motto: **"Helping Educators Do Their Work Better."**